Praise for

the
Engagement
GAME

"Buckle up. Reading *The Engagement Game* is like having brunch with your best friend, where she tells you all the crazy highs (hello, international travel and swoon-worthy dates) and excruciating lows (did he really just say that?) on her quest to marry a man she loves. Joi-Marie's transparency and incredible writing is a breath of fresh air in today's Wild West dating scene. Every woman should read this universal story of finding yourself in the journey to Mrs. Life."

—Charreah K. Jackson, *Essence* senior relationships editor and author of *Boss Bride*

"Joi-Marie McKenzie's debut memoir *The Engagement Game* is friggin' hilarious and a sometimes cringe-inducing time machine, shooting me back to my late 20s and those hours-long brunches spent dissecting what *he* meant by some text, G-chat, or Facebook poke (remember Facebook pokes?). It'll be a fun and eye-opening trip down memory lane for some and just last week for others. McKenzie expertly captures not just the heartache of sticking it out with Mr. Right Now but that triumphant Aha! moment when you decide to follow your gut and get to the joy on the other side."

—Helena Andrews, *Washington Post* columnist and author of *Bitch Is the New Black*

"Rarely do I see myself reflected in books: A young Black career-woman trying to navigate life and find The One at the same time! Joi-Marie McKenzie hilariously captures that adventure in this relatable, laugh-out-loud funny book."

—Arianna Davis, digital director, OprahMag.com

"*The Engagement Game* is a compelling tale capturing Joi-Marie's experience as a savvy, successful young woman looking to find and keep love. Ultimately, this journey provides her with an important life lesson on how to remain true to self while seeking marriage. Through her humorous and witty writing, Joi-Marie delivers an engaging read that celebrates independence and freedom among women everywhere."

—Lilly Workneh, editor-in-chief of Blavity and Shadow & Act

"*The Engagement Game* is not only an engaging read but coura-geous. So many women have been told they need a man, marriage, or motherhood to be happy. Joi-Marie McKenzie reminds us that what women really need is the freedom to define happiness on our own terms."          —Keli Goff, columnist, *The Daily Beast*

"Bubbly. Fun. But always real, Joi-Marie McKenzie's *The Engagement Game* is a memoir that reads like your favorite weekend escapist nov-el. As you dive in, the pages transport you from the humdrums of life to the fast-paced world of entertainment journalism; the New York and Washington, DC, dating scenes; and that dogged pursuit of a ring so many women fall into until they learn to invest in one's self over a man's affections. It's a tale of the 20s (and 30s and for some, even their 40s) that's relatable and relevant to every woman who's pursued a ca-reer while looking for an ending straight out of the movie *Mahogany*."

—Danielle Belton, managing editor of *The Root*

"Women like Joi-Marie seem like they have it all. But in this candid memoir, she peels back the layers of the glamorous life to reveal the anxiety and striving, the dodgy guys and the workplace absurdities. Still, her buoyant sense of humor makes it fun to accompany her on this journey through young adulthood."

—Amy Argetsinger, *Washington Post*

"*The Engagement Game* is a must-read for our time. It is a great tome for young women who need time to first discover themselves before they say yes to discovering someone else in marriage."

—Sophia A. Nelson, award-winning author of *The Woman Code: 20 Powerful Keys to Unlock Your Life.*

"*The Engagement Game* makes one thing clear (in alternately hilarious and heartbreaking terms): if the chase for Mr. Right and an Instagram-perfect life challenges a woman like Joi-Marie McKenzie, the rest of us mere mortals should see just how silly it is. McKenzie speaks clearly to those of us who've been made to feel that a 'MRS' title (and a properly large rock on our ring finger) means more than our professional accomplishments, our contributions to the community and even, perhaps, our happiness."

—Jamilah Lemieux

"A hilarious and unique take on dating that also reveals how sisterhood, daughterhood, friendship, and Spirit can lead to a deeper relationship with self and unbounded self-love."

—Chanel Craft Tanner, *Crunk Feminist Collective*; assistant director, Center for Women at Emory University

"Although I'm not single, I don't think you have to be to enjoy Joi-Marie's new book *The Engagement Game*."

—Jennifer Holmes, girlybookclub.com

"Joi-Marie McKenzie's debut effort is glamorous, well-paced, and just plain fun. But the attribute that most endears this page-turner to me is its honesty."     —Keyaira N. Boone, The C Letter

"In an age where looking for love means fielding meager advances made over DM and swiping aimlessly through apps and online profiles, Joi-Marie McKenzie's *The Engagement Game* offers a brutally, beautifully honest take on what it really means to be a smart, sexy, single-and-seeking twentysomething, navigating today's volatile dating minefield in a driven—at times even desperate—search for her fairy-tale ending."

—Janine Rubenstein, staff editor, *People* magazine

*the*

GAME

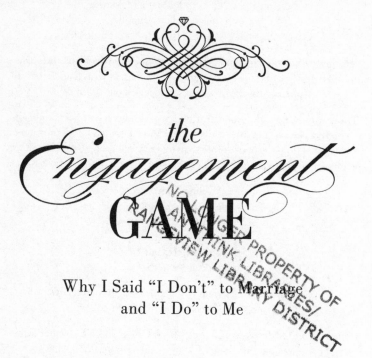

# the Engagement GAME

Why I Said "I Don't" to Marriage
and "I Do" to Me

## JOI-MARIE McKENZIE

CENTER
STREET

*New York   Nashville*

Center Street
Hachette Book Group
1290 Avenue of the Americas
New York, NY 10104
centerstreet.com
twitter.com/centerstreet

Originally printed in hardcover and ebook in March 2017
First trade paperback edition: March 2019

Center Street is a division of Hachette Book Group, Inc. The Center Street name and logo are trademarks of Hachette Book Group, Inc.

The publisher is not responsible for websites (or their content) that are not owned by the publisher.

The Hachette Speakers Bureau provides a wide range of authors for speaking events. To find out more, go to www.HachetteSpeakersBureau.com or call (866) 376-6591.

Library of Congress Control Number: 2016023224

ISBNs: 978-1-4555-9450-4 (trade paperback), 978-1-4555-9449-8 (ebook)

Printed in the United States of America

LSC-C

10 9 8 7 6 5 4 3 2 1

*For all the women who were ever
told they weren't the marrying kind*

# A NOTE FROM THE AUTHOR

The people, places, and events in this work have been re-created based on my memory, diary entries, e-mails, and text messages. Details, including physical characteristics, cities, occupations, and other identifiable traits have been changed in an effort to fiercely protect the privacy of my loved ones. Oh! And by no means is this a how-to book. Sorry, ladies.

# PART ONE

# Game Time

# Chapter 1

You're going to be my wife one day, you know that?" Adam asked.

A spark that felt like lightning ran down my back.

Was this a proposal?

I breathed in, out, in, out, in, out, trying to calm myself down just in case it was a proposal. Shit! What if he was proposing? No, he didn't seem nervous or fidgety. Aren't guys usually nervous when they propose? It wasn't a proposal. He wasn't down on one knee—but he was slouched over. I kept my eyes wide, in case his hands went to his pockets.

Adam and I were ringing in the New Year in a nightclub in Washington, D.C., our favorite city despite the fact that the New York area had held us hostage for the last four years. Adam was a lawyer and had passed the bar across the Hudson River in New Jersey, so he couldn't move unless he studied for the New York bar exam—and we weren't going through that again. At least not right now. Plus, I had finally settled into my job as an entertainment producer at a television network in New York City, getting hard-to-come-by celebrity interviews and breaking news on stories that mattered—like Justin Bieber's new haircut and Chris Brown's latest girlfriend. The stories of legend.

So when I mentioned spending the New Year in D.C., he didn't blink. I even convinced our best friends to book rooms in the same hotel just footsteps away from Georgetown University, where he went to law school. It would be nostalgic for him and a nice getaway for us.

By 11:53 p.m., Adam and I were way past tipsy.

"Yeah?" I slithered. A grin unable to contain itself appeared on my face.

"Yes!" he said, finally finding his balance and standing up straight. "We're going to get married, and you're going to be my wife. I love you!"

Okay. He was standing up, so this was definitely not a proposal. *It's not a proposal.* I found my breath again. My heart, which was beating inside my chest so hard that I could hear it in my ears, suddenly shrank back to normal. This was not a proposal.

Damn.

It was more like a promise, and I'd take that. If I couldn't get a proposal on New Year's Eve, I'd take a promise.

"I love you too, Adam," I said slowly, quietly, realizing the significance of this pseudo-proposal.

"Ten! . . . nine! . . . eight! . . . seven! . . . six! . . . five! . . . four! . . . three! . . . two! . . . one! Happy New Yearrrrrr!" the deejay proclaimed.

Adam planted a sloppy kiss on the space next to my mouth. I caught his wet champagne kiss, moving my head slightly so our lips actually met, and closed my eyes, letting the feeling of love wash over me.

I wondered if Adam would remember his marital declaration in the soberness of the morning.

I couldn't wait to tell my sister.

❧

"So what does that mean?" my older sister, Jasmine, asked.

I had just finished telling her the New Year's Eve pseudo-proposal story in great detail, hoping she could decode what Adam had meant, if he'd meant anything at all by it.

And Jazz should know. She had successfully gotten her boyfriend of three years to propose to her. Clearly she was an expert, and I needed expert advice.

"I honestly don't know. We have talked about marriage before, but it was always in general terms like, 'Yes, I see myself getting married and having two kids.' But never, 'I see myself marrying you.'"

"Well, then this is good. This is good," Jasmine said with the delivery of a stock market analyst. "Wait and see if he brings it back up again. Give him a good three months. If he doesn't, then bring it up. See where his head's at. I mean, honestly, Joi, it's not like you're getting any younger. You guys have been together for as long as Jimmy and I have been together and we're married with one on the way."

"Yes, I am highly aware of that."

"I'm just saying, you can't be afraid to have the conversation."

"Who said I was afraid?"

"All right, lover girl," Jasmine conceded. "Just keep me posted."

"I will. Adam isn't the type to say something and not mean it. He's always been a man of his word…Hell, at this point, I just hope he remembers his word."

"Well, you know what they say: You tell the truth when you're drunk. I wouldn't worry about it."

"You're right. You're right. Okay. Thanks, sissy. I'll talk to you tomorrow."

# Chapter 2

*Wamp! Wamp! Wamp! Wamp!*

With my eyes half closed, I threw my body over, flailing my arms like the dude in *Weekend at Bernie's*, in search of the alarm clock. I finally found my iPhone, which served many purposes, and tapped the screen to snooze. It was 6:00 a.m. and I really needed *ten more* minutes. I could really sleep in until 6:20 and still make it on time to work by 7:00. I closed my eyes happily, like a fiend who just took another hit.

I did not want to get up. I have never been a morning person, but when you work in news, you work odd hours. My shift now was from 7:00 a.m. to 4:00 p.m. It's complete torture to attempt to wake yourself up before the sun rises, but hey...at least I had a job. To think I complained when I had to go in at 9:00 a.m. Those were the days.

Unfortunately, my newsroom had downsized. We knew layoffs were coming—it's common in this industry. Still, for weeks, it was a wait-and-watch game to see who would be leaving. A few people texted me to see if I was spared. You okay? Hear anything? But I hadn't, so thankfully I was safe for now.

Consequently, I made sure I was always on time, always smiling, always polite, always responsive to e-mails—even if they were sent at 1:00 a.m. and I didn't get paid overtime. Plus, I vowed when I started working there two years ago that I would never be *that* person—the killjoy always too busy making deadline to make small talk around the coffee machine.

My job was supposed to be fun. I covered entertainment news. I went to red carpets and premiere parties and mingled with New York's celebrities and their clingers-on. There was just no reason to make the newsroom a living hell—for anybody.

But despite the glamorous people I covered, the actual job of chronicling the lives of Hollywood's glitterati wasn't really all that glamorous. I spent many nights waiting for hours in the cold and sometimes rain for red carpets to start. Plus, I had to look the part in cute and short party dresses but didn't get paid to look the part—my credit card was on the brink of I-can't-buy-you-any-more-shit-you-can't-afford. Yet, if I had a nickel for every person in the industry who didn't have a real job but posted pics on Instagram as if they were living the dream life, well, I'd really be living the dream life.

Instead of complaining, I fantasized about the day I wouldn't have to cover another red carpet again. I dreamed of the day I'd get actual invitations to attend the fabulous events, instead of invitations to cover them, paying my keep by tweeting and SnapChatting and writing a nonstory in the wee hours of the morning. I couldn't wait until I could assign that story to a newcomer so I could stay home with my kids and watch Disney movies. That would be a dream.

*Wamp! Wamp! Wamp! Wamp!*

I sighed deeply. I knew I had to get up this time. I looked under the covers to find my miniature dachshund, Arista, sleeping. When she noticed someone was waking her up, she yawned, licked her chops, and closed her eyes again. Spoiled ass. She was such a human—thanks to me—and I couldn't help but be jealous that she got to sleep all day while I had to get up to keep a roof over our heads.

I kicked off the covers, hoping the shock of the early-morning cold air would awaken my body as I tiptoed to the bathroom on the chilly wooden floors. I turned on the shower before I even plopped down to pee. My building, like many in Harlem, was old, and I knew the shower needed time to build up the hot water.

By the time I had gotten dressed, taken down my hair, and put on my Olivia Pope trench coat, it was 6:40 a.m. Sucks for Rissy! I usually walked her around the block twice a day—once in the morning and once in the evening after work. But there was no time to walk her this morning, and I honestly hated walking her at this hour. The only people out on the streets in Harlem at this time of day were drunk partiers finishing their night, winos, crack addicts, or fucking randoms.

Last week, when I was walking Arista down to the corner and back up on the other side of the street, I noticed a man staring at me. I didn't know why he was staring at me, and it looked like he was waving. Did I know him? I stared harder. It was dark, and I couldn't really see, but I was absolutely sure I didn't know this dude.

After passing a few more brownstones on the block, I realized the man wasn't waving at all. He had his pants down around his thighs, and he was whacking himself off—while staring at me.

I didn't have time to freak out or imagine what would happen if I walked past him. Instead, I sprang into action, crossed the street, now dragging Rissy by her pink leash, and ran up my building's steps. I prayed that when I went back downstairs to head to work he'd be gone. He was.

After clearing away junk e-mails—one from Tommy Hilfiger's publicist detailing which celebrity they had dressed on some red carpet, another attaching a folder of pictures from a celebrity-filled bash in Atlanta, and an invite to a party in the Hamptons from Jill Zarin—I saw one from a publicist friend inviting me to interview Spike Lee at his 40 Acres and a Mule Filmworks studio in Fort Greene. Yes! I kept reading…*Oh shit. It's today.*

Great. I hadn't put on makeup today, and my hair was snatched back in a ponytail because I was trying to give it a break from getting sew-in after sew-in. But I had to make this work—Spike would just have to meet me with puffy eyes and dry lips.

Honestly, this was my biggest interview in months. Recently, I'd been interviewing reality stars and *American Idol* rejects. It'd be nice to pick the brain of an iconic filmmaker on his latest, *Red Hook Summer.* The interview wasn't for another two hours, which gave me time to do some research before I trekked to Brooklyn.

"How you doing, Joi-Marie?"

I slowly moved my eyes from my intense Google search to find Mike. He was one of my safe havens here—always giving me advice. He suggested months ago that I should learn how to read from a teleprompter even though I worked for the digital team and offered suggestions on how to get noticed even though my desk was on the very far end of the maze of sad gray cubicles. He even told me to relax when I came into the newsroom on the verge of tears one day. He had noticed—a rarity in New York in general and at my job specifically—and asked what was wrong. I told him about how my boyfriend of three years didn't seem to be any closer to proposing and I didn't know if I should try harder or start over with someone else. Mike said he didn't propose to his wife until after close to eleven years. *Over a decade?!* I thought. I told him there was no way in hell I was waiting that long.

"Hey, Mike."

"I heard about your Spike Lee interview."

"Yup," I said. At this point, everyone had heard about the interview thanks to the e-mail I sent out, asking if the team had questions for him, before I started my flurry of Google searches.

I hoped Mike didn't want to do small talk right now. No offense, Mike was great, but I hated small talk when on a time crunch.

"If you don't want to do it, I can do it. I've interviewed Spike before, so it's probably best that I talk to him, since he knows me," he said faster than normal. He was probably nervous to make such a bold request. I'd be nervous if I were him too.

"Um, no. I've got it," I said, barely masking my how-dare-you attitude. "I've interviewed him before too, so I'm sure it'll be good for us to catch up."

"Oh, you have? When?"

"At last year's American Black Film Festival when he celebrated the twentieth anniversary of *Do the Right Thing.*"

"Oh. Okay, well…" He trailed off and moseyed his way to the coffee machine without finishing his sentence.

The nerve! Did he not think I could pull this off?! I did see Spike at the film festival last year. Although, in all honesty, it was hardly an interview. I was on the red carpet, squeezed in next to a green reporter from Global Grind and a videographer from *Ebony* magazine who was just getting b-roll of the carpet. Spike was making his way down the line of reporters, and since he had just announced *Red Hook Summer* was coming out, I wanted to get him on the record talking about it. No one knew what the film was about. We just knew it was going to be a Spike Lee joint. He started walking toward us, and the Global Grind reporter asked the world's dumbest question: "Are you enjoying yourself tonight?"

"Well, I just got here, so I don't know," Spike told her, pausing to see if she had a more poignant question. She didn't. So he looked away and I caught his eye—a red carpet sign that I wanted to talk to him.

Other celebrities had publicists who walked down the red carpet beforehand, asking publications if they wanted to speak to their clients, so it was rather easy to chat with them. But Spike didn't have that. He was a pro at navigating the red carpet on his own.

I pushed my microphone toward his mouth, just six inches away, holding up my mic flag with my thumb. The damn thing always seemed to slide down during interviews.

"What can you tell us about *Red Hook Summer*?" I asked Spike in a serious, I'm-a-real-entertainment-reporter-who-is-not-going-to-ask-you-about-the-weather-or-those-rumors-about-your-wife tone.

"Nothing," he said in a warning tone, as if he really didn't want to share.

He wouldn't get away that easy, though. As he started to walk away, I yelled, "Just give me one word about the film!"

"Gentrification," he said matter-of-factly before he walked to the next reporter.

After that awkward run-in, I was nervous to see Spike today. I hoped he wouldn't remember me from that red carpet, but I wasn't scared. I was going to be prepared with great questions. Mike could suck it.

After a few more clicks around the Internet, I printed off my questions about the film and one extra question about the Knicks to end the interview. I then e-mailed the questions to myself. I've been to enough on-location interviews to know to always bring a backup. Whenever I get there, my printed questions always seem to turn up missing, or I'm so nervous that I can't find them in the oversized hobo bag that I lug around all day. After tossing my equipment into my bag, I was out the door.

The forty-minute train ride from midtown to Brooklyn was a much-needed break from technology. The best thing about the New York subway is that you can ride and not feel guilty about ignoring that e-mail, text, tweet, or Facebook message. You just don't have service. What's left is reading the e-mails already loaded on my cell phone or closing my eyes for a little nap. I decided on the nap.

I woke up every time the train pulled into a station and more people crammed in. After ten or so mini-naps, I got off at the Atlantic Avenue stop in Brooklyn and walked another ten minutes to Spike's 40 Acres and a Mule studio. I had walked by this cultural petri dish many times before. In fact, when I first moved to New York, I came here as a tourist and took too many selfies in different poses in front of the garage, which always had some dope mural on it promoting Spike's latest film. But today I could actually go in.

When I arrived, Sharon, the publicist, was at the door with a clipboard. "Joi-Marie! I'm glad you could make it so last minute. Sorry about that."

"No worries. I'm just glad to get out of the newsroom."

"Great! We're running a little behind on interviews, but we have drinks and sandwiches downstairs. Come right in."

Everyone in the entertainment industry seemed completely jaded. To these people, the worst thing a journalist can be is a fan of someone's work. But at that moment, I was totally fangirling. My insides were about to burst out of my seams when I walked into 40 Acres and a Mule. All of the history rushed over me and I felt humbled to be there. These were the same hallways that birthed the careers of Denzel Washington and Rosie Perez. And now I got to be here, interviewing the visionary director whose movies shaped my cultural consciousness and made me fall in love with Brooklyn.

On one wall, floor-to-ceiling portraits of Michael Jackson and Michael Jordan hung next to each other. There was nothing fancy about anything—just tacky light wood linoleum floors with harsh overhead lighting. There was a table filled with Potbelly sandwiches and drinks. I grabbed a sandwich and a Coke and looked around for an empty seat.

Some journalists I recognized sat in metal folding chairs in a circle as if they were at a therapy session. I sat down meekly and whispered my hellos. No one stopped their conversations. No one bothered to look up.

I ate in the most uncomfortable position—with my plate in my lap, trying to squeeze mayonnaise on my turkey-and-cheese sandwich with one hand from that small metallic squeezy thingy. I was successful enough to put one thick stream of mayo on the part I was about to chow into and opened my mouth to enjoy it when someone finally said a few words in my direction.

"You're Joi-Marie, right? From TheySaid.com?" a journalist named Heather asked.

Heather was loud, opinionated, and beautiful—and looked like she had lived in Brooklyn all her life. Her jet-black curly hair fell in all the right places. It didn't seem like she used too much product to achieve her look. It was probably her natural curl pattern instead of the workings of Miss Jessie's and flat twists. She topped it off with a bright red lip that wasn't yet in season, but Heather managed to make it work.

"Um, no. Well, yes. I'm Joi-Marie, but I'm not with TheySaid anymore," I stammered, wishing I could just eat my sandwich instead of making small talk. "I'm at a network now."

Now the whole circle of journalists looked up at me with interest.

"Oh, really? That's hot, Joi! Remember me? I was friends with your old editor, Ronny. I'm Heather."

"Of course! Hi, Heather! You still working with..." I let my words trail off slowly so she could remind me of where she worked.

"Yup, I'm still at AngelaCorettaandYou," she said proudly.

It was one of the hottest blogs for black women these days. As I looked around at all the journalists in the metal chairs, I noticed they all wrote for blogs—hip-hop blogs, gossip blogs, no-name blogs—and realized why everyone now suddenly wanted to jump into our conversation. They were all bloggers and I was the magical unicorn journalist who had gone from small news blog to credible news network in a matter of months. I had made it, as far as bloggers were concerned, and they all wanted to know how they could make the same transition—or at least keep in touch for future job opportunities, a 401(k), and medical and dental.

When I was at TheySaid, no one included me on their e-mail chains, inviting me to the best events in the city. After I started working at a network, I had access to all the velvet-rope events that my blogger press pass could never get me into. I got easy accessibility from celebrity publicists, where before I had to prove our site's analytics and our reach before they would even consider my interview request. After years of scraping for celebrity interviews, they were now flowing to my inbox freely. But I still had a long way to go. Beyoncé's publicist still ignored me. I didn't get to interview Oprah Winfrey when she was making her rounds promoting *The Butler*, and—

"Joi. You wanted to be first, right?" It was Sharon, the publicist for the junket, interrupting my thoughts. She was speaking at lightning speed with her eyes darting nervously at the other bloggers.

"Oh yes! Is he ready?" I said, standing up from my seat and ending my thoughts of Heather and the three other bloggers trying to jump into our barely there conversation.

"Yup! Come on up. There are no pictures in here. Just wanted to remind everyone of that," she spat.

I hadn't even considered taking pictures of the place until she told me not to. I nodded while walking up the steps to the second floor. I looked around with my eyes wide as I saw memorabilia from *School Daze*, a silver bulldog on a windowsill, and the Sal's Pizzeria sign from Spike's film *Do the Right Thing*.

Sharon led me through an empty room that had round tables with metal chairs surrounding them. Spike was doing roundtable interviews with the bloggers later. She then opened the door where Spike was sitting in a director's chair. I was nervous, considering how my last interview with Spike went, but he seemed relaxed. His shoulders slumped a little like he was comfortable, and he had a slight smile on his face. Great—at least he didn't look pissed off.

I sat in the other director's chair facing Spike. He didn't say anything as I pulled out my now crumpled Word document filled with questions. I asked several questions about the movie, Brooklyn, and his legacy as a filmmaker. He seemed to appreciate every one, answering it like he had something to sell. Spike was charming, receptive, and attentive. I even made him laugh when I asked if he could ever see Carmelo Anthony playing for the Wizards, considering he was raised in Baltimore. He laughed really hard at that one. Brooklynites have long claimed Carmelo as their own since he was born there.

"Carmelo is from Brooklyn. Point-blank," he said in his thick New York accent.

"Yes, but he grew up in Baltimore. I remember him in high school," I said matter-of-factly.

When I was at Roland Park Country School, a private all-girls college prep school on the west side of Charm City, a young Carmelo—well, we were all young then—was playing basketball ten minutes away at Towson Catholic. Everyone knew then that he'd make it to the league.

I saved useless gems of information like this one if ever I could use it during an interview to get a reaction out of a celeb.

"Oh, you're from Baltimore? Well…Carmelo isn't," he said with a smile. Spike was that rude uncle everyone had in their family, and I loved it.

Sharon tapped on the door to let us know time was up. Perhaps she heard too many laughs, plus it had been about twelve minutes—two minutes over the allotted time.

I asked quickly if I could snap a picture with him. He obliged, saying we should take it right outside the door in a more well-lit room.

The high from the interview made me forget I didn't have a drop of makeup on and that the hair in my ponytail was now sticking straight up on my head like it was pointing to 12 o'clock. I looked twelve years old. I smiled with all my teeth as I towered next to Spike, who only came up to my collarbone.

As I walked down the stairs, camera in hand, I snapped two pictures: one of the silver bulldog and another of the Sal's Pizzeria sign.

# Chapter 3

It was 5:42 a.m., according to my iPhone. Great. That meant I had another half hour to sleep before I really had to wake up. In my newsroom, if you got in at 7:11 a.m., eleven minutes past the time I was expected to occupy my station at the far end of the connected cubicle maze, an e-mail went out to the entire staff announcing "Joi-Marie is out today."

It was now 6:12 a.m. But I couldn't get out of bed without checking the e-mails on my phone that had come in overnight, then my text messages (and there were a couple that streamed in after 10:00 p.m. when I'm usually out like a light), then Twitter, then Facebook. In that order. By the time I tapped Instagram, I was usually running late, so that normally waited until I was on the subway platform.

Still, this morning, which just so happened to be Valentine's Day, I got stuck in my inbox. An e-mail from my sorority sister came in, and the subject read, "So I'm in Paris and..." The preview already let me know what was behind the ellipsis. She got engaged! Her boyfriend—well, fiancé now—flew her to Paris and dropped down to one knee on the Pont des Arts, better known as the "Love Locks" bridge. I really don't think it gets more perfect than that. I let out a happier than happy squeal that no one heard, especially at this hour, except for Arista. She barely moved at the sound. I felt like I should celebrate this news with someone else, so I immediately texted Adam.

Aww, Lamar just proposed to Lindsay in Paris . . . , I typed.

I didn't expect to get a response, especially at this hour. I'm sure he'd take it as a hint, which it was, masked in an I'm-just-sharing-news type of text message.

But he knew me, and I'd been dropping hints ever since that New Year's Eve, when he leaned over to sloppily kiss me—a rare moment of PDA—in our favorite D.C. nightclub and told me, "You're going to be my wife one day." It was exhilarating, but I kept reminding myself that it wasn't a proposal. So every day I sat and prayed and hoped that he'd even remember that he said it.

But that was over a year ago.

Although we'd talked about getting married in the months after that, Adam never spoke about it with the same drunken enthusiasm he'd had that night. In fact, he stopped bringing it up at all.

*Shit.* I didn't want to do Valentine's Day. Even with a boyfriend, I just didn't want to do it. I'm nowhere near walking down the aisle—although twice a month someone tells me, "You're next!" The worst part was, if you'd asked me a year ago, I would've faked like I didn't believe you; now I actually don't.

*What the hell is taking him so long to pop the question?*

I couldn't help but think that Lamar and Lindsay met two years after I started dating Adam. In fact, I was there when they met inside an amazing Brooklyn house party where we made really bad cocktails in red cups and ate pizza with no plates. Although I wasn't looking, the house was filled with cute guys—so I pretended to be Patti Stanger and played matchmaker for my three sorority sisters who had joined me for the festivities.

Now Lindsay and Lamar were getting married, and I still wasn't—and now I really didn't want to get out of bed.

I did eventually and made it to work by 7:07 a.m. By the time I got there, I no longer felt the overwhelming wave of unhappiness—slightly mixed with anxiety and topped with cluelessness—that almost trapped me in bed on Valentine's Day. But in an effort to cheer myself up just a bit, I decided to play a practical joke on my sister, since I knew I wouldn't be sending a "Guess who's engaged?" e-mail for a while. I Gchatted Jasmine that exact message, snickering because I'd done this two times before, and she'd freaked out every single time.

WHO?! she replied in record time.

…, I typed back, trying to delay the inevitable, the re-realization that I still wasn't engaged.

My sorority sister Lindsay. Haha! I just wanted to make your heart jump.

LOL, she replied, probably already knowing that was coming.

Did it?! I teased.

I WAS preparing a SHUT THE FRONT DOOR response for you! HAHAHA, Jasmine typed.

Why do I find pleasure in this? I said, sniggling—the laugh you make when you're halfway between snickering and giggling.

Cause ur dumb lol

Lawd knows I may never get married at this pace—so I do this to scare you lol

It was cute. Plus I know you would never Gchat the news.

Yeah, I'm better than that.

# Chapter 4

The first time I saw Adam, I asked myself, "Who is *that*?" and was determined to find out the answer. He was in a bright Smurf-blue blazer, tailored across his broad shoulders. A mixed-looking blond beauty was holding his arm around her shoulder. The growing line outside Tuscana West, a now defunct restaurant-turned-nightclub in the McPherson Square section of D.C., parted for them. Girls like that didn't wait in line and neither did Adam. Someone tapped the bouncer to let the two of them in, along with anyone else they pointed out behind them.

As a person new to D.C. nightlife, I was utterly intrigued by it. I loved the fact that I could casually run into D.C.'s pseudo-celebrities—people who, by day, more than likely occupied a boring government job but by night became the District's scenesters. They ran the city in an allure that brought them local celebrity status. At only twenty-eight, Adam was one of the youngest players.

I had already tried my hand at getting into Tuscana West, only to be told it would be $40 each for my girls and me. Nope, there was no way I was parting with that much money to go party in a restaurant. Instead, I did what most recent college grads did—I waited outside for the Let Out.

The Let Out was when everyone who had been partying all night long inside a club left. They were looking sweaty and worn down and we were there looking ever fresh and ready to meet all the guys who were leaving. It's basically the same thing as being in the club, but instead you do it for free—outside!

I had already texted the guy I was dating at the time, letting him know I was outside. Brian and I had dated for four years throughout college, but he never wanted to put an official title on it. And me, being unsure of my worth and stupid as hell, never forced him to give me a title. I accepted the gray area that he put us in, even if I was pretty sure he wasn't dating anyone else. That night Brian texted me back saying he was on his way out. *Shit*. Just when I got that notification on my Nextel (remember when everyone had those?!), an awful-looking guy walked up to me. He had a familiar look in his eye—a look that said at the end of this conversation he wanted to walk away with my number. Not happening.

I really didn't want to be caught talking to this dude. Number one, he was unfortunate-looking, and number two, Brian was the jealous type. If I was caught talking to any guy, it would be three days before his anger wore off and he'd return my calls. I really didn't need that right now. Spotting Adam out of the corner of my wandering eye, I quickly turned my head and said:

"Adam! Hey, Adam. Remember me? It's Joi. You invited me to one of your parties at Cloud."

"Oh yeah, what's up?" He spun around slowly, looking uninterested. The blonde who had been on his arm had disappeared before the evening wound down, I guess.

Stepping into his personal space, I whispered in his ear, "Listen, can you get this guy to leave? My *friend* is coming out here at any second and he's the jealous type."

"Sure. Where's your boyfriend?"

"My *friend*," I corrected, "is coming out now."

"Okay," he said as he bear-hugged me, suffocating me in a cocoon-like grip that made me stand on my tiptoes with my arms bone straight stuck to my side. I tried to scream but nothing was coming out. In my peripheral, I saw Brian coming out of Tuscana West with a smile on his face that was immediately wiped off like something smacked him. Walking up right behind us, he stopped, only to look me deep in my eyes with envy-hate. Without saying a word, he walked off.

Knowingly, that was when Adam let me out of his death grip.

"You asshole! Why did you do that?" I said, my words dripping with fire.

"You're welcome," Adam said with a smile filled with audacity.

He friended me on Facebook the next day.

Falling in love with Adam was easy.

There wasn't much I disliked about him. He was everything a man was supposed to be: strong, attentive, decisive, protective, and fiercely loyal to his friends. Although he could be aloof to strangers—a quality that benefitted him in the courtroom—he was warm and inviting to me. And that endeared him to me. That I somehow was different.

In the weeks after our run-in outside Tuscana West, I found myself talking to him more and more—as his friend. And it was a sincere friendship. Somehow neither of us immediately thought to actually date each other. It wasn't until about two months later that I realized I spoke to him daily. I actually spoke to him more than I would speak to my own mother, and we chatted at least three times a week for hours. Somehow, Adam's voice had begun to put me to sleep every night and wake me up each morning.

It happened without my noticing, like a moon getting caught in an unseen gravitational pull. He drew me in with interesting conversation—not necessarily romantic, but stimulating. We would discuss and intensely debate everything from basketball to New York Fashion Week to the best way to smother chicken—with gravy from a can or making the gravy from scratch. And he always wanted my opinion on something. Initially, it was the D.C. night scene that intrigued him, and then it became any- and everything. Adam called at lunch to decide between the bento box or the chicken box. He called while shopping for socks to get my take on stripes or argyle, and he called while picking up dinner at the grocery store to let me weigh in on preseasoned salmon or baked chicken. It seemed he not only wanted my opinion, but he also started to need it. And his needing me made me feel special. I had never felt needed like that before.

Adam seemed less interested in how I looked and more interested in what I had to say. After one hours-long sparring about God knows what, Adam ended the debate with, "Your mind excites me." It's still one of the best compliments I've ever received.

He was a rare change of pace. He seemed to value every opinion I had, which only empowered me to consider him as a serious dating option. Why wouldn't I want a man like this, someone who wanted to know my mind and not just my body? This was the type of man I wanted as the head of my household, one who respected me immensely.

Adam fit. Without force. He just appeared in my life and I couldn't imagine what it was like before he was there because it seemed like he was always there...or at least like he was always supposed to be there.

I first realized I was in love with Adam after a night of partying in D.C. before we made it official. The two of us—along with my friend Felicia—decided to hit up Ben's Chili Bowl to grab food to soak up the alcohol we had in our system, and nothing does that better than cheese fries and a half smoke.

By that time, Adam and I had been friends for five months and we now referred to each other as "besties." But I didn't want to be his best friend anymore. I wanted to be his girlfriend, but I wasn't sure how to make that leap, especially without a little sign. A little sign that said he liked me too.

Felicia and I happily wobbled in our heels, like deer just learning how to walk, into Ben's. We sat down in a booth while Adam grabbed our orders from the counter. Lost in our intoxicated conversation, Adam startled me when he bounced down in the space next to me. Then he put his arm around me. It was the first time he did that.

Felicia looked at us with half disgust and half admiration as Adam threw his weight onto me. Putting his lips close to my ear so no one else could hear, he whispered, "You know that feeling you get on the first day of second grade when you're kind of nervous and excited? That's how I felt when I first saw you tonight."

I felt like Sandy in *Grease*.

Felicia didn't know that this was the moment we were finally giving in to our feelings. She didn't know it was the first time he was showing public displays of affection. She didn't know that, under harsh fluorescent lights, inside this cracked-leather booth, and surrounded by whiffs of chili and cheese, we had just quietly tiptoed across an imaginary line from best friends to more than friends.

That night, unlike previous nights, I didn't hide the love I had for him behind the browns of my eyes when I looked in his direction. I let the light I felt for him shine through. I didn't look away when his eyes met mine. I let my eyes nestle into his like leaves falling off autumn trees. I didn't turn off the warm flush that rushed up the inside of my chest when he grabbed my hand only to let it go a second later. I let it race up my body to my cheeks, hot in their defection. And I didn't stifle my laugh and pretend he wasn't funny when he made a good joke, teasing him like a best friend would. I let myself finally lose control. Finally trust him. Finally hand my heart over to him.

Felicia, who is at times painfully blunt, blurted out, "You guys are cute." Then she nodded as if her inner voice agreed with her like, "Yeah, girl, they are."

We made it official a few weeks later, on the same weekend Barack Obama moved into the White House.

# Chapter 5

Later that afternoon, Adam picked me up from work, which is super romantic considering it's New York and I walk everywhere. My throbbing feet and monthly MetroCard were proof. To actually sit down in a car was a luxury, and I guess he wanted to spoil me.

This was our fifth Valentine's Day together, and we had finally exhausted all the cliché shit that you see in movies. This year, Adam wanted to grab groceries and cook at home, and by home he meant my apartment. When Adam came back from D.C., he moved into a three-level home in Jersey with his cousin Sheila and her nine-year-old daughter, so we never went over there. Dinner at home actually sounded nice, so I didn't fight him on it this time. We were fighting too much about petty stuff lately, and today I just wanted to get along.

We drove to Fairway Market in Harlem to gather supplies for the night's feast. We decided on lamb chops—my favorite—and asparagus with wild rice. To start, we'd have Boursin cheese, another one of my favorites, and salami, his favorite. For dessert,

Adam picked out mini pecan pies. It'd be a perfect three-course meal.

What Adam didn't know was that the real dessert would be in my bed. We hadn't had sex in two weeks. I guess when you've been with someone for five years, two weeks didn't seem like a long time...but then again it did. I read in some magazine that men need to have sex every three days or their balls feel like they're about to explode. I'm not sure if that's true. Regardless, it's not like we were in our forties with two kids. It was just us...and my dog. There was no reason why the fire had run out already.

So, I began searching Pinterest for ways to spice up tonight's bedroom dessert and stumbled upon this really cute idea. Some girl had bought a pair of lace panties and put it on a breakfast tray—a play on "sex on a platter." It was more kitschy than sexy, but it was funny, and so me. I love corny shit. It was perfect for tonight. Hopefully Adam would crack up laughing, then grab me and throw me onto the bed.

As we were walking out of the grocery store, we walked past a flower stand. I spotted my favorite flower, yellow roses. "Babe, I want those. What do you think? My flowers are dead anyway."

"No, you don't need it. C'mon! Let's go. It's cold," he said in a rushed tone, which annoyed me.

"Babe! I really want them, though," I whined, knowing that if I kept at it, I'd get my way eventually.

"Joi. Is it really necessary?"

"I'll buy them if it's that big of a deal," I said, pulling out my black Marc Jacobs wallet.

Adam's head lowered. "Sweetie, I know those are your favorites. I already bought you some. They're in the trunk. It was supposed to be a surprise."

"You did?!" I squealed, a wide smile spreading across my face. If I didn't have two hands full of groceries, I would have hugged him for remembering.

Adam was the better cook, so I let him do his thing in the kitchen when we got home to my apartment. Meanwhile, I hurried to the bedroom to set up the "sex on a platter." I decided to take what I saw on Pinterest and add something—some Sweethearts. However, being the type A person that I am, I picked out the candy hearts that had sexy messages on them like "Let's Get Busy" or "Kiss Me." How could he not laugh and then grab me and throw me onto the bed?

I had been in my work clothes too long, and the band on my stockings was starting to pinch my rib cage. So I quickly changed into my red-and-white sorority sweatpants and a crop top. Even when I was lounging around the house, I tried to maintain my sexy. Hell, I wasn't married yet.

I placed the sherbet-colored lace panties I had bought from Urban Outfitters on the all-white breakfast tray. The Sweethearts added the perfect touch in the corners. I was so proud that I took a picture on my iPhone—not that anyone would see it. Maybe I'd show my girls afterward for bragging rights.

Proud of my accomplishment, I sauntered back into the kitchen to see how dinner was coming along. It was virtually done, but Adam wanted to plate it. I swear he thought he was Bobby Flay. Being a good sous chef, I took out the plates and the wineglasses and placed them on the two upscale TV dinner trays that I bought from Pier 1. Okay *fine*, that I stole from my mother's house in

Maryland. My apartment wasn't big enough for a proper dining table anyway. Damn New York living.

"Do you remember our first Valentine's Day?" Adam asked. His back was still toward me as he hovered over what would be dinner in a few minutes, but I could tell he was smiling at the thought.

"I do," I said. "We were still in D.C. We cooked breakfast and then went to the mall to buy each other presents because neither of us had bothered to buy a gift."

"We were so lame," he said, gently laughing. His laugh was inviting. It was the type of laugh I hoped he'd have later when I pulled him into the bedroom.

"We were. I think we fell asleep that night watching the NBA All-Star Game...," I trailed off.

"Yeah, that part was dope. You still get cool points for not changing the channel."

"Oh yeah?"

"Yeah...," Adam said, pecking me lightly on the lips.

His voice hinted that he had more to say. After a few moments of him expertly moving our dinner from pans to plates, he finally spat it out. "That year I also asked if you thought I was the one."

"You did?" I asked.

I wasn't actually wondering if he had asked me that question years ago. I just replied instinctively, hoping the question would hide my nervousness and stall whatever he wondered next.

The kitchen—which was really a kitchenette inside my living room—all of a sudden felt hot. I walked over to the window not utilized by the air-conditioner unit and opened it. I invitingly gasped at the cold air that rushed in.

"Well, what did I say?" I finally asked him once I gathered my thoughts.

"You gave this long, drawn-out answer that didn't really answer the question," he said carefully without looking up at me. He seemed to be concentrating on thinly cutting the salami. "But you did end your rambling with, 'Whatever God wants.'"

He abruptly turned to me and smiled. I guess to reinforce that he wasn't necessarily upset about the ghost of Valentine's Day past.

I returned his smile by forcing my lips upward, but inside I wondered what made him bring up our first Valentine's Day. I forced out, "That sounds like me."

The conversation stood still—thick with questions unasked—while Adam finished plating dinner.

"I'm just glad we decided not to buy presents this year," Adam said, breaking the silence first.

Adam and I decided we weren't going to exchange presents primarily because we had just celebrated our fifth anniversary the month before and we kind of overdid it on the presents. If I wasn't getting an engagement ring, I at least wanted a great anniversary gift. And Adam delivered—he got me a beautiful brown Gucci tote. I got him a suit—you know, the *good* kind. The kind that needed to be tailored. Plus, Adam said, "Every day is Valentine's Day with you," and with that we balked at the made-up holiday.

After dinner, I took Adam by the hand and led him to my bedroom. I walked in my sexiest "I am Beyoncé, bitch" walk and told him I had something special for him. When I flipped on the light, his eyes squinted to see what was on the bed. As he got closer, one half of his mouth went up in a smile while the other remained limp.

"What is this?" he said, not sure whether to laugh or not.

I started laughing, encouraging him that it was okay to laugh at me. "It's sex on a platter, babe."

In my mind, this was where he kissed me, grabbed me, and threw me on the bed. Instead, he looked down at my sweatpants, let go of my hand, and said, "It may have worked better if you weren't wearing those."

Then he walked back to the kitchen to grab the pecan pies. We ended up falling asleep on the couch with the game on.

# Chapter 6

Spring is the best time in Harlem. Lawn chairs magically appear on the sidewalk, and every third block or so, a card table pops up along with it. *Abuelas* sit watching their grandkids run aimlessly down the sidewalk, while another neighbor sweeps a patch of sidewalk clear of trash and bright green leaves.

It was the perfect sunny—but not too hot—day to take Arista to the dog park at 135th and Saint Nicholas.

New York dog parks are interesting experiences; either families come with their kids, making Fido play fetch, or a lonely guy sits there with his iPod, waiting for a girl with a teacup Yorkie or a perfectly manicured poodle to walk in. I always made sure I wore sunglasses and brought a book and an iPod to deter any confidence the lonely guy might have to strike up a conversation. It never really worked.

After climbing what seemed like a hundred stairs to the metal gate that led to the dog park—I didn't mind; it'd be the only exercise I'd have all week—I let my little doxie off her leash and she sprinted away, ears flapping happily in the wind.

I sauntered over to one of the benches, with my earbuds secured in my ear. My sunglasses blocked out any sign of a lonely guy as I raised my book to my face as a decoy. I wasn't actually reading. Instead, I was thinking about what Adam said inside that D.C. nightclub—over a year ago—that he hadn't mentioned since.

A few months after that New Year's Eve, I downloaded the Tiffany app to my iPhone in hopes of it being a gentle reminder. I forced him to—and he didn't seem to mind—peruse the options for engagement rings. I realized then that we had very different tastes on what an engagement ring should look like. He didn't mind three horizontal diamonds as an engagement ring, while I gasped at the idea—only a solitaire would count. He also liked a gold band. How 1970s. Only white gold or rose gold please, though platinum was preferred.

"How much should I spend on the ring?" he asked, genuinely wanting to know.

The second Valentine's Day we celebrated together, he ordered black diamond earrings online for me. Not knowing how much he should spend on them, what showed up were the smallest black diamonds the world had ever pressed together. The earrings were smaller than the point on a ballpoint pen. No bullshit. Ever since then I told him to check with me before buying diamonds.

"Definitely don't spend more than ten thousand dollars. More than that and we might as well use that money for a down payment on a house," I remember telling him. "But definitely more than five thousand—seven thousand probably."

Why hadn't he proposed yet or at least asked me my ring size? (It's a size 7 if my future husband is reading this.) What the hell was he waiting on?

All the while, every time I logged onto Facebook, I saw another photo of a perfectly manicured hand with a ring attached to it. If the ring was ugly, I didn't feel so bad that it wasn't me. But if the ring was perfection—a thin platinum band with a solitaire diamond bigger than one carat, cushion cut—well, then I felt an ingratiating pang deep in my insides, the annoying feeling of envy.

And I rarely felt envy. I was blessed beyond measure. I wouldn't dare call it lucky. I am who I am because of how I was raised and who I was raised by. My mother is a beloved preacher. Back when it wasn't necessarily kosher for women to pastor, she did. She was the pastor of three churches in Maryland until she successfully ran for bishop of the African Methodist Episcopal Church—the first woman to do so. Boss. My dad is a retired NBA player, and it's where I get my model height and physique from. I'm a non-awkward 5'10". I don't slouch; years of ballet made me appreciate my height. When I walk into a room, I'm often hard to miss because I am usually a head taller than everyone else.

We never struggled...at least financially speaking. Growing up, I usually got what I wanted. Now, I wasn't a spoiled brat. Mom would often tell us if we wanted the new Cabbage Patch Kid, or whatever the new hot toy of the moment was, we'd have to earn it by either helping our grandmother with some chore or by cleaning our room and keeping it clean. The "keeping it clean" wasn't the hard part since we always had a housekeeper.

In life, I had gotten everything that I set out to get. I breezed through college with a 4.0 while clubbing every weekend without fail. I was averagely popular at school, joining the best sorority on campus—the one with the prettiest girls, who were involved and who did community service. I got a master's degree in journalism—another task that I seemed to breeze through. That led me to get an amazing job as an entertainment producer at one of the top TV networks in the country. I had friends. I always had a boyfriend or at least a persistent admirer. I loved God and went to church regularly but wasn't too stuck up or too much of a holy roller not to stand on a couch on Saturday night and twerk with the best of them.

Although I was able to get all these things—a loving family, supportive friends, and a good career—without much effort, the one thing that I really wanted, which was a family of my own, seemed like the hardest thing to attain. The husband, the two kids, and the dog—my own team to be a part of, to contribute to the world, to have my back, to fill me up, was so far away from me.

I couldn't just make this happen how I made getting a job at the network happen—I stalked my boss until he finally broke down and offered me a part-time position. I turned that position down—Hello! I need benefits—until there was a full-time position available and I happily accepted. It took two years, but that goal was met.

I tried to remember that patience is a virtue, and old church sayings like "God is an on-time God" and "He's already ordered my steps" and all that, but nothing seemed to alleviate this ingratiating feeling. Like nails on a chalkboard, my body was in a constant wince of want.

It's the same feeling you get when you're the last to get picked for a softball team. There's only like three of y'all left and you're all looking at each other with that awful you-suck feeling. I guess that's the feeling of unwantedness. Even if you're not the very last person to get picked, you still feel bad because no one was excited to pick you.

I feel that way every day because every day someone else is getting engaged or getting married or having a baby or throwing their one-year-old a birthday party or posting professional pictures from a newborn photo shoot (like, since when did newborns get photo shoots?!) and I wasn't.

I was just working—the same old shit I've been doing since I left college seven years ago.

When I didn't see people I knew getting engaged, married, or posting about *every . . . little . . . thing* their kid did as if it were breaking news, I turned on the TV. With a casual flip through the hundreds of cable channels, I'd see *Say Yes to the Dress*, *The Bachelor*, *Bridezillas*, and any David Tutera spin-off and would still be reminded that I'm sitting on the couch, alone.

My thoughts of self-deprecation were interrupted by a text message. I put down my decoy book and stared at the phone.

My work wife is pregnant, Ashlee texted, with the iPhone indicating she was still typing.

Ashlee was my best friend from middle school. Well, she hated me in middle school, but by high school she realized just how cool I was and we've been attached at the hip ever since.

everyone is having babies and getting married and i'm just over here doing nothing, she said, unbothered by punctuation or capitalization.

lol yup, I typed, knowing all too well the feeling. i almost posted that on FB with a picture of me but then i didn't

good.

The period on the end of her text meant she meant that. Yeah, that wouldn't be a good look—as much as I was envious, I didn't need anyone to know that. I tried to one-up her news, and after seeing what I saw on Instagram that afternoon, I knew it wouldn't be hard.

remember leslie? I asked, equally unbothered by capitalization. the lesbian?

yeah well she just got engaged today. to a man. i just want u to marinate on that.

bye joi, she said—a contradictory statement because she wasn't actually ending the conversation. She just wanted me to know how ridiculous the news was.

Let me clear something up. I'm happy for Leslie, sincerely happy for *her*. My feelings of pissedoffness had nothing to do with her but everything to do with me and how the nuptial gods must really think I'm out here bullshitting if even lesbians can get married to men before me, a heterosexual through and through. Like, I didn't just join this team. I've been on this team. And I'm still out here ringless. It doesn't make any damn sense.

Just as I was about to go off the deep end, I called my sister. She could surely understand.

"Jasmine."

"Yes, sissy. How are you?"

"Girl, I'm over this."

"What are you talking about?" she asked. A tablespoon of exasperation was in her voice, but I was her little sister and I didn't care!

"It seems like I've been waiting forever for Adam to pop the question." (I thought I heard her say, "Here we go…" in the background, but I kept talking anyway.) "I've been on my best behavior. I haven't nagged him. I haven't even brought up New Year's in months. When he comes over and leaves his clothes in the middle of the living room, instead of yelling at him to put his clothes on the chair in the bedroom, I just pick them up and put them there myself. I don't say shit when he uses every utensil to cook dinner…so why hasn't he proposed yet? Serious-fucking-ly!"

"Oh, please," Jazz said in her usual know-it-all voice. "Men don't know what they want. It's up to us to tell them what they want."

"What do you mean?" I asked earnestly, mentally ready to take notes.

"If you want to get engaged, you have to step it up. You can't just drop little hints. There needs to be a real discussion."

"We've discussed it! He told me he wanted me to be his wife on New Year's, remember? We looked at rings together. Like, I'm not just sitting over here hoping and wishing and thinking."

"Okay, but you also need to play the game. It's time for the Engagement Game."

"What the hell is the Engagement Game?"

"Oh Lord, okay. Let me break it down. If you want to make sure you get a ring by the end of the year, you gotta do five things. Number one: Make a list of everything you want in a husband. Be as specific as possible. Then put that list somewhere so that you'll see it every day—post it on your mirror, put it on your dresser, wherever," Jasmine said, as if she were reading off a recipe for pineapple upside-down cake.

"Why do I need to make a list of my husband when I already know Adam is my husband?"

Jasmine sighed as if I was supposed to already understand. "You've been with this man for five years, but is he *really* the man you had envisioned for yourself?"

I sat silenced, pondering the question I somehow had never asked myself. Sensing this, Jasmine continued. "So, write that list to see if Adam even matches up."

"Okay...," I grumbled.

"Are you listening?!"

"Sorry, Jasmine. What did you say?"

"I saaaid...," she snapped. "Number two: As much as you take care of him, take care of yourself. No man wants a woman who doesn't have it together. Is your hair flawless? Do you have a manicure? How's your skin? You need to go to the gym or buy a DVD or something to get rid of that little pooch above your cooch, and you need to make sure you wax down there—regularly!

"Number three: Do you let him go out with his friends? Let him! Because before you met him, he had a life and you need to make sure you have one too! But more than that, you need to focus on your life outside of the relationship. When's the last time you've been on a date by yourself?"

"What do you mean?" I asked, seriously confused. Why would I want to go on a date by myself? Now, I love myself but that doesn't mean I wanna take me out. It sounded stupid.

Jasmine sighed before she rattled off, "Number four: Date yourself. What do *you* like to do? Instead of always forcing him to come along with you, go by yourself. You'll never be happy with someone else until you're happy alone."

"Yeah, that makes sense...Anything else?"

"Are you sure that he's the one?"

"Yes! At least I think so. I pray to God all the time to confirm for me what I already know. He's the best man next to Daddy—he treats me well, takes care of me, believes in me. He's my biggest fan. I love him, sissy. I really do."

"Okay! Okay. I just had to know before I told you the fifth and final step. And it's an important one. Do *not* do this unless you're for sure, for sure that he's the one."

"Okay...what is it?"

"Number five: Cook. And not just any meal. It's called 'Engagement Chicken.' I read about it in *Glamour* magazine, and basically it's this meal you cook to make a man marry you. I know it sounds crazy, but it's supposed to work."

"Are you fucking serious?" I said.

"Girl...just try it. But don't waste it. The chicken is the real deal. You pretty much just roast a whole chicken. And a man will think, 'Hey, if she can cook a meal like this, she can be the mother of my kids.' I don't know, sissy. I really don't, but I read it works!"

"Well hell, I'll try anything..."

"Well, you're going to have to. You're twenty-eight and you're not getting any younger."

That comment stung. I knew she meant well, but goddamn.

"All right, sissy," I said. "We'll talk later."

"Okay, love! Let me know how it goes. And congratulations!"

"On what?"

"Your engagement, duh! You're next!"

I smiled, then picked up the pink leash to lock up Arista and head home.

*Chapter 7*

W*amp! Wamp! Wamp! Wamp!*

Another Monday. Another day in the newsroom.

As I rode the train to work—my eyes puffy and back aching from this ungodly hour to be awake—I sat and thought about what Jasmine had said. I hadn't started the Engagement Game yet. I was too busy trying to book my interviews this week: I had two "Real Housewives" coming in and was trying to get confirmed to cover the red carpet premiere of *Scandal.* The third season was kicking off Thursday and I *had* to talk to Kerry Washington, even if it meant slumming it by working on a carpet, which I hated doing. These days, most celebs came to me to be interviewed in our studio, but for some—like Kerry—I'd do anything to chat.

I had never really asked myself what I wanted in a husband. I figured that when I met him, I'd just know. When I met Adam I wasn't even thinking about marriage—I was only twenty-three then—but I knew now that he definitely had the raw material to make a great husband.

Historically, I haven't been particularly picky, but I definitely had a type. I mean, I'm tall, so my husband had to have height on him. But I've dated a guy who, when I stood on the street and he stood on the sidewalk, was finally able to look into my eyes. (Don't laugh!) All of my past suitors have been ambitious, but not necessarily successful in the common sense of the word. I've dated air-conditioning installers, one dude who worked at Target, preachers, and even professional basketball players. I quickly realized I couldn't be a basketball wife like my mother. Nowadays, players think they're demigods and that not cheating on their wives is a moment to celebrate instead of normal relationship behavior. I've even dated guys who were between jobs—as long as they had enough money to take me on a decent date, I didn't really ask a lot of questions.

But with all the guys I've dated, I never felt like they were the one—until Adam. Adam was someone who walked in the room and captured everyone's attention. He conjured up a magical curiosity that made women want to get to know him. He had something better than swag. He had intrigue.

Shit. Deep in my thoughts, I didn't see that puddle at the edge of the sidewalk, a reminder of yesterday's thunderstorm. Now I'd have to sit in the cold newsroom with one wet shoe. Just great.

By the time I made it to my cubicle on the far end of the newsroom, I was ready to take on Number One of the Engagement Game and write my list of what I wanted in a husband. I reached in this week's workbag to find my journal. Today, my workbag was a gold metallic bag that I got as a gift bag from the premiere of *Being Mary Jane* last month. Oh, the perks! I looked for my black lineless journal but couldn't find it. *Hmm, that sucks.* I always kept my journal on me. The only other thing to write on in the bag was a DVD. It was an advance copy of the first few episodes of Bravo's

*Million Dollar Listing.* What the hell. The back of the screener was a good place to write down my list.

I wrote the list in all caps to let the universe know I was serious.

TALL DARK HANDSOME
DEGREED
GOD-FEARING/CHURCHGOING
AMBITIOUS
ENCOURAGING
AMAZING LOVER
AFFECTIONATE
PURSUES ME
RESPECTFUL/RESPECTABLE
NOT A SEXUAL DEVIANT
NOT ABUSIVE
LOVES ME + MY FAMILY
RESPECTS MY LEGACY

Focusing so intently on my list o' husband, I didn't notice Preston, another producer at the network, standing near my desk. No one told Preston that his glasses were entirely too big for his face and that was why they always slid down his nose. He always wore clothes in the khaki family, making his appearance mirror his personality, like it could be camouflaged in the background. And, honestly, if you squinted, he looked like Screech from *Saved by the Bell*—and was just as smart. Preston and I had this secret competition. It was so unspoken, he probably wasn't even in on it.

Preston looked harmless, but he kept me on my toes. He was hungry. Although he didn't have the looks, he had the credentials to back up his ambitions. Even when I didn't want to compete with him, I was forced to. He was always looking for and finding cracks in my professional armor.

"What's up, Preston," I said in a tone that implied I really didn't care to know what was up with him.

"Oh, Megan asked me to come over and say good job on your Spike interview," he said, referring to our boss. "How'd it go?"

"Why wouldn't she just ask me that?"

"Ummm, I'm not sure…Well, how'd it go?" Preston continued, unable to hide how pressed he was to see how well or bad it went. After interviewing the director back in February, the story had finally gone live on our website some months later.

"It was great. We laughed about Carmelo, spoke about the movie. Listen, Preston, I have a lot to catch up on. Can we chat later?" I asked.

"Of course. Oh, and Megan said to e-mail her the picture you snapped with Spike Lee. You *did* get a picture, right? With the mic flag visible in the shot? We need those pictures so we can promote our work," he said, trying to convince me of the importance of something I was already well aware of.

"Of course I got a picture. I'll send it to her. Thanks."

I said the last word in such a way that he knew it was his cue.

After I downloaded the picture to my computer, I winced at my bare face. Of course that picture was picked up by the trades the next day—me wearing a wrinkled orange shirt, without a drop of makeup on my face and my hair telling the world it was 12 o'clock.

I decided right then and there I'd never be caught at an interview like that again and would round up a few products—foundation, eyeliner, and mascara—from Duane Reade to keep at my desk for emergencies.

At lunch I randomly decided to remove my relationship status—which proudly declared I was "in a relationship"—from Facebook. Perhaps the move would send a ripple through the universe, inciting panic in Adam and making him magically propose to me.

It's crazy how a woman's mind works.

Now, every time I looked at my profile, right under my picture, the stupid website asked me in large font, "What is your relationship status?" Since there's no option for "Miserable," I left it blank.

This was a perfect time to quit Facebook. I'd joined Mark Zuckerberg's social network during my sophomore year in college. My forever friend Sydney, who went to Boston University, told me to join because it was the new hot thing on her campus, so I did. I joined and didn't log on for another semester. I didn't really know what to do with it—that was, until the rest of University of Maryland College Park caught up. Back then there were no photo albums or even uploading photos at all, really. You just selected what classes you were in and could see what classes others were in. There was no feed or mini-feed. There were no annoying game invitations and there were no corporate pages. Still, there was one feature that had been there from the beginning—the relationship status. Honestly, I'd never been concerned about it until I started dating Adam.

In college, I hadn't dated anyone seriously enough to warrant changing my relationship status. But with Adam I couldn't wait to change it. Of course, I didn't want to be too thirsty and turned off my notification settings so that, although I did change it, it wouldn't show up in everyone's feed. That's embarrassing. It just yells to your virtual friends, "HEY, BITCHES. I'M FINALLY HAVING SEX ON THE REGULAR!" Like, calm down.

But when I asked Adam to change his status, he refused. He said he didn't want people in our business. I told him we didn't have to link profiles necessarily (you know, have it say, "Adam Jacobson is in a relationship with Joi-Marie McKenzie") but he still refused. I eventually dropped the issue because I didn't want to get into a fight over a social network.

But now I think I'm going to stop logging on completely. Not because Adam still refused to cross the picket line and change his status, but because every day I log on, someone else was getting engaged, showing off their sonogram, posing for selfies at romantic locales, and I just couldn't take it anymore. Every time I scrolled down, it felt like someone was ripping out my heart. I couldn't even be happy anymore when someone posted the obligatory hand-on-belly "I'm expecting" picture.

I thought I could be stronger than this. Hell, my thighs don't touch. I have a master's degree from an Ivy League school, I have long natural hair and nails and eyelashes and eyebrows. I have edges! I don't have acne (anymore, thank God!) and I have good credit.

Since when did I become a bitter, self-involved, obsessive "happily-ever-after" junkie?

So, bye-bye, Facebook.

# Chapter 8

You never plan it like this, but when you have a boyfriend, he becomes your top calendar priority. You could be at home wearing sweatpants, with your feet up, hair matted, and there's a crisp scent of BO because you didn't bother to shower—the perfect Saturday morning. But if your man calls, asking if he can come over, you hop up so fast like a firecracker just went off under your booty. You sprint to the shower to take one-step-up-from-a-whore-bath, and rush to brush that guacamole taste off your tongue to prep for that quick kiss he'll give you when he walks in the door.

Having a boyfriend is the perfect excuse for getting out of all those girlfriend things you just don't want to do. I remember one friend asking, "Joi, you're the only person with a car in the city. Can you drive me to Ikea?" *Girl, no. Adam is about to come over and he wants to redecorate the apartment. I'm going to be occupied all day.* "Joi, don't you want to come over and watch *Scandal* with us?" *Girl. Can you believe I made Adam a fan of the show? He's coming over now to watch it. He hates when I watch an episode without him.* Knowing good and goddamn well he ain't coming over. I mean, can't a girl prefer to watch *Scandal* alone so she doesn't miss a second of Shonda Rhimes's dialogue? If you miss a syllable, you miss a lot!

Still, I had been using the Adam-get-out-of-jail-free card too often with my girls. So when I got an invite for Sydney's birthday brunch, I RSVP'd immediately—especially since brunch was the one activity that didn't require me to stay up late or get up too early. Plus, Syd had picked my favorite Harlem spot, 5 and Diamond.

I've known Sydney since before we could form real sentences. We went to elementary, middle, and high school together. One of those forever friends who you don't have to talk to every day, but when you do, you fall back into lockstep. She was the perfect type of friend, one who didn't require too much and didn't ask for too much. She understood me without me having to explain myself.

Sydney was celebrating her twenty-ninth birthday, a milestone for any human being but a scary moment for a single woman in New York City. If it took Carrie Bradshaw ten years to get engaged to Mr. Big, why should we expect any different?

It was the perfect summer day for brunch outside on the hot New York sidewalk. My tan had yet to stick, so I took the chair opposite the sun and rolled up my shorts to prevent as much farmer's tan as I possibly could. No one at the birthday girl's table knew each other. But we all knew Sydney, a dancer who had practiced ballet, modern, tap, and jazz all of her life. Syd and I had become friends over our love of dance, but while she went on to get her bachelor of fine arts in the art form, I traded in my pointe shoes for a laptop.

Even at a table of mostly complete strangers, after the second bourbon mimosa or so, the topic turned to relationships. Everyone at the table was single, except for me. I got the biggest groan from the group when I said I was happy in my relationship, although that wasn't entirely the truth. I tried to console them with the fact that I was technically single, since I still checked that box when I filled out my taxes. So really we were all in the same boat. Like my late aunt Lisa used to say, "You're not married until you're married." After that, they agreed that I could join in on the conversation of lamenting about being single, how to tell if he's serious, and when to text back after you texted him but he doesn't text back immediately.

We all rattled off our ages because that sort of defined just how comfortable you were with being single. Sydney was the eldest at twenty-nine. I clocked in right behind her at twenty-eight while the other two brunch guests—Naomi and John—were a measly twenty-three and twenty-four, respectively. They still had a lifetime to complain about being single, it seemed. Sydney and I, not so much.

"I'm sick of dating. I'm looking for a husband," Sydney said in her singsongy voice.

"Girl, me too!" I yelled a little too loudly, thanks to the bourbon.

John, a professional dancer with the American Ballet Theatre, turned to me in dramatic fashion, as dancers do, and let his sunglasses slide down his nose slightly. "Why are you worried about getting married? You look career-oriented."

I could've slapped the shit out of John.

What the hell did career-oriented look like? I was sitting there with hair that needed to be done, wearing a flowy white top from J.Crew, shiny shorts that came to a tasteful length, and nude sandals. One doesn't look career-oriented in a loose top, right? I looked more ready for Coachella than a boardroom. I could see him saying that if I was dressed in a suit for brunch, but I wasn't. And I hadn't even told the group what I did for a living yet. Seriously, what does career-oriented look like and how can I get rid of it? Why can't I look like a wife and a mother? Or why can't I be both? I don't want to be a woman who wants it all. I just want a career and a family—just those two things. Is the universe listening?!

Wanting just those two things was not new. In fact, it was the same thought I had when I broke up with Gary, the guy who I thought was my soul mate. I still think Gary is my soul mate, but perhaps we don't end up with our soul mates. I met Gary at a church down south that I was visiting with my mom years ago, while I was still in undergrad. I didn't know who he was, but he was breezy and held a quiet confidence that read he didn't have to convince anyone of how cool he was.

I was talking with some friends after the service was over, when Gary walked up to our circle. "Hi, Ariane. Hi, Laura. Hi, Felice." He stopped at me, barely passing me a glance, and proceeded with the conversation.

Not one to hold my tongue, I asked in a not-so-godly tone, "You're not going to speak to me?"

"Oh...I...I thought we did that 'I see you, you see me,' silent acknowledgment thing."

"No, I don't do that. I speak to people," I snapped back, forgetting God was in the building. It was actually nice to see this guy, whoever he was, thrown off a bit.

"I'm...Gary, Pastor Richardson's son," he offered.

"Oh!" My mouth was always getting me into trouble. "Nice to meet you, Gary," I said, catching myself.

Gary told me later that that was the moment he fell in like with me. As prissy as I looked, I had a certain bite. Most people from Baltimore do.

I wouldn't see Gary until a year later, at another church in another city. This time it was New York, where he had moved to go to divinity school. I was again tagging along with my mother to visit the church. We made a weekend out of it by visiting family in Rochester, then taking in a Broadway show.

Gary and I eventually had our first date in New York at some restaurant I can't even remember. I do remember that when we walked in we saw Michelle Williams from Destiny's Child, sitting facing outward at her table. I guess she was waiting for someone to recognize her. I couldn't even drink yet, not being twenty-one and all, but Gary had ordered me a cosmopolitan and I drank it. He kept my drink on his side of the table in case the waiter cared. He didn't.

At the end of the date, when men usually grab the check, rush you into a cab, and avoid calling you for another six days in an effort to keep their rotation intact, Gary asked if I wanted to do something. Unsure, but down to do whatever he wanted to do, I agreed to take the twenty-minute cab ride to Harlem, where he lived near school. We found a bench right on the edge of St. Nicholas Park and 135th Street and talked. We talked about everything under the sun: music, politics, poetry, and we didn't stop talking until we saw the sunrise. He never tried to kiss me. Gary genuinely wanted to get to know me. He told me he had a man journal and would sometimes write poems in it. I told him I was working on a book called Books Comes Before Boys, Even in the Dictionary. (Clearly, that book didn't pan out.) He said that was the most original line he had ever heard. I laughed with my head tilted up to the young sunrays.

When the sun decided to creep up above the trees, he looked at me in that weird way men look at you when you don't know if they want to kiss you or look away.

"What?" I asked, playfully inviting him into the moment.

"I don't know. Maybe you look extra pretty in the morning," he said.

My heart melted down my shirt and rolled into the street. With no traffic yet to run it over, it came back on the bench and sat in Gary's lap. He had me.

The sun came up and the hours continued to roll by. Neither one of us wanted to leave, for fear that this had all been a wonderful dream that was now over.

After that overnight date, I went back home to Maryland, but Gary and I spent every day talking endlessly on the phone like teenagers. In three months, we still hadn't kissed and had barely made it past holding hands. It was the longest foreplay I've ever had. It made just looking at him send an electric current up my spine. I even changed his ringtone on my Nextel to "Son of a Preacher Man" by Dusty Springfield.

Then Gary confessed. "Joi, I'm not gonna lie to you," he started. "You've got me inside out. I think about you all the time and when I'm not thinking about you, it's not because I don't want to; it's because other things in the day drag my attention away from you, but when it's over I go back to thinking about you."

The statement was so fulfilling I could've survived on those words alone for food. But I played it cool.

"You're mumbling. I can't hear you," I teased.

"Oh. Well, I have to speak up because I don't want to say this twice," he said steadily, before rushing out, "I want to be with you, so if you want to be with me . . ."

I don't remember how he finished the sentence and I don't remember what my reply to him was thanks to the excitement vibrating on the inside of my head. But he knew it was a yes. Imagine, a relationship proposal—and I use that word very loosely, unfortunately—so romantic and perfect you'd think the relationship would turn out to be so too.

But no.

I visited him frequently thanks to the Northeast Regional Amtrak train, but Gary got busy and started making excuses about why he couldn't see me . . . even though we lived just three hours away from each other. He said it was school. I imagined it was another woman but didn't have the proof to back it up. Perhaps more telling, though, I didn't have the energy to find out why.

Gary was a bright red balloon on a small white string, and I had let the string go. He was floating away.

No man had ever made me feel like Gary again. We had such a special kernel of intimacy it often felt like I was getting shocked by a downed live wire every time I was with him. He more than loved me. It was a love that dripped down to the darkest parts of the soul. It was so deep and careful and caring and loving; no man has ever cared to see me that deeply before. And I was afraid that no man would ever try again.

I broke up with him after he didn't pick up my phone call, but when I called from my dorm roommate's phone, a number he didn't have stored, right afterward, he answered. I figured right then and there that if he wouldn't take my calls, he wouldn't take a single thing from me ever again.

Although I broke it off, trying to maintain a semblance of self-respect, I was depressed because it just seemed like I was losing at every relationship I attempted to have. Because if you recall, I was still sort of dating Brian at the time too. (No judgment!) My friends tried to cheer me up the best way they knew how, but the cheer-up refrain that irritated me the most during that bounce-back was, "Well, now you can focus on your career!" As if to think I wasn't focused on school and my career before. As if to think that I couldn't do both simultaneously. I shouted back at them, "I don't want to just focus on my career! I want to focus on him too." It was almost as if they couldn't comprehend that giving both aspects of my life—love and a career—equal weight at equal times was possible. Why did I have to choose? Why did it have to be one or the other?

I knew it was possible. My mom was engaged to my dad before she even graduated from Morgan State University. By twenty-one and twenty-four, respectively, they were married and off starting a new life in Arizona, after my dad got traded from the Baltimore Bullets to the Phoenix Suns. Although my mom's life revolved around my dad's earlier in their relationship, eventually it balanced out when my dad retired from the NBA ten years later, and my mom began her eventual ascent to bishopdom. What they had done in between, however, was create a relationship where each was expected to thrive and contribute, not only on the job but also at home to raise their three children. And it worked. When Dad was in the NBA and couldn't change a lightbulb, Mom did it. (Back in the '70s, there was an actual rule for players that they couldn't climb ladders. So in the McKenzie household, Momma changed the lightbulbs.) And when Mom was working late nights at the church, Dad did our laundry and dropped us off at dance practice or the football game. My mom had it all—maybe not at the same time, but she had it.

I was so deep in my memories that John's "career-oriented" comment unwittingly set off that by the time I offered him the obligatory smile he expected, the conversation had moved on.

I decided to walk off my bourbon by trekking the twenty-seven blocks home. And since it had been on my mind since Jasmine first mentioned it, I Googled "Engagement Chicken." Part of me didn't want to believe it was a real thing.

When I began typing "Engagement Chicken," a number of entries popped up trying to help my search along. *So this is a real thing,* I said to myself wide-eyed as I saw "Engagement Chicken Book," "Engagement Chicken Recipe Barefoot," "Engagement Chicken Reviews," "Engagement Chicken Stories," "Engagement Chicken Glamour," and even "Engagement Chicken Howard Stern." That last one seemed odd.

I clicked on "Engagement Chicken Glamour," and an article called "How to Make Engagement Chicken" from 2006 popped up. After glancing at the recipe, I deduced that all you needed to make the man of your dreams propose to you is a four-pound bird, lemons, salt and pepper, and some fresh herbs.

Seemed foolish, but I had nothing to lose.

I kept scrolling down as I walked, and although I didn't want to believe it, the comments were making me a believer. One after the other, women were either asking if the chicken dinner really worked or they were telling their stories of how it worked for them.

That was when I read about one woman who said she made the chicken for a guy she was dating three years earlier. When he visited for the weekend, she decided to cook the chicken, but he ended up being a jerk and left abruptly. Well, that was when her neighbor came over and ate the leftovers. She and her neighbor got married last year!

Well, ain't that some shit. I was making this chicken.

# Chapter 9

She's sooooo cute," Jennifer cooed. We were both cupping my iPhone, looking at pictures of my niece.

"Thank you," I replied, as if I had anything to do with it.

"Were you there when she was born?" she asked. Her thick Chicago accent accentuated each syllable.

"I wish. I was at work. Here. In New York. I was actually interviewing Denise Vasi...," I said, but she couldn't seem to place the name, so I added, "Denise Vasi, from *Single Ladies*..."

"Oh! Yes! *Single Ladies*," Jennifer said in a burst of recognition. "Well, congrats on becoming an auntie. That'll be so much fun. My son wants a sister, but..."

"Hey, J. Hud. We have your next interview coming in," Jennifer's publicist blurted out loudly.

Publicists always had impeccable timing when it comes to interrupting a conversation, especially ones that border on the personal. I never could tell if it was the publicist being overprotective or if the celebrity tells them beforehand, "Cut me off if I get too personal."

I wasn't mad at the publicist for doing her job, even if she did cut off probably the most interesting part of my interview with Jennifer Hudson—the fact that her son, little David, wanted a baby sister.

I was running late for the *Scandal* red carpet anyway, and thankfully I wasn't too far from Saks Fifth Avenue, where the premiere event was being held.

Before I grabbed my bag and left the twenty-ninth floor of the Waldorf Astoria Hotel, which had been turned into a makeshift interview room for the Oscar winner to promote her latest film, *The Inevitable Defeat of Mister & Pete*, I asked Jennifer for a selfie. In a rushed tone, the publicist suggested she take the picture instead. Again, I couldn't tell if Jennifer had told her to take the photo if anybody asked for one or if the publicist was being extra helpful.

After a quick snap on my iPhone, which didn't flash, so I knew the picture was going to turn out horribly blurry thanks to the room's soft lighting, I double-checked that I had my recorder and microphone and headed for the door. Behind me I heard Jennifer say to someone, "Doesn't she remind you of my cousin? She could totally be my cousin."

I smiled at the thought of being Jennifer Hudson's kin as I kept walking out the door, then out of the hotel and onto Park Avenue. I then texted my mom to tell her I just interviewed my first Oscar winner.

By the time I stumbled into my apartment after the red carpet, Adam had already put the dinner that he cooked into a Tupperware.

"How was it?" he asked, smiling.

"Exhausting," I pushed out, throwing my body onto the couch.

I didn't feel like talking or running down my day—it was one of those days—but Adam sat down next to me anyway, putting his arm around my shoulders. Our cuddle was interrupted by Arista, who jumped excitedly onto the couch, wiggling her long body in between our laps.

"I saw Jeremy tonight."

"He was at the *Scandal* red carpet?!"

Jeremy was Adam's friend, who used to be in the army or Secret Service or something and now was a bodyguard for celebrities. The last time we saw him was at a Jay Z concert, getting free tickets from the rapper himself.

"Yes! He was escorting Kerry Washington down the carpet," I said, kicking off my black ballet flats—a very important part of every New York City woman's survival kit. Adam grabbed my feet and placed them in his lap. Through my tights he began to rub them in places I didn't know existed—hidden, magical places. "I tried all night to make eye contact with him but he was ignoring me. Sucker. I guess he was trying to be all professional."

"Well, you gotta respect a man about his business," he offered.

"Oh, I do. And can I tell you how amazing Kerry looked?! She was even more beautiful in person," I said, not bothering to breathe. "The lighting from the red carpet hit her magically. She was glowing, babe!" (We'd later find out that Kerry was actually pregnant, which might have had something to do with that glow.)

"Did you get her to talk about her husband?"

"Oh yeah, I forgot I told you I was trying to get her to *finally* say something about him."

Kerry notoriously kept mum about her mythical but very real husband, a topic she hadn't yet discussed in the press.

"I tried my best, babe, I really did. The most she gave me was, 'You know I don't talk about my personal life.'"

"But that's something, right?!"

"It's something," I sighed.

"Well, then, let's celebrate," he said, putting my feet on the floor and springing up from the couch. He reached into the hallway closet, which had over the years turned into his closet.

"What's this?" I said, wide-eyed. I had a feeling all thirty-two of my teeth were showing.

"My babe can't have her feet hurting out here. These are for you...so you can keep up with Oprah."

He handed me a tan-and-orange box that read *Nike* on the side. Inside was a pair of neon-green running shoes...with arch support.

*Chapter 10*

New York had turned cold again. It now took an extra thirteen minutes to prepare myself for the elements.

Surviving winter in New York required the masterful technique of layering. After I dusted off my knee-length army-green down coat—a subconscious nod to the fact that trekking through 14-degree temperatures in the city often felt like fighting in the War of 1812—I pulled all thirty pounds of it over my cardigan. Next came the ultra-long hand-crocheted maroon scarf that my sister made me while she was on bed rest before delivering my niece. It was so long it wrapped around my neck three times.

Shit. Why didn't I put on my boots beforehand? I glanced at the clock on my cable box. There was no way I'd have time to take off my armor just to put on my boots. But there was so much *faaabric*. It was like I had a mattress on, and it was hard to bend over it to reach my feet. It was getting really hot inside all my layers, but I managed to scrunch it all down to tie on my tan Steve Madden boots with red laces.

Where was my hat? It wasn't really a hat, actually. It was more like a fur donut that covered my forehead and ears. I waddled to the living room, darted my eyes from the couch to the floor to the desk filled with random bills and last September's *Vogue*, then back to the floor. Nothing. I waddled back to my bedroom, looked on the unmade bed, then to the floor, back to the bed. Still nothing. Fuck. *I'm just going to have to go without it*, I reasoned, to get to work by 7:07 a.m. Seven minutes late isn't that bad.

I waddled to the bathroom to take a quick peek at myself before walking out the door when I spotted my fur "hat." It was on the back of the toilet on top of my shampoos and assorted soaps basket. *How the hell did it get there?* I grabbed it, double-checked that I had my keys, and sprint-walked to the subway.

After switching my Pandora radio to the Gospel Today station— the only way to start my day so I wouldn't snap at someone in the newsroom—I finally had time to check my phone to see if Adam called. Hmm, nothing.

A gnawing feeling was rushing over me like high tide. Not only did an early-morning wind whip down my spine, but it also seemed like Adam was farther away than ever. I couldn't understand why we saw each other only on the weekends when he lived just thirty minutes away. I brought it up to him before, but he said he was working late on another trial. Not to mention, he said he had to pay $14 to see me every time he crossed the George Washington Bridge. He told me I didn't understand the sacrifice he made every time he came to Harlem.

Thankfully, we had this conversation over the phone so he couldn't see me roll my eyes. I didn't bother to mention that I *did* understand the sacrifice he was making. Nor did I mention the fact that I'd love to go to Jersey to rendezvous, but that option wasn't on the table because his cousin, whom he lived with, said she felt uncomfortable when I spent the night. It set a bad example for her daughter. Okay. Fine. I got that. But that meant all of our time together was spent in my cramped one-bedroom apartment. My fridge had become his fridge. My closet, his closet. I was the only one paying rent but slowly, yet surely, and without me even noticing, my apartment was becoming our apartment. Except he could go home and escape when he wanted to.

It was like the time I had returned from a trip to Maryland one weekend to find that my living room had completely been rearranged. Adam was there watching Arista for me, bless his heart. So when I arrived on a late train, trying to squeeze in as much family time as possible, I came home to find my TV table, which made perfect sense under my mounted flat-screen, moved to the far side of the room. Wires from the cable and Internet boxes that had previously been hidden by the table now hung jarringly against the white walls.

I had never bothered to paint, because I didn't want to repaint the walls when I moved out and into an apartment with Adam.

The couch was pushed all the way back to sit underneath the two windows, but that meant I couldn't reach my desk, which was now squished between the windows and the couch. Adam's reasoning: I never used the desk anyway. He didn't realize that I didn't use the desk when he was there because I didn't work when he was there.

The room looked bigger, sure. But I had to remind him: He didn't pay the bills here. These are my things. This looks a fucking mess. Thank you, but no thank you.

As you can imagine, that was an epic fight that ended with him leaving. He offered to rearrange my home, my sanctuary, my tiny one-bedroom apartment before he left, but I told him I'd manage. I should've taken him up on his offer, though. My back killed me for a whole week from trying to move the wooden TV table back to its rightful place—below the TV!

Adam usually sent me a "Good morning dearheart" text and briefed me about his day. Clutching my phone, I reminded myself that I probably had nothing to worry about. Perhaps he just wasn't up yet.

My morning was consumed with celebrities' lives, but thankfully I got a break around lunchtime. Having still not heard from Adam, I decided to call him.

He was usually really good at calling, and when I didn't answer, texting. But after last week's talk, when we tried to decide where we would spend the holidays, I guess he was in no rush to reprise it. I wanted to spend Thanksgiving at home in Maryland with my new niece, while Adam wanted to stay here. He was taking a trip for Christmas (without me) and said he wanted to spend at least one holiday with his mother. But we needed to sort this out because it was getting closer to Thanksgiving and I wanted to book our train tickets home. And by home, I meant my parents' house.

Adam, like most men, was extremely last-minute, which didn't bode well for my type A personality. I kinda wanted to get this handled. No Olivia Pope.

He answered. "Hey," I said quickly, leaving out all hints of cheeriness. "So I really just wanna get this straight. You don't wanna spend the holiday with me?"

"I didn't say that! It's just that last year we spent Thanksgiving with your family so I thought this year we'd stay here."

"Yes, but that was before Jasmine had the baby; you know that. Plus, you're going to spend Christmas on vacation with your family, so you'll see them then."

"My mom can't go on the trip…"

"So…"

"So I won't see her on Christmas."

"When do you leave to go to Barbados?" His aunt and uncle, two of my favorite people, were going to visit relatives back in their homeland. I was invited on the trip, but I didn't have any vacation time left. If I had known about the trip earlier in the year, I could've planned better.

"Christmas Eve."

"So spend Christmas Eve Eve with her. I just do not want to spend the holidays alone. Please don't do this to me."

"Don't do that," he said calmly, which further irritated me.

"Do what?!"

"Do that!"

"What!"

"You're making this about you."

"You're damn right I am. I don't want to spend the holidays alone. *Couples* don't spend holidays apart. Couples, who plan to get married, damn sure don't spend holidays apart. I have to see my niece. My goddaughter. I can't stay here. And I won't see you on Christmas?"

"Dearheart, can we please talk about this later?"

"Sure, if later you'll say you're coming home with me for Thanksgiving."

"We'll talk."

*Click.*

*Chapter 11*

Adam was headed to D.C. for the weekend. Or I should say Adam was escaping to D.C. for the weekend—just one week before he was supposed to go with me to Maryland for Thanksgiving. I was pissed when he decided to go without me and instead with his friends to the city where we fell in love. He bought a bus ticket without so much as a consultation with me. So I "let" him go.

I tried to ignore the feeling that he always put his friends before me—a feeling I shared with him and he replied with, "My ex said the same thing," as if that was supposed to erase my irritation.

I didn't let my irritation show, though, because letting him spend time with his friends was Number Three on the Engagement Game list and I wasn't deviating from the plan. The plan that worked for at least one woman in the invitation-only Mrs. Club. So, while I "let" him go, I really didn't want him to.

I knew what happened in the D.C. club scene. Before we became official, I was part of the What Happens in D.C. Stays in D.C. Fraternity with Adam and his friends, a group of guys he had collected from high school and college. They'd always rent a hotel suite near Dupont Circle, drink way too much, hit up three, four, five clubs at least, with pretty women—pretty *drunk* women—in tow. They'd have the type of nights where someone would collect cell phones during the pregame festivities so evidence couldn't be found in the morning.

I was particularly annoyed because it was one of those weeks when I didn't see him. A red carpet, then an arraignment, then quality time with his mother, then an open bar industry event kept us from seeing each other, so I was kind of looking forward to doing nothing on the couch with him. That'd have to wait.

"Babe, I can't believe you're going to D.C. right now. Isn't this all sort of last-minute?"

"Yeah, but my brother wanted to go, so I said I'd roll."

"I haven't seen you all weeeeeek, though. You sure you don't just wanna stay here? I'll make it worth your while," I sang out invitingly.

"You're not fuuunnn," he said, matching my tone, which ironically made me laugh. "You're the fun poliiiiiiiiiice. I want to have fun with my boyyyyyys. Plus I'm already packed."

I couldn't stop laughing. Adam had mastered the art of the polite put-down.

I'm not sure when I went from being his fun buddy to his patroller of fun, but I was no longer his accomplice and had instead become his adversary when it came to the topic of fun. At one point in our relationship, you could find me and Adam rubbing together in the corner of a D.C. nightclub on any given Saturday night. Now we pretended we were chaperones at the high school dance. I rationalized it by telling myself we were being polite to the people around us. Because, I mean, c'mon, who wants to be around the couple who makes out all evening? I didn't know how we got here, nor did I know how to fix it.

For some reason, when I used the defense of "But I am fun," it just further proved how unfun I was. Insistence always had the opposite effect, so instead of getting upset about it, I just laughed it off. Because at the end of the day, he deserved to have fun...even if it wasn't with me.

Plus, with Adam going away for a fun weekend without me, I could use the extra days to knock out Number Four of the Engagement Game—"date yourself."

I had already taken care of Number One and written my list of what I wanted in a husband, and Adam seemed to match up perfectly.

I didn't need to worry about Number Two very much—the "take care of yourself" directive. Keeping myself up was one of my favorite hobbies. Plus it was critical to my job as an entertainment producer to keep my skin clear, my nails done, and my hair tamed. Although I was 140 pounds wet, I did notice a growing little bump right under my navel. But only when I sat down. The fat seemed to disappear standing up, so there was no need to work out just yet. (I know I sound annoying and people seem to think skinny people can't complain about their weight, but is that really fair?) I wasn't giving up carbs just yet either—I loved tortellini and macaroni and cheese too much. Instead, I decided to drink less Pepsi. Anytime I craved one, my plan was to chug water. I once read that Gabrielle Union drinks a gallon of water a day and if my skin could look like hers in my forties, I'd consider myself touched by an angel.

As far as Number Three of the Engagement Game—"let him go out and have fun"—well, that seemed to be taking care of itself, now, didn't it?

I still had yet to tackle Number Four in the plan, and this weekend looked like the perfect opportunity. I had been dying to see *Saving Mr. Banks* anyway. After sending a group text to my girls asking if anyone wanted to go with me, they all declined and then proceeded to make fun of my choice to see a Disney film as a near-thirty-year-old without a plus one under the age of eight.

The idea for Number Four seemed simple enough: Take yourself out on a date. Great! It's not like I hadn't been places alone before; I had. To the bathroom. To a party where friends would eventually meet me. To Starbucks to pick up coffee on the way to work.

But the idea of going to a place traditionally reserved for couples seemed unnerving. God, I didn't want to do it. I'd have no one to talk to when I got bored with my own thoughts. People would look at me sympathetically because I was alone—like how I look at people who eat at restaurants alone. Ugh! Why did I have to date myself? Hell! It's myself! I'm with myself all the time! I don't need any more time to myself! I think I've got that covered.

Then my sister's annoying voice rang through my head like the Wizard in *The Wizard of Oz*: "You'll neeeeever be haaaappy with someone elllllllllse until you're haaaaappy alooooone."

Fine. I'm doing it. I'm an adult. I can do this.

I guess taking myself to the movies where the lights would be off most of the time and no one would be able to see me there, alone, should be easy enough. Right? I won't get to the movie theater until after the previews have already started. I'll order my ticket on Fandango because I sure as hell ain't waiting in line to buy a ticket by myself for myself and then have to announce to the ticket agent and to the impatient line growing behind me, "*Saving Mr. Banks*. For one. Just one!" I cringed at that thought. And I wouldn't dare pick an evening showing. I'll do a matinee. Perhaps then people would think I had to watch the movie for a class at school—I hoped. And I'd drink a couple glasses of wine before I trekked there—Hey! It's myself! And myself deserves to be wined and dined. Great. At least I had a plan. Sunday at 2:00 p.m. *Saving Mr. Banks.*

There is a sacred moment every week and it's called Sunday morning. I don't know what it is about the stillness of a Sunday morning, but every seventh day I feel it. Arista doesn't bark. I can't hear the people ordering in the drive-thru at the McDonald's next door, and I can't hear any sign of my neighbors, which is a novelty in my prewar building with walls as thick as bedsheets. It's the time that I can be the most at peace with myself. No one calls. The only texts I get are to see if I'm going to church or brunch, and it seems that I can finally live the full width of each minute.

I opened the top to my mini Keurig machine by its silver plastic handle to throw out the previous coffee pod from last Sunday. I tossed it into a white plastic bag that once carried my groceries. It had found its home on the corner of my kitchen chair, repurposed as a trashcan.

I had long gotten rid of my trashcan because I was too afraid of the bugs it attracted. As a Marylander, I had never seen a cockroach before moving to New York City a few years ago, and I was frightened to pieces when I noticed an entire colony had taken over a toaster I had stored above my cabinets in the kitchen. Adam had warned me to get rid of it months ago, but being the stubborn lover of toast and crispy bagels that I am, I had refused. Until one day I saw two stragglers climbing my walls, looking for their crumb-filled oasis. There were enough crumbs in that years-old toaster to last those critters a few lifetimes. I cried as I pulverized the lot of them with Raid, then had to psych myself up to put a plastic bag over the boxed toaster and carry it seven feet—but what felt like seven miles—to the trash chute in the hallway. After that I threw away anything that could attract bugs, animals—anything. I was not emotionally equipped to deal.

Placing another coffee pod inside the machine, I pulled down the silver handle and stared at the brown stream of coffee as it filled the red mug that I stole from my parents' house. A noisy gurgling, as if the coffee were drowning in itself, let me know that the coffee was done. After a quick step over to my refrigerator to grab my special creamer, I plopped onto the couch because I wasn't making it into the sanctuary today; I'd stream the sermon while simultaneously watching Oprah AME Church, more often referred to as her popular TV show, *Super Soul Sunday.*

I got up a little later today than I would've liked. It was already past noon. Soon I'd have to get ready for my date. I should at least shower for myself, right? I was still debating that as I thought about what to wear. I didn't think I should dress up for my solo date. I barely got super dolled up for dates with Adam. He always thought I was overdressed or dressed incorrectly, but after one too many fights about the buttons on my pants and "appropriate shoes," he had resorted to buying me things he'd rather see me in. My bank account wasn't complaining. I hadn't gone shopping in months, but I did stay with a new wardrobe. Adam wasn't shy about saying he preferred women who didn't need a ton of makeup. But thanks to bad acne as a teen, I was still dealing with battle wounds (read: hyperpigmentation) that made me rely heavily on MAC's full-coverage foundation—my skin savior.

After getting halfway through Oprah's sermon to my soul, I skipped the shower and decided to just get dressed. I pulled out the silk button-down shirt Adam had purchased for me on my birthday from C. Wonder and the complementary bordeaux-colored pants. He even had my initials stitched into the back pocket of the pants in gold bold letters. Since Adam wasn't around to make fun of my fashion faux pas, I put on a black fitted cap to complete the look. I needed something on my head to cover up the fact that my hair—with its naturalness rebelling against blending into my two-week-old extensions—needed to be graced with a flatiron. *And* I needed something I could pull down low over my face in case I needed to hide.

I timed my subway ride down to the AMC in Times Square—I figured this movie theater would be the most crowded—perfectly so that I could waltz right into the theater well after the lights had already dimmed. I climbed the dozens of softly lit movie theater stairs and found a seat on the end, close to the well-lit red EXIT sign. You know, just in case I needed to make an escape.

Taking a sip of the wine that I brought in my silver travel coffee mug, I settled into my seat, placing my purse and coat two seats down, creating the illusion that I was expecting someone to fill that seat and that I hadn't come to the movies alone.

By the time the house lights came up, I had become so at peace with myself and my own thoughts I forgot that I was alone. I didn't hurry out of the theater like I had rushed into it, head down, clutching my to-go coffee cup filled with Riesling. I didn't look around to see who was looking at me. I wasn't worried about who noticed me, alone or otherwise. I had managed to enjoy an activity—a simple one at that—without someone else. It seemed so difficult, but it was super simple.

I took the long way home, strolling through my favorite part of the city, Times Square, and even stopped to treat myself to a caramel latte at Starbucks. Though based on my bank account balance, I probably shouldn't have. I decided to call Jasmine to give her an update on my progress. I had gotten through one of the toughest tasks so far in the Game.

"*Saving Mr. Banks* turned out to be the perfect first date for myself. I thoroughly enjoyed the experience."

"First date, huh? So, will there be a second?" she teased.

"Oh, I don't know. I haven't asked myself yet. I'll wait the customary three days. We'll see," I teased back. "Seriously, I loved it and I really loved that movie."

"What's it about? I saw the previews for it but didn't really pay attention."

"It's about how Walt Disney created *Mary Poppins* and how the author really didn't want to turn her children's book into a movie, but eventually gave in to the Disney magic."

"Hmmm," Jasmine said.

"Mary Poppins wasn't really a singing, flying nanny after all. She was sort of this badass nanny. It was *so* interesting. One of the lines made me take out my phone and write it down. The author, P. L. Travers, said, 'Mary is…' Oh God, let me put you on speakerphone so I can read it to you."

"Ooookaaaay…," Jasmine said, mustering up her patience.

"Can you hear me?" I yelled against the New York City traffic.

"Yes! I can hear you!"

"Okay! Good! So she said, 'She's truthful! She doesn't sugarcoat the darkness!' And I said, Aha! If only children's films didn't do that—sugarcoat the darkness!"

I took her off speakerphone so I could hear her reaction. "Yeah, but so what if they do? Wouldn't you rather go into life with blind optimism rather than a bleak sense of reality?"

It was a really good question. Knowing what I know now about life and how hard it is to fix it into what you imagined it to be as a child, I just didn't know. So I told her as much.

"Sissy, having hope isn't such a bad thing, you know. Even if you don't get what you want."

# Chapter 12

I am a daddy's girl through and through. Before my parents knew what they were having, my dad wanted a boy. I already had an older brother and sister, but for some reason my dad wanted another boy—a football player.

Sadly, the universe paid my dad no mind and I was born on a cool Sunday afternoon in October after my mother preached the Women's Day sermon at her small church in Christiana, Delaware. My dad drove ninety miles an hour all the way to Baltimore so my mom could deliver me—a whole eight pounds, eleven ounces—the biggest baby my mom had carried. My dad, proud that I was the heaviest load, lovingly called me his "little linebacker."

It didn't help that I was a spitting image of my dad. We looked and acted exactly alike: same nose, same smile, same sense of humor, same ability to anger quickly. I hated that we were basically twins growing up because my parents' friends would call me "Little Stan," and when I was younger I couldn't for the life of me figure out why people insisted on calling me a little man. That was the way my brain worked then. I didn't understand that they really meant that I looked like my dad. So I resented my dad for a while, and during my teenage years I plainly treated him like shit. I was so bad that when I matured, I promised myself to make it up to him. I've grown to appreciate my dad and just how amazing he is. He's a man of few words—I'm sure he gets that from the Bahamian side of his family—and he doesn't want much: just a lovely wife and a great family.

When I heard stories about other people's parents fighting, splitting up, arguing, I couldn't even wrap my head around it. I never even saw my parents bicker until I was in my twenties. I've never seen them full-out argue—ever. And they've been married for more than forty years. Perhaps they kept that part of their relationship behind closed doors. I don't know, but the only thing my siblings and I saw were the loving and supportive moments of their relationship. I'm unsure how well that prepared me for my own relationships, but it definitely gave me a good foundation for what a partnership should look like.

"Mom is redoing your room, so you're sleeping on an air mattress in the computer room," Dad said when he picked me up from the train station the Wednesday before Thanksgiving.

I groaned, knowing my back was going to be messed up all weekend.

"You'll be fine, Joi. You don't need much sleep, especially since you ain't cooking in the morning," he said flatly...then broke out into a full smile.

"Hush, Daddy," I laughed.

Dad said we were meeting Mom at my favorite restaurant in Columbia—Clyde's. It was such a nice wintry day. The humidity that often hung in the Maryland air, so thick like molasses, had disappeared for the season, which made the restaurant by the man-made lake packed with diners. The hostess asked if we wanted to sit outside on the heated patio at a table overlooking the lake, where tables were immediately available.

"No, inside," my dad answered for all of us.

He led the charge, slowly, and we dutifully followed behind him like ducks. I noticed Dad was slower than normal, and when he climbed the six or so stairs to our table, I saw he had a small limp.

"Dad, you okay?"

As soon as I asked, it seemed like the question exacerbated the issue.

"Ahh." He winced, his face wrinkling up in pain and his arm reaching toward his knee. He started swinging his leg from the knee down to relieve whatever was bothering him.

"What happened?!"

I must've looked horrified because Dad averted his eyes from me.

"Dad's been having some knee and hip trouble," Mom chimed in. "He's been to the chiropractor and they're going to make sure he's A-okay."

"He's been to the doctor already and you all didn't tell me?!" I said. Tears tagged with an unknown address welled up in my eyes.

"Oh, because we didn't want to worry you, sweetheart," Mom added in her most saccharine affection. "Look at you now. Just calm down. Dad will be fine. They're going to set his hip and it should all work itself out."

"Can y'all please tell me when something is wrong with you? I told you this the last time. If we aren't kept up to date with what's wrong with you guys, if you're in trouble we won't know what to do, what to tell the doctor. You can't keep hiding this stuff from us."

Mom and Dad kept their eyes down, letting me talk some sense into them—an odd role reversal.

"I'm fine. Let's eat!" Dad said, smiling his widest beguiling smile.

I ordered my favorite: the chili with sour cream and cheese along with a salmon burger. But as our entrees came, I couldn't shake seeing the limp out of my mind. Why did parents do that, not tell you about their ailments? I suppose they don't want us to worry, but it only makes us worry even more. What other health problems were they hiding? I wondered.

Once, my dad had his attorney mail his cemetery plot paperwork to me. It came to my small Harlem apartment totally unexpected, and for some reason I thought it contained the latest issue of *Lucky* magazine or something. When I read what was inside the envelope, my heart dropped. My thoughtful father had purchased cemetery plots for all of us—so we could be together for eternity. He had purchased his, my mom's, my sister's, a spot for her husband, my brother, a spot for his future wife if he ever decides to marry, and mine with a spot for my future husband. It was the most considerate yet scary piece of mail I had ever received, and I immediately called him to yell at him for making me think of the inevitable and not warning me that this emotional (yet practical) paperwork was coming. By the time I hung up the phone, hot tears were falling down my cheeks.

Thinking about death always incited a panic I just couldn't shake. To know that one day everything that I've ever known will cease was just too much to handle. I could never wrap my mind around the concept of not living. And the thought of my dad dying—although inevitable—seemed like too much to bear.

After we all returned home, Dad wanted to have a glass of wine to cap off our long day of catching up. So I sat out with him on our backyard patio, which overlooked hundreds of pine trees and bare treetops where only branches remained—a reminder that trees have to let go every winter. The sun had already set and there was a light buzz in the air from the neighbor's generator. Dad and I talked about everything and nothing at the same time. After discussing basketball and random church gossip, my dad got up slowly, with a groan and a grab to his knee that he probably didn't want me to notice.

"I'm going to bed," he said, patting me on the shoulder. "Get some sleep."

I got up too and decided to start the arduous task of pulling out the airbed and finding proper sheets and pillows. I set up my bed in the computer room and decided to call it a night after discovering that the only outlet in the room to charge my iPhone was way across the room—and I wouldn't be able to lie down, charge, and scroll aimlessly on Instagram.

Why did it feel like I was twelve years old again, sleeping in my parents' house? Like I hadn't grown up and moved out and graduated twice. Well, three times if you count high school. I often felt like this when Adam didn't come home with me. It was always my mom with my dad, my sister with her husband, and me—the fifth wheel. Alone. With my brother being forty years old, we no longer expected him, a proud bachelor, to marry, but he did always seem to have a girlfriend. I wondered if this was how it was always going to be. Would I just become the cool aunt Joi-Marie? The one who never got married or had kids and just spoiled everyone else's? God, please don't let that be my life.

By 7:00 the next morning, sunrays were fighting through the translucent curtains that hung in my new room. I had apparently forgotten to close them. The air in the air mattress had leaked out a bit overnight, so my butt was now resting on the hardwood floor. In my haze of normal morning discombobulation, I looked around for Arista. I didn't see her. Right, I had forgotten that I had left the little one back home in the care of her dog walker.

When I tiptoed out of my airbed to yank the curtains closed, the room spun—a reminder that I had finished off the bottle of Bordeaux last night. And a reminder that I can finally share a drink with my dad without feeling completely weird about it. Adulthood had some privileges.

I grabbed my cell phone, which had dutifully charged on the other side of the room, and slipped back under the covers, shifting around a little to warm up the spot I had let get cold. I checked my phone to find a text from my sister, telling me that she, her husband, and the baby would be over at my parents' house by 11:00 for Thanksgiving brunch. A second text reminded me that I was responsible for making the pecan pie, which had miraculously— knowing my cooking skills—become a holiday favorite.

After responding "K," I decided to check Facebook before I closed my eyes again. (My Facebook ban didn't last long thanks to my innate curiosity and the need to fill up time when I'm walking to work, while I'm at work, when I'm leaving work, while I'm at home, while I'm working out. You get the point.)

This Thursday morning, a random person invited me to play Candy Crush Saga for the 508th time, one of my childhood friends liked my post telling them Happy Birthday—a wish I had only given because the social network reminded me to—and some random blogger in D.C. had invited me to their shoe party.

The last Facebook notification intrigued me, though—my mom's best friend and my de facto "auntie" had tagged me in a post. Like my mom, Rev. Dr. Cecelia Bryant is a beloved preacher and had been posting prayers of thanks all month in preparation for the Thanksgiving holiday. I sat up a little to read the prayer, hoping it would help me comprehend better.

*LORD JESUS CHRIST, MESSIAH AND FRIEND.*
*I am PRAYING that each WOMAN will receive the Baptism of*
  *Intercession.*
*I am PRAYING that each WOMAN will experience the*
  *INDWELLING of the HOLY SPIRIT.*
*I am PRAYING that into each life YOU will bring a Relationship*
  *worthy of being a COVENANT SPOUSE.*
*MAY each WOMAN know Wellness, Serenity, and true*
  *Abundance.*
*In the Name of JESUS.*
*AMEN.*

I sat dumbfounded and touched that she had even thought of me in her prayers. I folded my legs Indian style until they found their rightful place under me. My heart started to quicken and I felt a sudden unexplainable flush. I had to read the prayer over again.

The words *covenant spouse* stuck out to me. *Covenant spouse. Covenant spouse.* How did Aunt C know this was at the top of my list too? Here I had been praying for a husband all these years, but perhaps I should've been praying for a covenant spouse.

A husband is only defined in relation to his wife, but a covenant spouse is defined by his relationship with God. And that's the type of partner I'm looking for. That's the type of partner I hoped Adam would be.

Although I have to drag him to church, he does let me pray over our food before we eat it, and he's never been disrespectful about my spiritual life. He's just never been that interested in it either. Admittedly, I'm not a "put a banner on my doorstep" type of Christian, but it's definitely important to me. Adam knows that. I mean, look who raised me for goodness' sake!

My eyes couldn't stop rereading the words *covenant spouse*. I lay down with the phone still clutched so I could continue scanning over those coupled words when I started to drift back to sleep, feeling happy that it felt like the universe was looking out for me, for my future.

When I trekked to the grocery store later that afternoon to buy what I needed to make my world-famous pecan pie, I saw a chicken thermometer, which reminded me I needed to make that damn chicken when I got back to New York. I threw the thermometer in the cart along with the light corn syrup, dark corn syrup, pecans, and brown sugar.

*Chapter 13*

I've missed you," Adam said with the most adorable pout on his face, stepping out of his black Audi. He really must've because he volunteered to pick me up from Penn Station in the heart of Manhattan as soon as I got home. After a hug, he unlocked my car door to let me in before throwing my pink luggage in the backseat of his two-door.

Although he had automatic locks, I reached over the center console and unlocked his car door. Adam told me years ago that he preferred it that way. It'd be an issue if I didn't unlock them. He said he saw that in *A Bronx Tale* once, where an old Italian man explained "the door test." Basically, if a woman—after she gets let into a car—doesn't then reach over and unlock the door for the man, she should be dumped because she's selfish, as if this makes sense in the day and age of automatic locks. Still, I've learned to adapt rather than fight his movie-tale notions of love.

Adam made it a point of pride that I was his first official girl-friend...at twenty-eight. Although he had dated women in the past, some for years, for some reason no one had made it past the friend zone threshold. I, in my naiveté at twenty-three, was actually proud to be his first girl instead of concerned.

I knew what love was. I had seen it—not just in gangster films like *A Bronx Tale* or romantic comedies. I saw what happily-ever-after looked like after the credits rolled, after the movie theater lights went up, and after the attendant came and swept up the popcorn from the floor. You know, the not-so-fun part of being in love that mostly revolves around the mundane—that delicate balance of worrying about yourself and taking care of your partner.

Adam and I seemed to have different ideas of what marriage was supposed to look like...offscreen. Although his parents were divorced, which was obviously no fault of his own, I watched my parents dance the monogamy dance without (seemingly) breaking a sweat for forty-seven years.

I had also tried to love other men before Adam. Although the relationships weren't successful, the love was. After every relationship ended, I said this prayer: "God, give me a clean heart." I also asked him to bar bitterness from my heart so I can accept the man God has in store for me. I'd ask God to light my path so I don't waste time with people who don't deserve the pleasure of my company. Then I'd ask God that if I should meet a man and if that man isn't the one for me, to change my desires to match his will. Then I'd end the prayer, asking God to prepare me for the man he has for me so that I can be ready to receive him.

Thankfully, this strategy has worked—even when I dealt with Brian's inconsiderate ass, the pastor with the wandering eye, the college basketball player who broke up with me via text, the sorta-famous singer who had one hit song on the radio, the Alpha I fell in love with after graduating from Maryland, and the other basketball player—point guard—who left to go play overseas.

Wow. That was all the loves and the pseudo-loves of my life neatly fit into one paragraph.

As we started driving, Adam reached over and palmed my thigh. His usual driving stance. "I missed you too! How was Thanksgiving with the fam?" I asked.

"Grandma asked about you. She said where is Marieeee Johhh-hhh," he mimicked in a fake Bajan accent.

Adam's grandmother never got my name right, but I didn't mind because she was one of the sweetest people I had ever met. Or perhaps I just liked all grandmothers, especially since both of mine, Grandma Ida and Grandma Olive, had died by the time I was ten.

"How was your Thanksgiving?" Adam asked.

I didn't want to tell him about Dad's new limp or that I felt like the fifth wheel all holiday long because he had left me to endure it alone. Instead, I focused on the positives.

"Well, everyone loved my world-famous pecan pie—" I started, before he cut in.

"YOU cooked?!" he teased.

"Oh stop. You know I have five good meals."

"What are they?" he asked in fake (or not-so-fake...I wasn't sure) disbelief.

"Really? We're going to go there," I said with a smile. "Fine! My world-famous tortellini. I can make a good lamb chop. I can stew chicken in my Crock-Pot and I can do a breaded chicken. Five good meals. Bam!"

"Babe, but that's only four...," he teased again. A laugh from his stomach rumbled over the car's radio.

"Oh shoot. Okay, then...add the pecan pie. Dessert counts as a meal, right?"

"I'll let you slide," he managed, squeezing my thigh.

Adam was undoubtedly the better cook. He could make soups from scratch, his gravy never came out of a jar like mine, and one time he even boiled live lobsters that he bought from Queens for us and his friends.

But as a Bajan man, he expected me to cook and take care of the household in general. After he declined my suggestion of playing to our strengths—meaning if he was the better cook, then he should cook—I've been trying my hardest to become interested in cooking. I bought a Crock-Pot and two cooking books, and I've even started perusing Recipes.com. But I'm still not interested in standing over a stove for a couple of hours just to prepare one meal. It doesn't seem efficient—at all. Especially when you can purchase extremely good meals that require no work at all. Who cares about the art of cooking? I just want to eat.

Not with Adam. He loves cooking. He prefers fresh ingredients. He bought special cutting knives that are so sharp they once cut into my gel nail by accident when I tried to slice garlic—a task I wouldn't dare do if Adam wasn't there—and he even bought a special steamer for the lobsters.

In my opinion, he overseasons everything, but what do I know? I don't even wait until the water is boiling to put noodles in. Adam said apparently that's a no-no. I could overcook the noodles . . . as if I'd even know what overcooked noodles tasted like.

However, tonight, after some days spent apart, I thought it was the perfect time to head to the kitchen—to cook Engagement Chicken. My sister said to make sure that I cook it for the right person, and after spending the holiday alone, I was sure. Adam was the man I wanted to be with, who I wanted to get on my nerves for all eternity, whose children I wanted to have. Hell, we'd been at this for years now. There's nothing I don't know about him and nothing else to get to know. All in all, I loved who he was.

We've been through a lot together too. I knew he wouldn't bail on me when times got hard—like me switching careers, his great-grandmother dying, and him leaving his job.

Tonight was the night. Not to mention, I had already made a list to take with me to Fairway so I wouldn't forget to buy my chicken and the side dishes—asparagus and potatoes. I just had to sneak away to the grocery store to buy my happily-ever-after.

"You want to get burgers?" Adam asked nonchalantly as he drove up the West Side Highway to my apartment.

"No, actually I was thinking about cooking tonight," I said matter-of-factly.

"You? Cook?" he teased again. "Babe, seriously. You don't have to do that. Plus, you just got back from Maryland. I found this really great burger spot on the East Side. Let's try that."

"No, that's okay. I want to cook," I lied.

"We're already in the car. I can just drive us there," he said with a noticeable tension growing in his voice.

On any other night I wouldn't have cared where we went to eat. But tonight was Engagement Chicken night. We're going the hell home.

"Adam, babe, I've already thought about what I'm cooking. Trust me on this. We don't have to waste money and eat out tonight," I said, probably for the first and last time.

Adam didn't even reply. I could see the knot in his jaw and the vein pulsing in his neck. He was pissed, but I couldn't understand why. He's been complaining that I don't cook enough, that I don't even like to cook, and the one night when I want to cook he's trying to force some East Side burger joint on me. What gives?

When he turned off the West Side Highway onto 125th Street, he drove past my cross street—Lenox Avenue. Instead, he kept driving, crossing over into East Harlem. The nerve! He was driving us to that burger spot.

"Where are we going?" I spat.

Adam kept his eyes intently on the road, refusing to answer me. I didn't need an answer, really. He and I both knew he was driving us to that damn burger spot after I told him I had planned to cook.

"Can you stop driving to this burger spot? I thought I said I was cooking. What's the matter with you?" I asked, enraged.

He continued to ignore me, which only further infuriated me. I felt like my head would explode if he drove any farther. I had to get out of the car. He was ruining my night, our night, our happily-ever-after. I reached for my door handle with the car still in motion. It popped open like a Snapple bottle. Wind rushed in and almost slammed the car door shut, but I held it open for effect.

"Joi, are you *crazy?*"

"Stop! Driving!"

He slowed to a stop while I gripped the door handle. I knew that if I let the handle go, the car door would've gone with it at the rate he was driving and I didn't want Adam to kill me for wrecking his Audi. I just wanted him to listen to me. To stop driving.

"Are you insane?" he asked, without really asking. He looked at me like I had seven heads. "Joi, let's talk about this when I pull over. You can't just hop out of the car like that. Do you know where we are?"

I didn't, so I closed the car door and said, "Were you really just gonna drive to the burger spot, like for real?"

"I only looked up burger spots because I know they're your

favorite. I just wanted to treat you to something," Adam said, his voice lowering.

*Fuuuuuck.* Why did he have to be thoughtful Adam today? There was no way out of this nicely; I was officially the bad guy. It's not like I could tell him, "Hey, sweetie, I really want to go home and cook because some magazine said if I cook this meal, you'll propose to me." Like, I couldn't say that out loud without appearing even crazier.

So I did what any woman in my position would do. I leaned over and gave him the most passionate kiss my pride could muster up. He pushed me away. I tried again and he let me. After I let him up for air, I apologized. "Babe, that's the sweetest thing. You know I love a good burger. Let's go."

I could tell in his eyes that he didn't want to go anymore, but we parked around the corner from the greasy no-name burger spot anyway. The inside of the place looked like we were on the set of *Alice.* Everything looked dated—the countertops, the booths, the cups. There was even an old jukebox in the corner.

And when our burgers came—his burger with Monterey Jack cheese, salsa, and a fried egg, and mine with Swiss cheese, avocado, and curly fries—they tasted like shit.

# Chapter 14

Something had been telling me to ask for a while now, especially since we had spent three holidays apart. He ended up spending New Year's with his boys, and I trekked to Brooklyn to ring in the New Year with one of my sorority sisters. Alexandra and I had so much fun that night—having random men buy us glasses of champagne and dancing all night in our bar stools. We ended up walking back to her Clinton Hill apartment, watching the sunrise. I hadn't stayed out that late since my high school prom.

I didn't want to ask. Perhaps because I already knew the answer and the credits would finally roll on my wannabe fairy-tale life. But when I woke up this morning—the morning after another Valentine's Day and more than two years after that drunken non-proposal in our favorite D.C. nightclub—I knew I had to.

In fact, I heard a really tiny voice that told me to ask. The voice, nagging in nature, was a familiar one. A direct one. It never minced words. And although it didn't yell, for some reason I always heard what it said.

It was the same voice I heard when Mom asked nearly six

months ago, "How are things going with you and Adam?" I was driving to Jasmine's house in Prince George's County, Maryland, and Mom was trying to be casual...too casual. Clearly she had been thinking about this conversation for a while. I was sort of taken aback because we weren't even discussing my love life at the time. It was raining for goodness' sake! Why couldn't she just let me concentrate on the road? I had thought then.

The voice told me then, "Not well." But how does one say that about a man they've been dating for five years? Shouldn't he be "the one"? If my mom could figure out in nine months if she wanted to marry my dad, why couldn't I be sure about this?

"Things are going well. I'm really just waiting on my ring. I told him I didn't want to move in with him until I had that. And we've talked about it, so I'm just waiting. I'm happy, if that's what you're asking," I pushed out. I said every word too fast. I was nervous. I hated when Mom played Oprah. She sized up every sentence I said.

"Do you love him?"

"I do!" I said, forcing my cheeks into a smile.

"Well, okay." She shut down, but I knew she had more to say. I hated when she did that.

"Mom, whatever it is you're thinking, you can tell me."

"Well, remember when I asked you to send pics of you and Adam..."

"Yes, and I sent them!"

Since we all live in separate states, Mom has this thing where she makes us exchange selfies. She'll send one with her and Dad on a plane or someplace, and she makes us send her one in return no matter what we're doing. It's always fun to see what the family is doing at the time. Oftentimes I'm on the streets of New York with my earbuds in, my brother is checking out some tourist attraction, and my sister is in the kitchen with her husband. And I'm not just saying that for stereotypical effect, but that's really what my sister is usually doing.

"Yes, and remember when I asked you to send me pics of you and him on your five-year anniversary...when you all went to..."

"We went to Lure Fishbar in SoHo."

"Yes, well...he never looks happy to be with you, Joi'Rie," she said, adding my childhood nickname, probably to soften the blow. "In every picture, he doesn't look happy. I don't think he's the one."

My stomach sank, but I tried to pretend it didn't.

"Mom! He just doesn't like to take pictures. Why would you say something like that? And it's not your relationship; it's mine. We're fine. We're happy. We're getting married. Did Grandma like every guy *you* dated?"

She looked at me like she'd risk it all to slap me.

"Okaaaay..." Her voice trailed off. Mom didn't fight with Dad and she surely didn't fight with me. She just let my words hang in the air and swirl around a bit. She knew, like I knew, I'd choke on them just a tad. Left with my own thoughts, we drove in silence for a while.

"Mom, you like Adam, right?"

"Yes, I do. I really do. I just want to make sure *you're* happy."

I turned to her and asked, "Don't I *look* happy?"

What is it about motherhood that gives you the ability to know best in your children's lives?

Mothers be knowing.

Back inside our—correction, *my*—apartment, I knew if I didn't ask today, I might ask at an inopportune time like at a very important dinner with his colleagues. So I asked.

"Where are we going?" I asked directly.

There was no tone in my voice. I was very careful to purge any indication of an attitude from my voice because that could affect the conversation. If he thought I was off-the-bat pissed, he would get defensive and I wouldn't get the loving Adam that I needed him to be right now. I'd get the asshole Adam. If I asked in a pleading way, he might think I was desperate—and didn't necessarily want to marry *him* but wanted to marry anyone. Although I'm not so sure there's much of a difference right now.

Adam was lying down with his eyes closed, his face sunken into the new flannel sheets I had bought from Target in hopes of keeping me warmer in bed. He didn't open his eyes, but he willed his body to an upright position to match mine and sighed a deep sigh that told me everything I needed to know.

"Where are we going?" he repeated.

"Yes, do you have intentions for this relationship?" I asked levelly.

Adam read through the lines. He knew I was asking why it was taking him so long to pop the question. He knew "Do you have intentions?" meant "Do you intend to marry me?" Although he didn't want to lose me, he answered honestly.

"Dearheart, I'm burned out."

"Burned out?!" My voice teetered on a scream. I couldn't help it. As level as I'd wanted to be, I hadn't expected this response from him, again.

I had heard these words before. Two years ago he blindsided me and said he needed a break because he was "burned out." Apparently I had been too much for him and he had reached his breaking point, unbeknownst to me.

Admittedly, I wasn't concerned about him then. I couldn't be.

After leaving my full-time job in D.C. and spending over $50,000 of my parents' retirement money to get a master's degree, I focused on proving that degree's worth and proving I could finally live on my own in New York. You know, be an adult. I got a cheaper apartment, saved for cheap furniture from some store in the Bronx, and got a job writing from my Harlem apartment. With all of my school behind me, I was working on becoming a real adult even if I couldn't afford the previous luxuries I had before the master's degree, like $13 cocktails at a bar, J.Crew, and Starbucks. Now it was flasks, H&M, and a Keurig coffee machine that I got for Christmas.

Just when feeling like an adult finally felt normal, Adam broke up with me without warning. Well, really, I suggested a break after a small fight, but I didn't expect him to happily accept. Besides, the fight was over the stupidest thing. I was cooking one of the five meals I know how to make—breaded chicken over fettuccine. I realized I didn't have enough noodles for the both of us, so after boiling some noodles for about seven minutes, I added more.

Oh no. Adam, being Bobby Flay Jr., said I couldn't just add noodles to the pot because the original noodles would be overcooked. As if anybody could tell the difference. I said if he was going to look over my shoulder in the kitchen, he should just cook. That turned into a four-hour power struggle that ended in us eating the overcooked and al dente noodles over breaded chicken and vodka sauce.

After twenty-three days—I was counting—I told him, "Look, dude, we're off the break." And he quickly told me, "We'll talk about it later." That was the same day he won his first grand jury trial and instead of calling his mother first to share the good news, he called me. Clearly I was still the most important person in his life, break or no break. But he wouldn't budge. For nine weeks I called him, every Sunday, asking if he had changed his mind. And for nine weeks he told me he hadn't.

During one of those phone calls, I told him I should've seen it coming. It's not like this relationship was his idea. Before I moved to New York for grad school, Adam came to visit me in D.C. every weekend. And every weekend, he'd stay with me or in the Beacon Hotel near Scott Circle. Either way, I'd pick him up from the bus station and we'd spend the whole weekend together. We did that for about two years until he started to become exhausted with the travel. I didn't blame him, but at the same time I didn't want to come up short after investing those years.

While Adam was the one to initiate our relationship by putting his arm around me in that booth, it was me who technically solidified our relationship status. On the weekend when Barack Obama was inaugurated, after a long night of drinking champagne out of orange bottles and celebrating the first black couple in the White House, I asked him, "Are you in or are you out? Are you gonna be my boyfriend?" I'm not sure what gave me the balls to ask a grown man to be my boyfriend, or where exactly my pride went. But when you love someone, and you want to be with someone like I wanted to be with him, pride really didn't matter. Thankfully, he didn't hesitate to say yes. But we were so drunk the next morning I had to ask him again to make sure I remembered it correctly.

After those nine weeks in Breakville, my dignity rolled up its sleeves and took back its rightful position. I had kicked the habit of crying myself to sleep after a glass of Riesling, another episode of *Sex and the City*, and another Facebook album of someone else's wedding. I got my life back on track. I started off small. I woke up every morning to scripture, thanks to my trusty Bible app, and a prayer. Although I felt my life had fallen apart in front of my eyes, I tried to identify things that I was grateful for: my life, my health, my parents' health, me living my dreams in New York City. I did things that genuinely made me happy, like keeping fresh flowers in my apartment. I changed the energy in my room by getting new candles, new sheets, and new pillows. I bought tickets to plays and visited museums. I went to the dog park, without any decoys, and even did the one thing I kept asking Adam to take me to do: bike in Central Park.

And just when I got back to liking myself again, the universe must've tapped Adam on the shoulder and said, "She's moving on! You better catch her before she leaves your ass for good." Adam came back, apologizing, explaining, needing, wanting. That wasn't before he had the chance to introduce whoever the hell he was dating during the break to his cousins. He'd later tell me "out of respect." I told him then that he could have a second chance, but he wouldn't get a third.

Now, two years after that break, here we were again.

"Well, we just fight all the time. And at first our bickering was cute but now...I just feel like—"

"Feel like what?" I cut him off defensively.

"Like if we have another fight, I'm out."

"So why didn't you tell me this before it came to this?" I said, loud enough to stop the thoughts pouring into my mind— thoughts that said I'd be alone soon.

"I've tried," Adam said, pleading. He grabbed his head in his hands and scratched it violently. "I've tried, but nothing has changed. Honestly, we haven't been the same since you opened that car door."

I shuddered at the thought of those grease-soaked burgers on what was supposed to be Engagement Chicken night. I had yet to reschedule our feast to scratch Number Five of the Engagement Game off my list.

"So what are you saying?" I asked slowly.

I wasn't going to let him off the hook. If he wanted out of this relationship, he was going to have to man up and break it off. He needed to say the words.

"I'm saying...I don't know what I'm saying."

I stopped breathing. My heart was breaking and I couldn't breathe.

"What do you want to do? I'm twenty-eight. You're thirty-two. My father is seventy years old. I want him to walk me down the aisle, Adam. I don't have time for 'I don't know.' What have I done to you? What did I ever do to you? I tried to be the woman you wanted me to be. I kept lemonade in the fridge. I learned to cook because you wanted me to..."

"And that's the thing," he whispered.

"What? What did you say?"

Adam sighed, on the verge of tears. "That's the thing. I never asked you to do that for me, Joi. I wanted you to do that for yourself."

Now I was fucking confused, and the look on my face said it. I was confused. Angry. Upset. Sad. Heartbroken.

"I'm a simple man, Joi. I don't require much. I don't care that you don't cook or any of that stuff. I just wanted the woman that I married to *like* cooking. The type of household that I want to run, it requires a certain type of woman."

"A *cooking* type of woman?"

"I just don't know if I could run a household with you."

Shit. This was worse than I thought.

"I understand that this is a marriage-or-bust situation," he analyzed.

"Yeah…well…I guess I'm not the partner for you," I said, trying to sound matter-of-fact.

The one thing I learned from our last break was that I would never again convince a man of my worth. I would never convince a man to stay when he wanted to leave. I wouldn't dare convince a man to love me. Ever again.

Suddenly it all made sense. All the trying in the world couldn't turn me into the woman Adam wanted me to be—some mystical cooking, independent yet desperately dependent on him, debater who didn't teeter on the line of bickering, sex kitten, Michelle Obama–prototype type of woman. I could only be myself.

"You should go."

"You want me to leave?" Adam said. He genuinely seemed shocked, but it didn't matter. He needed to leave.

"You should go," I repeated, dead-voiced.

"I didn't want it to end this way," he said.

I willed my face to look indifferent. I couldn't even look at his side of the bed.

Adam got up quietly and pulled on his sweatpants. Then pulled on his T-shirt carefully, unrushed. He walked to the hallway closet to where I'd hung his overcoat and threw it over his shoulder, careful not to put it on, just in case I changed my mind. He looked back at me to see if I was looking at him. I wasn't. I just stared down at my hands, picking at my nails. With the bedroom door now open, Arista sprinted into the room, finding her spot on the bed.

"Okay, Joi. I'm going…I want you to know that I didn't want it to end like this."

"Yeah, and I didn't want it to end at all," I said.

Making his way slowly to the door, he looked back once, took a deep breath, and closed the door. As soon as I heard his footsteps get fainter and fainter, I burst like a balloon—heaving and crying and wailing. A grief deep inside me pushed itself upward. I hadn't felt pain like this before, not even when my grandma Ida passed away. Fearing I was too loud, even though he was probably in the lobby of my building by now, I grabbed a pillow and screamed into it. Mouth open, tears pouring, fingers clenching.

If he was going to take my future, he sure as hell wasn't going to take my dignity.

# PART TWO

## Fouled Out

# Chapter 15

It felt like a pinch. The really bad ones that make your eyes water and your nose scrunch. It felt like someone just punched me in the chest and I'm holding back the tears so no one else knows just how much it hurts.

Every step I took from the 1 train on my way to work the morning after Adam told me he was burned out hurt. My legs felt like they wanted to give out, but I forced them to put one foot in front of the other. I stumbled when I walked off the sidewalk, into the middle of the street, at Amsterdam and 66th. At this time of day, only trucks were on the road. I could barely see them through my eyes, which after a night of crying, the ugly kind, had swelled up like two marshmallows.

I watched as one truck approached. I'd have to wait until it passed so I could finish crossing the street. But that morning, something deep within me that I didn't know existed pushed me to walk in front of the truck. I started counting under my breath—nine...eight...seven...six—to figure out how many seconds I'd need to end up under that army-green Mack truck. If I could just will myself to walk in front of the truck, I'd feel another pain. A pain much stronger than the one in my heart, and perhaps for once, I could stop thinking about it and focus on something, anything, else.

But I couldn't do it. I couldn't move. I *really* wanted to, but my feet suddenly felt like they were trapped in quicksand. I slowly watched as the truck rolled by, looking at it longingly. It would've been my out, my heart's refuge.

I came home after a very long day at work where I'd pretended that I was okay. I quickly got comfortable tearing up on the subway and even bawling while walking down the street. It might have been winter but the cold didn't freeze my tears. They still fell. And they burned. A deep burning I wanted to scratch out.

As soon as I turned the key, I cried. I cried because the only other person on the inside of my door to greet me wasn't even a person at all—it was my dog. She was just as desperate to see me as if I'd left her for dead. She jumped on the couch, back onto the floor, her unclipped paws jumping on my tights. Usually I would jump around as if I'm standing on hot coals so she wouldn't rip my tights but today I didn't care. I just let her jump on me. I let her show me how much she missed me. She was the only being who would act like they missed me all day.

Losing a lover is like a death in the family. It's a grief felt only when you've lost something you once treasured. And the worst part was that I was even more upset that I lost my dream—the dream of getting engaged within the year, the dream of having children by thirty, the dream of sharing a life with someone. I had already imagined what our kids would look like. Adam would take pride in dressing them because he seemed to care more about appearances and style—it was a Caribbean thing—and I'd make sure they were loved with kisses, hugs, and encouragement. I couldn't wait.

Now I'd have to.

After making dinner for the night—an ice-cold glass of RELAX Riesling—I looked down at my phone to see that I had already mistakenly answered it. I hated when I did that. Thank goodness it was only my sister.

"Hello?" I answered with a question, a question that infers, *Why are you calling me when I just want to be left alone in my own shit?*

"Hey. Just checking on you."

"I'm fine. Thank you," I said almost too robotically. "Sis, I'm just getting home. Can I call you back later?"

"You know you're not calling me back," she said, matching my attitude. In the background, I heard my niece crying. "Just make sure you Gchat me tomorrow when you get to work, okay?"

"Okay! Bye, sissy."

*Tap! Tap! Tap! Tap!*

I froze. Who was that knocking on my door? It sounded like someone's nails were grazing my door…but I wasn't expecting anyone tonight. Shoot—I hated answering the door if Adam wasn't here. I was home alone; anyone could overpower the door and do God-knows-what with me.

*Tap! Tap! Tap! Boom! Boom! Boom!*

Ooooh, they'd started police knocking now. I tiptoed to the door, careful not to step on any known creaks in my wooden floorboards. Placing one leg in front of the door, just in case they could sense me on the other side, I carefully—without taking a breath—looked through the peephole.

I saw my neighbor, standing there in anticipation. I never could remember her name, even after coincidentally sitting beside her at an ASCAP awards dinner earlier that year. Since then, she had dyed her dreadlocks to match her bright red lipstick.

I tiptoed back into the living room to check my cable box to see what time it was—11:00 p.m.?! What could she possibly want from me at this hour? I had a mind to ignore her. She'd go away eventually...but something told me to see what this late-night drop-by was all about.

Unlocking my dead bolt and undoing the gold chain, I cracked open the door—if only to hint that I didn't want to be disturbed—then opened the door wider. "Hi," I answered.

"Um, you're very loud. I can hear your dog running around and I can hear you walking."

Was she serious?

Perplexed, I asked her to clarify. "I'm sorry, what? You can hear me *walking*?"

"Yes, I hear footsteps. All day and all night. And the dog, I hear her nails on the ceiling. Can you just keep it down?"

Every time I come home, my dog allows me approximately seven minutes of alone time before she finds her squeaky ball and lays it at my feet to throw. I feel bad for leaving her cooped up in the apartment all day so I throw the ball, with her running feverishly after it, until she gets tired. Apparently, my neighbor couldn't take my eight-pound dog's little paws scratching on my wooden floors.

Little did she know I didn't give a shit, especially not today.

"I'm sorry that you can hear me walking, but I'm not sure I can keep that down. I need to walk around."

"Try," she said. That one word dripped with attitude.

I smiled tightly, no teeth. If she wanted to be a bitch, I could show her one better.

"Have a good night," I said with fake cheer before slamming the door in her face, *Martin* style. It felt good. I've always wanted to do that ever since I saw Martin Lawrence do it on his hit TV show.

By the time I made it back to the couch and flipped on the TV, I had tears in my eyes. Nothing was bothering me; I couldn't care less about the neighbor. It was just that these days any emotion made me cry uncontrollably.

Of course the television was turned to TLC and another marathon of *Say Yes to the Dress* was on. At the sight of Kleinfeld Bridal, I threw the remote so hard that the batteries popped out of it.

I was sure the neighbor heard that.

# Chapter 16

I had become the woman I thought I'd never be. The woman who reads relationship blogs and articles on her lunch break in hopes of finding a morsel of truth to apply to her dire situation.

It'd be better if Adam just up and disappeared, but he didn't necessarily go away when he walked out of my apartment that cold February day three weeks ago. He still called regularly—at least three times a week. We never spoke about much and everything seemed forced—forced niceness, forced small talk, forced, forced, forced.

This method of keeping tabs was exactly what happened during our last breakup. Adam would continue to do this until he was up and ready for our relationship again. He didn't want to be in a relationship with me, but he also didn't want to give me time to be in a relationship with anyone else. It's the classic case of wanting his cake and eating it too, and I wasn't letting him this time. I told him the last time he broke up with me that I wouldn't be giving him a third chance, and I meant it. Just because he couldn't be a

man of his word didn't mean I couldn't be a woman of mine. I had
to cut this off.

My back was aching. I really needed to buy a new bed. I'd had
the same Ikea bed with a wooden wicker headboard since I moved
into that apartment off-campus senior year of college. Walking up
the stairs to my apartment would be hard today, even with the
neon running shoes Adam had bought me.

Before I trekked up the two flights of stairs, I walked over to
my mailbox, only to discover mail that had already been opened.
Again?! I flipped over the envelope—yup, it was addressed to
me—but the flap now sported a scrunched-up hole, large enough
for an adult finger to fit through.

Only in Harlem.

I always tell people to mail important stuff to my office because
I didn't trust my mail carrier. Around my birthday last year,
every card that was delivered to my locked mailbox came already
opened. I wouldn't know if anyone gifted me a check, cash, or a
gift card. My godmother Marie's birthday card did get there with
her $20 still inside, but only because she put large, two-inch-wide
tape over the flap after she heeded my warning.

*Boing! Boing! Boing! Boing!* It was Adam's special ringtone—
speak of the angel.

"Hey . . . ," he said. His voice held hope.

"Hey."

"How are you?" he tried.

"Adam. Hey. I was just thinking about you, actually."

"You were?"

He sounded excited.

"I don't think we should talk as often as we do," I continued.

"We're broken up and I feel like if I'm going to move on with my life, then I should create some distance between us."

"You want to move on?" he asked, almost incredulously.

"I think that's the only option I have, Adam, since you know, you're burned out. And that's a valid feeling. I don't want you to think you did anything wrong. You didn't. You told the truth about how you felt…but I also have to be truthful to myself and the truth is I need space."

"So what does space look like for you?" Adam said. His voice resonated with irritability, which surprised the hell out of me since breaking up was his idea.

"Just don't call as often as you do, maybe?"

Adam agreed that he would try it my way and with that I rushed off the phone.

I got an e-mail later that night from him that I didn't read. I did allow my eyes to land on some words…something about him hoping we'd remain friends. I rolled my eyes but couldn't bear to delete the e-mail. I just let it live in my inbox until I was really ready to read it.

Adam knew I wasn't friends with any of my exes. He is, but I'm not. We've discussed the topic heavily. He thinks that if he doesn't remain friends with them, then they weren't really friends to begin with. Whereas I'm in the school of thought of I didn't get into a relationship with you to be your friend. I don't need any more friends. You were supposed to be a boyfriend, and if you don't want to be that anymore, you don't get the privilege of my friendship. Sorry, not sorry!

My Adam-thought was interrupted by a light buzzy vibration emitting from my iPhone. Dominique, my sorority sister, was texting to tell me that she's in town. Come with me to dinner tomorrow, she typed, more like a demand than an invitation. Without waiting for me to confirm, she wrote that she was sending the restaurant's address and that my ass better be there.

Dom had no clue that Adam and I had broken up. I wasn't the type to put #*single* under my latest Instagram posts, or even subtweet, emo tweet, none of it. So although my life had drastically changed, the world didn't know.

I was kind of thankful Dom was in town. It was a much needed distraction from the thoughts in my head. I kept asking myself, did I do the right thing by pushing Adam to marriage? I mean, there are couples who never get married and they're perfectly happy and content. I did consider that option. However, if I gave him an out, it would again be deferring to what he wanted. And for once, just this time, I wanted to get what I wanted out of life. Yes, I'm talking about a ring, but I also wanted Adam to love me enough to give me what I wanted. Because he felt like I deserved it. But now that we were done, it still didn't feel right. I still felt unsure. I still wanted our future.

Yes, ma'am, I replied to Dom, complete with a rosy-cheeked emoji.

Thank God for the universe. It won't let you wallow.

By the time Dominique texted me the next day after her various meetings in the city, asking if we were still on for dinner, I was already home and had taken off my bra. It's the universal sign for all women that I was not leaving the house anytime soon, probably until the morning. I texted her back, saying the couch had sucked me in.

Booooooo, let's go! Get up.

I took my bra off, I typed back immediately.

Oh.

The little ellipses icon on the iPhone let me know that she was still typing. Well, fine. Then I better see you tomorrow, girlfriend. Try to get some rest!

I wrote back a heart emoji. I hated being too mushy—she knew that—and even when my heart probably needed it the most, it wasn't happening.

Already on my second glass of Riesling, I opened my laptop. I felt like a ball of yarn with the string undone, so I figured I might as well dive into the deep end and read my diary. I always read my diary when I feel completely sad. I call it emotional cutting.

I missed him. I missed Adam like crazy and perhaps I could read back to times when we were happy to will this latest episode away. Before I settled in to read, I opened iTunes and scrolled down to the Etta James tracks I had downloaded. I double-clicked on "I'd Rather Go Blind." *Perfect.* It would be a successful night if I made myself cry.

I've kept a diary since I was in high school thanks to Diaryland .com. All the girls in high school had one and we all read each other's. It was part voyeuristic, part gossiping without having to make a phone call. We talked shit about each other on them and spread rumors about tons of kids on them. It was like the first generation of blogs, and although most of my friends stopped writing in theirs, I kept mine up to date and put a seventeen-character password on it, of course.

I scrolled all the way down to 2009 to when I still lived in D.C. Adam had just moved to Jersey to start using his law degree. I'm sure we were happy then, I thought. I clicked on a post titled

"Faith" that I wrote in September of that year. After skimming a few lines, this part stood out:

*We had a talk about our relationship the other day and it's more evident that he's really trying to work on this long-term relationship thing that he's never been in. And although I was proud of that fact months ago, now I see why it doesn't work. Because when I tell him, "I miss you. Can't wait to see you," and all he says is, "I appreciate that," sometimes I want to punch him in his fucking face. I just want this to work out and it still may . . . I guess I just have to have faith.*

Before Etta could finish her song, the tears had already started to fall. Perhaps if I had paid attention to the signs, I could've gotten out of this sooner. But even if I had seen the signs, would I have wanted to? Sure, it wasn't the picture-perfect relationship all the time, but when it was good, it was really good.

Adam is a good man. He has a good job. He loves his family. He cares for his friends like they're his brothers. He's responsible. Even if he doesn't love me the way I want him to all the time, does that make him unfit to be my husband, my lover, the father of my kids? Am I making the biggest mistake of my life?

I didn't bother to answer my own questions. It was not like they would make much difference now anyway. I didn't leave me. *He* did. I didn't say I was burned out. *He* did.

I clicked on a post from November 30, 2010, called "This Time Won't You Save Me," which is clearly a reference to how much I loved Nicki Minaj at the time. How overdramatic of me. I laughed as I grabbed my glass of wine, which had now turned warm, and read:

*The man that I absolutely adore . . . well, quite frankly I love him, he's in my bed. The worst thing about him being there is that he probably won't touch me all night. As much love as I have for this man, he won't love me the way I want him to, the way I need. I'm always the one asking, "Hey, put your arm around me," or "Hey, can we snuggle?" Perhaps he doesn't know how and quite frankly I am tired of teaching.*

Adam had improved on showing affection since then, but I was still complaining about a man who just couldn't love me the way that I wanted him to. I don't even fault him for that. Perhaps he just can't.

After getting stuck on the couch for two days, I finally made a dinner date with Dominique. She was leaving Thursday, and although I eventually told her that Adam and I had broken up nearly a month ago, it was no longer an excuse not to see her before she trekked back to Maryland.

I thought it would just be her and me at Jado Sushi, but it ended up being her, her business partner Ashley, her manager Cody, and a potential job candidate whose name escapes me. Apparently, her small business making graphic T-shirts was doing so well she was looking for a virtual assistant.

So there I was thinking I was going to get a night of drinks, guy talk, and keekee—you know, the uncontrollable laughter that makes your stomach sore—when I found myself wedged in between the nervous job candidate and Cody. At least there were still drinks.

"Where did you go to school?" Dom, in her most businesslike voice, asked the job candidate.

"I went to Hampton."

Cody excitedly jumped in and turned the conversation over to me. "Joi! Where did you go to school?"

"Um"—I looked to Dom to make sure I could have the floor—"I went to Maryland. Home of the Terrapins."

"Oooooh, nice!" Cody replied enthusiastically.

*What is this dude's deal?* I asked myself. Surely he couldn't be flirting with me. I had just scraped myself off the couch after crying there for the better part of forty-eight hours. My eyes were still puffy. I don't think I even put on eyeliner.

I nodded a few times and looked back over to Dominique. I didn't want her to think I was turning this sit-down into *The Joi Show.* I wanted her to get the job interview over with so we could get a good keekee in before it was past my bedtime.

"You don't remember me, do you?" Cody asked while Dom continued with her questions to the hopeful. "We met at BET's Black Girls Rock taping."

I whipped my head back over to him after an internal *fuck* ran through my head. I hated when I did this. I have the worst memory and I'm not even sure why. It started right after I moved to New York. Perhaps I lost my memory because of the anxiety the city gave me, but if I don't write it down, I won't remember. If it's not in my calendar, it's not going to happen. If I don't tell Siri to remind me to do it, it won't get done.

Cody continued. "Yeah, I was like who is *that*? You looked beautiful that night."

I didn't have to whip my head back around to see that Dom was smiling in approval. All of a sudden, without warning, my face started to get flushed. The corners of my mouth curled up without my permission. Shit, I was blushing.

"Um, thanks," was all I could muster before staring down hard at my plate of sushi and sashimi.

"So you live in Harlem, right?" Dom asked, continuing with her job interview. "What church do you go to?"

"I go to First Corinthian Baptist Church," the young lady said.

"I go there too!" I chimed in, too happy to change the topic of conversation.

"Oh really?" she replied. "What service do you go to?"

"Nine thirty."

"Oh yeah, I'm an eleven-thirty girl."

"Eleven thirty is too much of a club for me. It's like going to a Morehouse Homecoming. Everyone there is trying to see and be seen."

"True."

I wanted to keep talking to them, to keep my attention away from Cody, but it was impossible thanks to his constant stream of conversation.

When it got to be around 10:00 p.m., I knew it was past my bedtime. No one in this restaurant had to be at work earlier than me, so I said my goodbyes to Ashley, who was still in the booth with me. The job candidate was replaced by another one, and this time Dom took the newest candidate to a separate table. Thank God. It was so freaking awkward. Cody was over there too . . . until I got up from the booth. That was when he hopped up from his seat.

"Did you have a good time tonight?" Cody asked. His smile was so wide and sparkly. It was almost as if it was encouraging me to smile right along with it, but I couldn't find the strength. I didn't have it in me.

"Yeah, um, it was fun. Sure," I said nervously.

Cody walked with me to the restaurant's coat check. Before I could even give my ticket to the attendant, who was doubling as the hostess, Cody went behind the hostess stand and picked up my black knee-length puffy coat and helped me put it on. A gentleman: I could dig it.

"Thank you," I said politely, bending down to put both arms in my coat as he pulled it up over my shoulders.

"Oh, a lady who wears fur, eh?" Cody asked.

I had just pulled out my fur "hat," which was stuffed inside my coat sleeve.

"It's not real," I said a bit too sharply, volleying his attempt at a compliment. I hadn't flirted with someone other than Adam in years. Compliments from Cody somehow felt wrong. After opening the door and letting the Harlem chill whip my face, Cody said good night.

I left the restaurant full of sushi and vodka, wanting to know more about Cody. I wouldn't dare ask for a business card to keep in touch; I was in no mood to pursue. But when I got home I ended up friending him on Facebook and then proceeded to spend forty-six minutes going through and dissecting every photo he had ever posted. Literally. I clicked on his profile photos, checking for any sign of a girlfriend, drug paraphernalia, and children. So far, so good but wait…hmm…his sixth photo was a picture with him and three little girls. Shit. Does he have children? I hurriedly began to read the caption. Whew! Those were his nieces.

I had to call Jasmine to detail the entire evening.

"You thought he was flirting with you? Child, please. He was just being nice," she concluded after I told her the entire story—how Dom set me up, how Cody was being too friendly, and how he had even helped me put my coat on.

"I don't know, sissy. I haven't flirted in a long time, but I think I was being flirted with."

"Think again," she quipped. I could hear my niece crying in the background.

"What's wrong with BB?" I asked in a faux-baby voice, referencing my sister's newborn, whom she named Brandy.

"Oh, she probably needs another bottle. BB, just hold on a second," my sister said as the cries got louder. "Just one second, okay? *Okaaaay?* Let me call you back."

I heard the line cut off before I could reply.

With my Facebook investigation on Cody completed, curiosity finally caught up with me. I lay down against my flannel sheets and decided to finally read Adam's e-mail. After pulling it up on my iPhone and scrolling down to see how long it was, I immediately regretted it.

Dearheart,

I was hoping we could talk in a couple days, but I've been all consumed by this. Let me start by saying, I want to be the best person for myself and who I am with. I assume you wanted the same. It just seems like in the past few months, you've been really sensitive to my constructive criticism and it's led to more arguments. The truth is there is no reason why cooking or checking out a new burger spot should ruin our day. I don't want to fight with you, and I feel more isolated the more we argue. I may have reacted in a way that was detrimental to our relationship. The fights made me angry, dejected, and unmotivated to even be with you.

You said you tried to be the perfect girlfriend so that eventually I'd think you'd make the perfect wife. When you told me that, I immediately regretted asking you last February if I should buy a ring. Maybe you wanted to be perfect to get me to propose? After so many years together, you had every right to ask where this relationship was going. I'm sure you feel the pressure to get married from your family, just like I do.

I am not perfect and I don't expect my partner to be, but we've had such highs that the lows become harder to take. So many things in life are mediocre; love shouldn't be one of them.

I write this from a positive place and hope we can remain friends.

And in no way do I think our breakup was a reflection of your love for me and my love for you.

# *Chapter 17*

So we're going to brunch after church on Sunday?"

"Um, who is this?" I asked incredulously. I usually didn't answer unknown numbers, but it was Saturday and I'd just had the most amazing sleep. Not once did I wake up to cry or panic about life. However, even in my good mood I was annoyed by the call. Who had the audacity to just start talking after I picked up?

"Cody. So we're going to brunch after church on Sunday?" he asked in a rushed tone.

The city screamed behind him. He sounded like he was hustling across Fifth Avenue.

"Um, okay."

"Yeah. I'll pick the place. I'll text it to you when you get out of church."

"Um . . . okaaay," I pieced together.

*Dammit, Dominique, for giving this man my number.* And in the amount of time I had to process what was actually happening—that perhaps he did like me, that perhaps Jasmine was wrong and he was flirting with me, that perhaps he went through some sort of trouble securing my telephone number to boldly ask me out on a date, which really quite turned me on—he was gone. I heard the iPhone tone three times, signaling he had hung up. What a tease.

Was I really going on a date after church? No, I wasn't asking hypothetically. I honestly didn't know if this was a date. It didn't feel like a date. And because I was unsure if Cody had actually asked me out on a date, I didn't dress like it was a date. I dressed like it was a job interview—I threw on my Rachel Roy knit dress that came down to my knees and my ballet flats. I didn't want to look like I thought it was a date . . . you know, just in case it wasn't.

I still wasn't sure if I was indeed going on a date when I showed up to 5 and Diamond. Coincidentally, he picked my favorite restaurant to have brunch. I took it as a good sign. I was walking up to the corner of 112th and Frederick Douglass when I spotted Cody outside. Sheesh. Those sacred moments when I smooth down my flyaways and reapply my lipstick were now impossible.

"Hi," I said. "What are you doing out here?"

Cody smiled and opened both of his arms wide as if he were a circus ringmaster and said, "Waiting for you. Have you been here before?"

"It's actually my favorite place," I said, giving in to a smile.

Cody smiled back mischievously. He looked amazing in a three-piece blue pin-striped suit. His tailor had made sure the suit jacket hugged his muscles, which he had obviously spent lots of time toning in the gym. He looked like a chocolate Ken doll.

"I just got mad points, didn't I? Does this mean I get a hug at the end of this?"

*This is definitely a date,* I said to myself.

I didn't notice when the entrees came to our corner table. I was entranced in our conversation. We traded statistics in rapid fire. Pretense had been left at the door.

"I'm thirty-six. No kids. No STDs. I've been engaged once. We broke up because she cheated on me . . . with one of my friends. "

"Wow. I'm sorry to hear that," I said somberly. "I'm twenty-eight. No kids. No STDs. Never been engaged. Got real close, though."

"What happened?"

"I'm still trying to figure that part out," I told Cody honestly.

He nodded as if he understood everything I didn't say. And that was how the conversation continued. For four hours, it felt like Cody was on the same wave as me. We floated together. We laughed together. We reminisced about '90s sitcoms together. We didn't want to leave. We had to order a second dessert so they wouldn't kick us out.

"What do you say we do this?"

"What?" I asked, genuinely confused.

"We do this. Talk. Eat. At every restaurant in Harlem."

It sounded good. It actually sounded great and I should've been jumping at the chance. But for some unknown reason, Cody's proposition made me think of Adam. I wished it were Adam who was sitting across from me, asking if we could have intimate conversations in every restaurant in Harlem.

Sigh.

*But it's not, Joi,* I told myself. *It's not. He's gone. He's burned out. Again. So now what? What are you going to do? What do you want to do? Joi! Answer. He's still looking at you. He's smiling and looking at you. You have to say something. Say something! Now!*

"Sure," I pushed out with a forced smile. "Sure, Cody!"

By the time I got home from our date, the sun was long tucked under the covers. My cheeks hurt from smiling and my voice was raspy from all of our getting-to-know-you chatter. I ran up the two flights of stairs, threw down my coat, and did a little dance as if I had just carried the ball into the end zone. I had to call my sister to tell her about the best first date I've had in a really long time.

"Jazz!"

"What, girl? What!"

She could sense the excitement in my voice.

"I just got back from a date with Cody!"

"Cody, huh? I guess he *was* flirting with you, then..."

## Chapter 18

For the next nine weeks, Cody and I made good on what we'd promised each other on our very first date at 5 and Diamond. We visited every restaurant in Harlem—Corner Social, Lido, The Cecil, Park 112, and even Chéri, the living-room-turned-upscale-eatery with the fixed menu.

We saw *12 Years a Slave* together, and every time I closed my eyes or tried to conceal my running tears, he comfortingly put his hand on my thigh. I even bumped into him occasionally at church. He always managed to find me after the service to comment on my nails, or my dress, or my hair. He wasn't stingy with a compliment. He laid them on thick like day-old mashed potatoes. I never understood why he thought I required that much and I was still unsure about taking them. It still felt odd to be dating, no matter how charming Cody was. And he really was charming.

One of my favorite dates was when I took him to my alma mater. Martha Stewart was giving a lecture about her magazine at Columbia University Graduate School of Journalism, and he, being a nerd like me, wanted to come with. The date was really special because it would be the first time he met any of my friends. Two of my classmates from J School were meeting me at the lecture and they were dying to meet him. Of course he was his normal, extra-hyper, super-friendly self, and my girls texted me before the lecture was even over to tell me they approved.

As we were walking off Columbia's campus to head home, he was texting feverishly on his own phone, so I knew he had somewhere to be. He usually kept his phone in his pocket during dates. Selfishly, I wanted to make our time together last longer, so I suggested we grab Starbucks and stroll home. And he sort of obliged. We got caramel lattes at the Starbucks across Broadway, and as we began to stroll, we walked past a bookstore. There's never been a quaint bookstore I could pass without going in, so we did. I thumbed the latest in fiction, then crossed over to the nonfiction table. Glancing up at him, he looked like a cross between bored and well meaning. "Want to go?" I asked.

"Oh no, no. Have fun. It's just that I don't read books."

My mind immediately zoomed back to the time I went over to his beautiful multistory apartment in Harlem, complete with an outdoor patio perfect for entertaining. It'd take me years to afford an apartment like that. When you walked in, there was this beautiful black bookcase. We spoke about that bookcase in detail because it was so beautiful and held such an interesting collection. I remember fingering some books, pointing to one and asking him to tell me what it was about. It turned me on.

Was Cody lying then or was he lying now? Or was I looking for inconsistencies? Was I just hoping he wouldn't measure up to Adam?

I kept my questions to myself because I stumbled upon the latest book from Chimamanda Ngozi Adichie, *Americanah*. I got so excited about the book that he insisted on buying it for me.

When we walked out of the bookstore and headed south on Broadway, I cheerily asked him, "So where to next?"

"Oh, I'm sorry, babe. I can't. I'm gonna put you in an Uber and I'm going to walk home and smoke this."

He pulled out a long cigar, wrapped in a Ziploc bag. It looked as if it had been in his pocket all night.

"You are?" I asked. My question could not hide my shock. I looked at the cigar uncut. I thought about asking him how he could possibly walk around smoking an uncut cigar but decided against it. Then the words tumbled out. A tiny flash of *I'm caught* ran across his eyes. It didn't make it down to his face, though.

Cody said he needed to go with such conviction that I didn't bother fighting him on it. I just followed him to the corner of 110th and Broadway and waited for my ride.

When the black car pulled up four minutes later, Cody opened the car door and gave me a tight hug. I had just bit into the brownie I bought at Starbucks when he kissed me gently.

"Good night, Joi," he said.

When I closed the car door, I knew that was our last date. I couldn't deal with habitual liars, especially men who lied about things they didn't have to lie about. If you can lie about whether you're going to walk around Harlem and smoke a cigar, you can lie about a shitload of other things. And Lord knows, I don't have time to figure out if you're lying or not. I'm busy!

Plus, in that moment, I realized Cody had done this before. He called one Monday, saying that he wanted to send me off on my weekend vacation with the girls in style. I thought it was sweet he had thought so far ahead. But the days in between that conversation ran long and tired and wanting. I texted him. I called. Everything went unreturned; I should've known he'd renege on my big send-off. But I prepared anyway—cleaned my apartment, got my nails done, and shaved my legs just in case he proved me wrong. I desperately wanted him to—this man who so carefully pursued me.

Perhaps he wasn't being careful at all. Perhaps he wanted to prove a point. He was so used to women liking him immediately, did he only pursue me because I couldn't remember meeting him? Did he only pursue me because I had looked past him?

When I finally saw him and got up real close, I saw his cracks, his shortcomings, his flaws, his insecurities. I mean, he *was* always looking over at my phone. Although I could love Cody past all of that, I decided not to. Because life changes love. And my love was no longer unbridled and free. It was a careful love, measured love, afraid love.

So we were over.

# Chapter 19

It's depressing to spend a holiday alone. Granted, it was only the Fourth of July. Thank goodness it wasn't Thanksgiving or Christmas or, worse, Valentine's Day. But it's still a holiday, and holidays are meant to be spent with family or friends.

My family was in Maryland—creating memories and sharing them by uploading photos on Facebook. My friends either didn't want to leave their respective boroughs or had other plans that didn't include me. So there I was, trying not to let depression creep up on me as Arista and I sat in bed. Although it was nearing 90 degrees outside, I had on socks and sweatpants. I was sipping on a sweet cup of coffee and searching for my happy.

The most embarrassing thing to admit to yourself is that you're lonely.

Lately, after long days in the newsroom, I come home only to tear up because no one is there to greet me. Well, that's not true. The dog is there to greet me, but that's even sadder than having no one there to greet me. And what's even sadder than that is that I'm happy Arista is there.

It didn't start off this way. Loneliness never does. It's like roll-ing down a hill. At first it's fine. You're rolling down. It's fun. It's more than fun. It's I-can-walk-around-naked-in-my-apartment-fun and I-don't-have-to-do-the-dishes-today-fun! But eventually every-thing starts whizzing by you too fast, and you feel like you're losing control, like you're about to head over a cliff at any minute. Your momentum is so drunk with gravity that you can't even control yourself to stop. You've fallen down the hole, Alice, and now you have to deal with that damn rabbit, a fucking tea party you're not dressed for, and that Cheshire cat. You didn't ask for it. You tell your friends you're sad, and they say you're probably PMSing. They don't understand, but you can't blame them because neither do you. How did being alone become so intolerable that it felt like someone was choking me every time I crossed the threshold into my one-bedroom apartment?

And it was not being alone that bothered me. I was technically not alone. Both of my parents were just a phone call away, friends texted me constantly, I mentioned the dog.

I just felt lonely.

A couple of weeks ago, on one of the hottest days of June, the familiar fog of loneliness followed me all around New York, from my Harlem apartment to the 2 train downtown, to my job near Lincoln Center. By lunchtime, the feeling had irritated me so much that I cried all the way to my vegetarian spot, Maoz. As I asked the cashier to wrap up my falafel sandwich on white pita to go, tears streamed down my face. Crying openly is so common in New York—there's never any expectation of privacy here—that she didn't even blink at my tears when she passed off my sandwich to shaking hands.

I imagine that when I have a family of my own, loneliness won't have room to grow. I pray so much that God would send me a husband and future children that I'm sure he's memorized my request.

Sometimes when I wake up, it's impossible to lift my head. It's so heavy from the cloud, the dark cloud, readjusting itself over my head for the day. I always wonder if tomorrow will be the day it won't come. Sometimes I wake up in the middle of the night scared, suddenly not believing that it'll get better tomorrow. One really, really, really bad night that happened and I started hyperventilating. I ran to the bathroom because I could no longer breathe lying down and it was the coolest room in my prewar apartment, so I figured I could catch my breath there. I clutched the sink, sucking air in, forcing it out, in, out, in, out. My heart was pounding so hard that it felt like my ears were bleeding. But instead of solace in the chill, I was shocked by my reflection in the mirror. I didn't even recognize myself.

Thinking I might die and needing a witness to know if something did happen to me, I called my mom. When she answered, I couldn't even talk. I was sobbing and breathing uncontrollably, but she knew it was me.

"Joi, Joi, Joi, calm down. Breathe. It's going to be okay," she said with her usual soothing voice.

She didn't even have to ask what was wrong with me. I am my mother's child. She knew what was wrong.

"It's going to be okay, baby. You're going to be okay," she affirmed.

Eventually, after following her instructions to splash cold water on my face, I told her I felt better and said goodbye...still sobbing.

I'm not sure what type of faith my mom had to not call NYPD to do a welfare check on me, but she didn't. I guess she knew I really would live through this. She knew I'd eventually go back to sleep and wake up with renewed faith. She knew that I'd get through this change in my life. She knew there was no other option.

That night I prayed, "I hope I'm happy tomorrow." I decided to make that my nightly prayer until I didn't have to say it any longer.

*Boing! Boing! Boing!*

Ugh. It was Adam. Why was he calling so early . . . and on a holiday? It was barely 10:00 a.m.! I kicked off my duvet and decided to answer before the call got sent to voice mail.

I wouldn't have to wait long to find out why Adam called. He didn't waste any time telling me he had run into my sorority sister Rebecca in Brooklyn the night before. Apparently, he was out with his "homegirl." That's code for "girl I'm dating."

"So what did Rebecca say to you?"

"Oh, dearheart. It's not important, but she did give me a look like 'What are you doing here with her?'"

I could only offer a sound: *humph.*

Adam pretended not to hear it and continued. "It didn't help that the girl I was hanging out with said, 'I thought you had a girlfriend.'"

If she thought Adam had a girlfriend, why was she on the date with him? That question bobbled around in my mind as I let him ramble.

"I still have your ring money," Adam blurted out. He sounded nervous. Good.

"What?"

"Your ring money—the money I was going to spend to buy your engagement ring. I still have it. You know, if you still want it," he said as if he were telling a joke.

"Is that supposed to be funny?"

"Kind of. I guess."

"Too soon, my friend. Too soon," I allowed before trying to rush him off the phone. I needed to walk Arista anyway. She had already trotted to the door, waiting to be leashed up to relieve herself. Now she was just staring at me impatiently while she waited.

"Wait! Understood. You were a great woman to me, dearheart. I should have expressed that more often. If I knew we weren't going to be together, I would have cherished the silly moments more... like you dancing in your living room."

Ordinarily, I'd consider this an endearing rare moment of sincerity. But since the split, Adam had been much more open with his feelings, a lot more open than I had. I was still angry at the way it all ended. I was irate, really. Funny enough, although he pulled the plug on our relationship, it seemed now like the other way around. I couldn't move further away from him fast enough, but he, on the other hand, seemed like he was ready to come back. And every time I thought I should consider it, especially since I was still truly in love with this man, something unnamed stopped me.

"Adam, I should go," I said abruptly. "Have a good holiday."

With that, I hung up.

I found it hilarious that Adam felt the need to call me first thing the next day, just in case Rebecca had contacted me the night before. She hadn't. Perhaps she had asked around and someone told her that Adam and I had broken up.

I still haven't made any type of social media breakup announcement. I would never. It's just not my style. I haven't started using hashtags like #singleandreadytomingle or any of that. The closest I got to that was putting the hashtag #sorrymichelleobama on all my photos.

What's #sorrymichelleobama? Think about it: Our First Lady is a vision of perfection when it comes to what men look for in a wife. Her garden party dresses never have one wrinkle in them, her hair is always laid, she's always smiling, she never has lipstick on her teeth, and Barack is always on her good side. She's the perfect wife and a really great mother. At one point, she was the type of wife I desperately wanted to be—supportive, giving, comforting, proper, smart, sophisticated, mature, buttoned up, enviable, perfect.

But as much as I tried to be Adam's Michelle Obama, I couldn't be picture-perfect anymore. In the process of becoming his first lady, I had lost myself.

Adam didn't like women who wore a lot of makeup, so I hadn't. He hated my belly button ring—said it was so 1990s—so I took it out and let it close up.

And I'll never forget the time when I wore my first crop top to a Jay Z concert. He had never seen his rap idol perform in person, so when the rap god was performing a series of concerts to open the Barclays Center in Brooklyn, I scored us two floor seats thanks to my prowess of incessantly refreshing the page on Ticketmaster. I got all dolled up with a Rihanna-esque crop top, high-waisted leather skirt, and five-inch royal-blue heels. To make my way inside the Barclays Center, I had to carefully maneuver my way around the potholes on Flatbush, clutching Adam's arm for support.

"You wouldn't have to grab me so hard if you wore other shoes. Why'd you even do all of that?" he asked loudly in front of our friends. Well, really, his friends.

Adam had a habit of airing me out in front of company. I had told him about it repeatedly, that I found it embarrassing and could he please stop, but he continued to do it. He would say things like, "Joi can't cook. Can you believe she was about to put gravy from a jar on the smothered chicken?" I'd try to laugh as his friends side-eyed me and my cooking skills. Or lack thereof. I'd playfully retort, "Well, isn't that cooking, Adam?"

He'd laugh and say, "I've never met a woman who used gravy out of a jar."

"My mom does!"

"Well…I can't say nothing bad about your mom," he'd say, laughing.

I'd laugh too…pretending to be in on the joke, instead of the butt of the joke. But I was the butt of the joke and it hurt my feelings. Yet, night after night of bringing up to Adam just how hurtful he was being at my expense, I just eventually pretended not to care.

With his face scrunched up in clear disapproval, I was too mad to even speak as we walked arm in arm to the Barclays Center. We had been here before. We had had this fight before. So instead, I just looked down at my new cobalt blue heels and concentrated on avoiding the pockmarked pavement.

"I wish my wife still dressed up for me," his friend Derrick had muttered, probably in an effort to smooth the tension.

I shot a look of "thank you" to him and he nodded ever so slightly.

I hadn't even noticed that in the five years that we were together I had become someone different. At one point, our relationship was fun: It was laughter and it was staycations and it was boiling lobsters from scratch because I loved seafood and it was stolen kisses and it was passionate.

And then it wasn't.

But neither one of us wanted to let go because we didn't see the shifts happening. They were so gradual and so slow—like tectonic plates—that we didn't realize we weren't in the same place anymore until a crash, an explosion, an earthquake happened.

I looked back at all the times I smiled with my mouth but not with my spirit, when I let what he said go because it was better to be silent than to have another argument, when I chugged that glass of wine before he came over so I could remain Zen when he stopped by, when I ignored the fact that he didn't kiss me goodbye or when he flinched when I grabbed his hand to hold it. I started to ignore this because after all, I still loved him. And ignoring it was better than being alone and dealing with the realness of myself.

No wonder Adam was burned out. He was tired of this dance we tried to choreograph.

But now I wanted to reclaim myself. I had to reclaim myself.

# Chapter 20

As the holiday weekend dragged on, I wished I had somebody's Netflix password. Instead, I was laid out on my bed with Arista, letting the hum of the fan drown out my thoughts of nothingness.

I hadn't felt desired since I ended things with Cody. My need to post another #sorrymichelleobama moment on the 'gram, led me to meet Chinedu—an American-born Nigerian who grew up in London.

*Ding. Ding.*

The respectable iPhone chime alerted me of a text from my sorority sister Kaya. She wanted to go out "now." Apparently, she was bored and about to lose her mind. Her brother and his kids—two utterly adorable yet demonically rambunctious kids— were home for the July Fourth holiday weekend and she needed an excuse to escape.

Come to Harlem, I texted her.

Corner Social? she replied, suggesting Cody's old favorite watering hole on 126th and Lenox.

K, I said, lying back down to let the bed swallow me.

Kaya lived in Queens and I lived ten blocks away, so I at least had another hour before I really had to move.

Of course, by the time we walked into Corner Social, shortly after midnight, it was packed, and I immediately regretted leaving my bed and Arista. But I was forcing myself out of the house these days. If I didn't, I would let the dark cloud pull me back to places I needn't dare linger.

After getting Adam's favorite drink, which had somehow become my favorite—a vodka gimlet with simple syrup—at the crowded bar, I finally looked around the dark room. Reggae, curated from the deejay booth positioned right by the door, blasted any chance of small talk inside the restaurant-turned-hot-spot.

Then he caught my eye. Chinedu was dark with a chiseled jaw, covered in a well-manicured beard. He wasn't that tall—definitely not taller than me—but his tailored suit hinted that he worked on Wall Street and his striking confidence made me look twice. I actually did a double take. Like, who actually does that in real life...but Chinedu was alarmingly handsome. Think a thinner, shorter Idris Elba complete with the British accent.

But he wasn't enough to make me stay. I was ready to go home. I had had a long day of watching TV, then lying in bed reading. As another person said "Excuse me" to rush to the bar, all I could think about was slipping back under my covers. So I gave Kaya the let's-go look and thankfully she obliged. I shot back what was left of my gimlet, licked the sugar rim, which I had specially requested, and made my way past the deejay booth toward the front door.

"Joi! Joi!" I heard someone scream over Sizzla's reggae classic "Dry Cry."

It was my sister's old roommate from Howard University, Jessica.

"How are you, Jess? Who are you here with?" I yelled at her.

"Jake!" she said, referencing her boyfriend, whom she had been with since she lived with my sister in the Towers. "He just passed the bar, so we're celebrating by doing shots. Where's Adam?"

I knew Jess, whom I hadn't seen since I moved to New York, didn't mean any harm, but she had accidentally ripped my Band-Aid off, removing the scab. Her question hurt.

"Um...um, actually. Actually, Jess..."

My stammering gave Jess enough time to look to her left and her right for Adam, who wasn't there.

"We broke up," I finally managed to say.

"Ohmygod, what?" Jess said, shocked.

I was embarrassed. I was less embarrassed that I was single. More so I was embarrassed that I had failed at something so many people seemed to do with ease—be in a relationship.

"Yup. Months ago, actually. It's just not something you announce."

"Totally! Are you *okay*?"

"Of course! Look at me!" I faked, then expertly switched subjects. "This is my friend Kaya. We were actually just about to head out. I'm exhausted."

"Yes, yes! It was nice seeing you," Jess said. Her well-wish didn't match her face, which was still stuck in a state of shock by my news.

As disappointed as I was, I hated to see others disappointed by my news too.

If you don't announce your breakup on social media, which I refused to do, telling people felt like my very own version of coming out of the closet. One of my gay friends—who would probably want me to refer to him as a friend who just so happens to be gay—once told me that he was in a constant state of coming out.

People think that when you come out, you do it once. Like ta-da! I'm out. Case closed. But that's not the case. Usually, you come out over and over again to different family members, to friends, to colleagues, to old acquaintances. That's how it felt to reveal my newfound singleness. It wasn't enough to tell my mom, my sister, my closest friends...but I had to tell my work colleagues, people I hadn't seen in years, and sometimes even *his* friends.

As I walked out into the summer night's air, little did I know Chinedu had followed me.

I had already hailed a cab to drive me the thirteen blocks to my apartment, but Chinedu—thinking it was his last chance at a summer romance—yelled in a Nigerian-English accent, "Hallo! You're *leaving?*"

"Yes, I've had a long day," I said dryly as I peeked in the cab to let the driver know that despite this small talk, I still planned to get in.

"Why so soon?" he asked with a smile that made my stomach drop. "You don't have time for one more drink?"

The cabdriver was staring a hole through the side of my head, but I didn't know what to do. I really did want to go home, but something about his audacity made me want to get to know him. Chasing me out of a restaurant took balls, after all. Plus, when was the last time I'd been actively pursued?

Leaning inside the cab, I told the driver he could go. I hoped I wouldn't regret that.

Chinedu and I texted lightly after that fateful meeting outside Corner Social. Although I remembered him being really cute, it wasn't enough to accept his last-minute invitation to dinner on a Tuesday, nor to a late brunch on a Sunday, nor to drinks at Ginny's Supper Club on a Friday. I told him, "You do things too last-minute for me. Make a date and I can do that." But three Thursdays later, he ignored my request and instead called to ask if I wanted to grab drinks that evening.

"Do you not realize there's a hurricane coming?" I asked pointedly. "Today may not work."

"Oh, it's just a little rain," he said with the air of an aristocrat. "How about nine?"

Nine?! That seemed so late, but I couldn't be difficult again. I had given him the runaround for weeks now, and he had been patient…so perhaps I should. Considering the weather, he'd likely cancel on me anyway.

After waking up from my daily nap—when you wake up as early as I do, naps are imperative—I peered outside my window to see if the hurricane that was steadily approaching had done any damage. It had stopped raining, but I did notice a tree was now horizontal in the middle of the street. That was all I could manage to see from my apartment window.

*Ding! Ding!*

I know it's our first time hanging out but want to come to my place?

As I stared at Chinedu's text, I raised an eyebrow. *Really*, dude?

I had barely thought of an appropriate response before another text pushed through. This time it was a picture of his apartment. His living room had floor-to-ceiling windows, showing off the Harlem skyline. From the looks of the view, he must've been on the top floor.

I really didn't want to go, but I was bored and wanted to figure out once and for all if this guy was worth my time. Plus, I had thought about Adam too many times today.

sure send address. just need to get dressed, I replied.

By the time I had showered, gotten dressed, applied makeup, and sprayed on my Gucci perfume—a scent Adam bought me—it was already 11:00 p.m.

Chinedu didn't make me feel bad about taking my sweet time to trek to his apartment, which was only seventeen blocks away. Instead, he told me he had just finished cooking and asked if I was hungry. I didn't really feel like eating, considering how cute I looked. I had pulled out my low-cut, off-the-shoulder, long-sleeved shirt for the "date."

He made us tequila cocktails—served in wineglasses—although I told him I'd sworn off tequila after one bad night that ended with me throwing up in the bathroom and my sorority sister rubbing my back and forcing me to drink water.

"Break your own rules," he said, smiling.

That'd be the first of many times he'd tell me that.

We barely watched *Vicky Cristina Barcelona*, which he probably turned on with the intention of ignoring it. At least we were on the same page. *No, get your mind out of the gutter.* Instead, we talked. We talked about everything—our siblings (he has six), our parents (his, like mine, have been married for over forty years), and what we do (he owns two businesses, which he runs from his apartment). Based on his kitchen and view of Harlem, I believed him. He told me he went to high school in London, then got a degree in engineering from Berkeley before getting his MBA at Harvard. He said his father was a diplomat back in his homeland, but I have no idea what that actually means.

"Can I kiss you?"

Ohmygod, ohmygod, he actually *asked* to kiss me. Who *does* that? It's adorable but a bit creepy.

"No!" I said aloud, laughing.

His head lowered and my heart quickened. Okay—wait. I did actually want to kiss him but who *asks* that?

"Just...um...wait five minutes," I sputtered out.

"Need to refresh your drink?" he asked, picking up my glass and walking briskly to his kitchen. I watched him take the silver and lime-green Patrón bottle out of the refrigerator and pour three seconds' worth of it into my wineglass. He then put the bottle back into the fridge, only to take out a box of juice. Pouring that into the glass, he replaced the juice and walked back over with a tight smile on his face.

It hadn't been five minutes, but when he sat down on his brown leather couch next to me, placing his hand on top of my knee, Chinedu kissed me. It was the most delightful, delicious, hungry, passionate, lip-biting, boob-grabbing, tongue-tickling kiss.

It was undoubtedly the best kiss I'd had all year. I needed to be touched, needed to be wanted, needed to be adored, and Chinedu did that for me. In that moment I didn't want him to stop. With my eyes closed in want, I didn't see him when he put his pointer finger in my mouth. It was so unexpected and salty that I didn't have time to react. In fact, I was so surprised I almost bit down on the digital intruder, so I did the first thing that came to mind. I started sucking his finger from the top of his knuckle until the tip of his finger left my mouth. His finger left an undesired tangy aftertaste in my mouth. Taken aback and a little grossed out, I grabbed my wineglass filled with tequila to wash down what lingered.

"So you'll spend the night, yes?"

Although his voice rose at the end of his sentence to infer he was asking a question, Chinedu was telling me. The faux question dripped with nerve.

"No, Chinedu."

I looked down at my iPhone to check the time. Ohmygoodness, it was almost 3:00 a.m. and I'd told myself that I wouldn't stay long. There was no way I was sleeping over at this man's apartment no matter how sexy he was.

In his Britishy accent, Chinedu interrupted my thoughts and tried to delay my exit by asking me, "What are two things you know for sure?"

I allowed myself to smile. It was a question that I'd usually ask my suitors and it was nice that the tables were turned for once.

"Finding two answers may be hard...," I stalled. "But I do have a good one."

I paused.

"Chinedu, I was a bit unsure when I left my apartment. I'll be honest with you. But I'm happy I came over. What about you? What are two things you know for sure?"

He didn't hesitate. "I know for sure your eyes are beautiful. I know for sure you're beautiful. You're the best kisser ever. You have a body I could adore—"

"Stop, stop, stop..." I pushed him away. He somehow had managed to inch his warm, muscular body closer with each compliment in cadence. But I couldn't take it anymore. I could feel my face getting flushed. I hated that feeling. I hated to blush, to lose control over my body.

"What?" He cocked his head to the side. A faint smile appeared on his face.

"I really don't need all of that, Chinedu."

"But it's true," he said softly. Then he abruptly walked to the kitchen to refill his glass.

When he came back to the living room, he told me he'd be leaving for three weeks. For one of those weeks, he'd be attending a wedding in London. He didn't tell me what he'd be doing the other two weeks and I didn't ask. Then all of a sudden I got sad.

"I may miss you," I said.

"I don't understand you women," Chinedu said, shaking his head. "Why would you say 'I *may* miss you'?"

"Well, when I speak to you next, you may piss me off and then I wouldn't miss you anymore."

"If I did, I'd make it up to you."

"Don't say things you don't mean," I said squarely.

I wanted him to be telling the truth, though. I wanted him to be telling the truth so badly, but it was just too soon to tell.

After a few more stolen kisses and a handful of rough ones, he ordered an Uber for me. Before he walked me downstairs, he tried to pull my head into his to steal one last kiss near his door, but I felt his hand creeping up the back of my neck. God! No! My naps! You know, those little unrelaxed hairs at the nape of my neck! I pulled my head back so hard that it hit the wall behind me with a resounding thud. I might've just given myself a concussion. It was that bad. The pain shot down my spine, and I heard a faint ringing in my ears, but I brushed it off.

He's such a gentleman; he didn't even laugh. Hell, even I would've laughed at me.

When my Uber arrived, Chinedu opened my car door but didn't let me go just yet. We made out like teenagers with strict parents. From the corner of my eye I could see the cabbie getting impatient, but we were hungry for each other. Or perhaps I was hungry for someone. Anyone.

When I got back to my apartment, I texted Chinedu to let him know that I got home safely. He didn't reply until the morning, telling me that he was at the airport.

I never heard from him again.

# PART THREE

# Back on the Court

*Chapter 21*

There it was. Not noticeably at first but then definitely. I felt an undeniable shift. I didn't have to pause when I got out of bed in the morning. I just stretched my body, from my navel to my toes, and hopped out. I got dressed with interest and intent and made the train on time. When I did my daily eight-minute walk from the 72nd Street train stop to my job, I noticed things I hadn't seen in a very long time.

Sunrays shone through the trees, creating hazy diagonal lines to the ground. A bird that looked like an oriole flew and landed on the grass. (Hmm, didn't orioles only fly near Maryland? What was it doing here?) I smelled the distinct scent of freshly cut grass, and it smelled good. When I walked into work each day, I actually cared what the security guard said back to me when I said my obligatory, "Good morning."

For the first time in a long time, I was happy. I was present in this pocket of time. I had been kind of lazy-rivering it, just trying to stay afloat for so long, that it felt good to be awake. To be here. To participate.

I've come such a long way since February when I split with Adam—from enduring sleepless nights, losing twelve pounds, drinking wine for dinner, crying helplessly on the streets of New York, and not being able to be happy for other people in relationships. That was who I was right after the life I thought I was going to live disappeared right before my eyes. Six months and five days later, I felt lighter. My heart was happy. My soul was full and so was my calendar.

And I had a new prayer: "God, surprise me." My simple prayer was much more than yet another request for God on my long list after the husband and a couple of children. It was much more than wanting my eyes to widen in joyous wonder, matching my mouth agape in amazement.

For me, it was proof that I was open to his ultimate imagination for my life. It was proof that I was taking my hands off the wheel and trusting him to direct my path. It was proof that I was finally open to the life he envisioned for me instead of the one I had so desperately wanted for myself. Asking God to surprise me was telling him I no longer wanted a say in the way this played out because I trusted him so implicitly. So wholeheartedly. Completely. It was confirmation of my humility. I wanted no say. I wanted to shatter the limits of my expectations to heighten my reality.

I have this horrible habit of trying to control everything in life. It was my fear of losing control that had made me desperately afraid of letting Adam go. I figured if I let him go, I'd never convince another man to fall in love with me or even think about marrying me. For some reason, with all of my amazing qualities—and I do have some—I just didn't believe that a man would fall for me again. Me, beautiful, tall, smart, independent, sexual, hood, bougie, giving, swallowing, *me*.

I've always had a hand in a man falling for me. Almost every boyfriend I've ever had, I've asked him to be my boyfriend and not the other way around. My very first boyfriend, Matheo, didn't want to date me initially because he had just broken up with a girl from my school, but I didn't care. We got along so well, he was cute, and he was one of the few boys taller than me in high school. So I asked him out, and we dated for four years. Then there was Brian. I definitely came on to him in the diner on campus. He was trying to get some freshmen to buy him a meal with their diner points when it happened. And despite Gary, the preacher's kid who did actually ask me to be his girlfriend, there was Adam. And yup, I asked him to be my boyfriend too.

So perhaps my new prayer will open my eyes to possibilities I never considered before. I was already less stressed, less anxious, and less depressed—because what I wanted before wasn't God's will. So I had already lost before I began.

There's a blessed freedom that comes with taking a step back, especially when you're used to being in control. Everything in life can't be manipulated. There are some things, the best things, that are God given. I call them divine. If you think you can create a divine life with your might, prayers, vision boards, and diligence, you're sadly mistaken. Don't believe anyone who says they willed their lives to happen on their own. They're taking credit for what God does. And you can't trust any person who doesn't give God credit for what he's doing.

It was good that I woke up in Happyland that August morning because when I arrived at the newsroom, I got an unusual request. Our country music producer, Hilton, wanted me to interview a band for him since he was out sick. The band was Rascal Flatts. I had heard of them before, but I'd never listened to their music.

Thank God for Spotify. I hate to interview musicians without ever hearing their music, so I dedicated an hour before my interview to familiarize myself. It was the least I could do, right?

I heard song after song, but one stood out: "Payback." The guys crooned to some girl in a bar that they could help her get payback on a man who had "done her wrong." After a night of drinking, snapping photos for Instagram, and partying, she would show her ex exactly what he was missing.

I mean, was this *not* what I was going through?! If only Adam knew what he was missing.

Although it wasn't one of the questions Hilton had prepared for me, I just had to ask about this song. What I didn't foresee slipping out during the in-studio sit-down was me saying, "Ohmygod, this is the exact same thing I'm going through right now."

I didn't think anything of my flippant admission until Joe Don Rooney, the lead guitarist, brought it up as I walked them to the door to meet their waiting black SUV.

"I wish we could stay here all day," Joe Don said.

"Well, I'd love it! It'd make my day go by faster," I replied. And, no, it wasn't a line. I mean, c'mon. He was married and had a baby on the way, but it was the truth!

With a sincere look on his face, which also included a lot of caked-on makeup—perhaps they were doing television interviews later that day—he patted me on the back, like a father, and said, "I wish you the best of luck on your relationship. Were you engaged?"

"Very close," I admitted. "We dated for five years."

"Wow! Really? Hope you're okay," he said with a flash of sincerity.

I love Southern people.

"Oh, no. I am. I'm actually enjoying dating again. I mean, I'm learning a lot. A lot has changed since the last time I dated. Twitter didn't even exist before my last relationship and online dating was relegated to weirdos and the sexually addicted."

He laughed from his belly.

"Okay, good," he said. "Hopefully you'll find a man who will blow you away. And you'll do the same to him."

I felt a chill run down the length of my back while I looked into Joe Don's eyes. It was such a prophecy from such a random moment. But it felt genuine. Real. It was what I needed. Hope.

As I held open the door so the guys could go to their probably fourth interview of the day, I told them to come back any time. When I said those words, I meant them.

# Chapter 22

Posting international vacation pics is to single women what posting baby pics is to new mothers. We love that shit. Nothing says "I have an amazing job that gives me the luxury of expendable funds, vacation days, and fabulous friends" than a trip out of the country.

My "mom" friends can never make the trips, which are often planned at the last minute. We'll allow a married friend or two on the rare occasion that said married person hasn't transitioned into an all-I-can-talk-about-are-married-people-things zombie. It just ruins the vibe when they push into every conversation their husband and other adult topics like life insurance policies, home improvement projects, and how they're trying to have a baby—complete with sharing the exact calendar days that they're ovulating and specifying how many times they've had sex and in what positions.

In the last several years, my single friends and I have become world travelers. Our previous college trips to Jamaica and the Bahamas don't count for some reason. But we've dabbled across the pond in France, Italy, South Africa, and even Romania.

But it was our trip to Istanbul, Turkey, that took the cake. The occasion? Ashlee was celebrating her thirtieth birthday in the country that bridges Europe and Asia. We had already spent days in Romania, visiting my two sorority sisters who had moved to Bucharest, or, as the locals call it, Bucureşti, to teach at an international school there.

After getting drunk in downtown Lipscani, eating gelato on the cobblestoned streets, and having a three-course dinner on the edge of Herăstrău Park at Casa di David, later that week we took a tram to the top of the Buşteni Mountains. I immediately regretted wearing sandals on our mountain hike because it began to snow. We ended three days of sightseeing by eating in a countryside log cabin where we could watch sheep grazing in the grass nearby.

A quick flight later and we were in Istanbul to begin the second leg of our trip.

Oh, I forgot to mention the part where I was mistaken for an international basketball star. An elderly Romanian man was startled one morning to see me coming out of my sorority sister's building. He didn't speak any English, but he knew how to fake dribble with his hand. He did the motion twice—dribble, dribble—then pointed at me, smiling. I shook my head hard to let him know the assumption couldn't be more incorrect. Sadly, I couldn't think of any hand motions for "tourist," so we parted ways.

To say Istanbul was a culture shock would be an understatement. I don't think I've ever been so far away from home, and barely any of my street knowledge from Baltimore and Harlem translated here.

One of my six friends on the trip suggested that instead of paying for two cabs to take us to our boutique hotel near the Galata Tower, we should catch a bus for five euros. It sounded like a deal, so we all hopped on what looked like a more comfortable city bus. It was a nice introduction to the city we'd spend the next four days in. Little did we know that the bus didn't actually take us to our hotel, and we'd have to drag our nearly fifty-pound luggage across Taksim Square in the still, dry heat. Sweat showed up in perfectly formed beads on my forehead and lower back as we made our way onto a little red trolley and down many cobblestoned streets to our actual hotel. We made it—barely.

After some much needed rest, we woke up the next morning ready to tour the city sights. Ashlee, who moonlights as a travel blogger, suggested we try this walking tour she found online that guided you to Istanbul's must-see sights, including the Galata Tower, across the Galata Bridge and into Old City, where the fish boats are located, so we could try the famed fish sandwiches. We'd then head to the Grand Bazaar and lastly to all the mosques.

What the walking tour failed to include was just how long it'd actually take to get to all these places with six talking, gossiping, laughing, picture-happy tourists. So after trekking two hundred feet up the Galata Tower to get some scenic photos for Instagram, and walking across the bridge above the Golden Horn where fisherman after fisherman after fisherman outright stared at us—I don't think they'd ever seen six black women traveling together without any men—and maneuvering our way through the maze that is the Grand Bazaar, we were ready to call it a day. But it was Istanbul, so under the oppressive summer heat, we kept pressing until we reached at least one mosque.

I had read up on enough mosque etiquette to know that I had to wear a dress that covered my knees. Thanks to H&M, I showed respect for the culture in a short-sleeved magenta maxi dress. I brought with me a matching bedazzled pashmina that I got in a Dubai souk to cover up my head and arms, which was also necessary.

Of course we arrived at the Süleymaniye Mosque during prayer time, which meant we couldn't go in until it was over. Devout Muslims here pray five times a day and many times it's within a mosque. Although we had read in a tourist guide that prayer time could sometimes last over an hour, we had made it this far, so we weren't turning back. Instead, we toured the picturesque grounds of the mosque with its gardens of familiar flowers to waste time until we could go inside.

My friend Farrah and I sat down in the mosque's courtyard to rest our feet, which were now throbbing after hours of tourist attractions, while the other girls searched for a WC—a bathroom. I exhaled. On this sacred ground, I felt a sudden sense of calm. It felt familiar. My usual anxiousness that I've gotten expertly good at masking didn't exist here in this ancient space. It felt like home . . . to me, a Christian.

With most of the girls gone, I had time to look around and take in my surroundings. Here I was, sitting on cool marble that had been laid centuries before me underneath the hot Turkish sun. I looked down and touched it. It was dusty under my fingertips, but it was still there. I wondered if anything I'd ever create would last this long. I stared at incredible domes that sat atop perfectly symmetrical outdoor archways that reminded me of St. Peter's Square in Vatican City. Different religions, same beauty. I couldn't wait to get inside the mosque to see more of it.

After making Farrah, who I've known since before I could read, take several photos of me wrapped in my pink pashmina, I noticed a man staring at us. I felt my energy shift as I stared back at him— Baltimore-style—to let him know his stare was uninvited. But something got lost in translation because he then approached us. Farrah and I could both sense something we didn't want to happen was about to happen. She grabbed her iPhone, which doubled as our camera for our impromptu photo shoot, and draped her purse over one shoulder just in case he tried to grab it and run away. Thinking quickly, I used the oldest trick in my book to deter him from striking up a conversation.

"Dad?" I said, holding up my phone to my ear, which was conveniently on airplane mode so I wouldn't incur any unnecessary charges while I traveled. "Yup, Dad, we're right here in the courtyard," I said to no one at all. "You want us to meet you where? Where, Dad?"

Farrah caught on quickly as I got up to meet "Dad." Thankfully, as we wandered outside the courtyard, we found the other ladies, who had just returned from the bathroom. We had strength in numbers.

After about an hour or so of waiting, we finally took off our shoes and entered the mosque, snapping photos of every nook and cranny. It almost lived up to the beauty of that quiet moment in the courtyard.

The forty-five-minute walk back to our hotel didn't seem as long, especially after stopping to stuff that fish sandwich, sprayed lightly with lemon, into my mouth. When I got up to throw away my garbage and pay a child on the street selling tiny bottles of lemonade, I felt two hands on my ass. Undeniably, two hands with fingers spread wide apart found their way on both of my cheeks… at the same time. A hot flush ran through my entire body. It was rage. I don't remember yelling, but I must've because Farrah turned to me, asking, "What? What? What happened?"

"That man just grabbed my ass! Full-on just grabbed it."

"Ohmygod," Farrah said, looking to her right and left to see who had done it.

I whipped my entire body around to see my assailant face-to-face. I wanted him to see in my eyes how violated I felt so I could curse him to high heaven...but then I remembered where I was. And I remembered that I was with six women who had never been here before. I got frazzled. My Baltimore curse-out wouldn't work on this disheveled bearded man with the blackest, curliest hair I'd ever seen, wearing days-old clothes. He probably didn't even speak English. And he clearly didn't understand body language either because he began to follow Farrah and me.

"Leave me alone!" I yelled with my gut. Farrah held her arms out to me and I rushed into her human shield of protection. "Leave me the fuck alone!"

I only knew three Turkish words—how to say *cheers*, *thank you*, and *stop*. "*Dur! Dur!*" I yelled at him to stop. And then he did.

Still hugging me, Farrah whispered in my ear, "I didn't want to say anything before because I didn't want to ruin the trip, but when we were in the Grand Bazaar, I felt one finger on my butt. It wasn't even a grab; it was just one finger going right up my butt cheek. By the time I had turned around, I didn't see where he had gone. It was like he had vanished."

She looked down at her sandals, while I stared at her embarrassed face in disbelief. I wasn't the only one violated that day.

"Well, we're not gonna let this ruin our trip, right?" I said, still shaking.

"Right." She nodded. "We're not."

A couple of long sightseeing days later, it was finally Ashlee's thirtieth birthday. She had decided that for dinner, we'd head to Suada Club, a privately owned island in the middle of the Bosphorus River, full of restaurants, a nightclub, and an Olympic-sized pool. It was our only night out in Istanbul, so the plan was to dress up. Our travel guides told us that it's not disrespectful to ditch the pashminas and dress to the nines at night in certain parts of the city.

My hair was getting worn down from the trip, so before I took my shower, I twisted my long weave—fresh for the trip—into eight twists. Further twisting those twists created bantu knots, making my head resemble Medusa's. After trying to sing Brandy songs in the shower, I took thirty whole minutes to do my makeup. I wanted my face to look like it'd been touched by the hands of God, or maybe Sam Fine. By the time I shimmied into my black semi-sheer bandage skirt and matching crop top, I felt my hair had been knotted long enough. Thankfully, when my hair tousled down, twist by twist, I looked like I had been on the beach all day—but sexier, sultrier.

I was ready to meet someone.

We took a cab down and up the winding Turkish streets that would make Six Flags roller coasters feel like kiddie rides and finally arrived at Kuruçeşme Park. Every girl, in five-inch-high stilettos, tiptoed onto the boat—the evening's public transportation—that would take us to the island for dinner. A uniformed attendant helped us out of the boat and directed us to one of six restaurants on the island.

We had the best seats in the house—right in the middle of the outdoor restaurant, in the middle of the island. In the distance, the Bosphorus Bridge beautifully lit up the night sky and the now dark river. Heated lamps provided a bit of warmth while we ordered our first round of cocktails. The bar that overlooked the pool had several televisions on it, playing a soccer match, or *futbol*. Because it was dinnertime, the pool was closed, but the purple and aqua lights glowing underwater gave the island an exotic glow.

By the time we ordered our small plates to share and some kebabs, word must have gotten out in the restaurant that the *Real Housewives of America* were eating outside because the owner came over to introduce himself. A charming, tall, intimidating guy who looked like a Turkish George Clooney sat down at the head of the table explaining how Suada came to be. We were so intrigued by this little gem in the middle of the river that we pelleted him with questions. But with so many beautiful women interested in his club—his words—he didn't seem to mind. In fact, he said he wanted to join us for dinner and called over the waiter so he could get his own place setting. After dinner, he promised he'd give us a tour of the island. And he did. He walked us around the pool to the event space—where a wedding was being held—and to his office, which had its own private dock for his boat. His dog even had a boat. We thought the language barrier was failing us when he said that.

"A dog boat? What's a dog boat?" we each said in surprise.

"My dog has a boat!" he said confidently while opening his deck door like a Turkish Vanna White. There it was. In the dark, out on the water, a floating doghouse bobbed up and down.

"Is your dog in there?" I asked incredulously, thinking of my own miniature dachshund back at home. She'd totally freak out if she had to live on water. She didn't even like taking baths!

Our George Clooney laughed, throwing his head back to seemingly confirm my question. Then he closed the patio door and continued his tour. At the end of it, he said he didn't want the night to end. It was Saturday, after all.

"My boat will take you to my club, Reina. Yes? It's right across the river. It's your birthday right?" he said, looking at Ashlee. "I'll get you girls a table and a birthday cake on me. I'll take care of you. Come!"

We didn't even hesitate. A boat to the club? Yes, please!

By the time we tiptoed to the restroom for a quick touch-up and a couple of mirror selfies, a tan sports yacht was docked outside the restaurant, waiting for us. I felt like a celebrity while other tourists looked on at us, wondering who we were to have our own boat as they crammed onto the public transportation boat. We hopped on, one by one, with help from the attendant and proceeded to jet the ten windy minutes across the river to Reina. The Bosphorus Bridge was the perfect backdrop for our impromptu selfies to capture and brag about this moment later on Instagram.

By midnight, the club was in full swing and we were the owner's guests. Huge velvet curtains that took two people to maneuver swung open in unison as the boat pulled up to the club's dock. That was what you called making an entrance. We were helped off the boat, just as we were helped on, and led to our table.

"Wait, this is it?" Ashlee said when the hostess finally arrived at our table.

Table service in Istanbul was nothing like table service back at home. Our "table" was not a dining-room style table with couches like we were used to in the United States. Instead, it was a cocktail table with snacks. It came complete with what looked like mini-apples, mini-oranges, and an assortment of nuts. Well, that was thoughtful. If we were going to be drinking all night, at least we had snacks to curb any hunger pangs.

After downing our bottle of complimentary champagne, courtesy of the bronzed George Clooney, we danced to EDM songs I had never heard before. We were relieved when the deejay finally started playing Rihanna and Pharrell Williams's hit song of the moment, "Happy."

After another touch-up in the bathroom, we headed back to our cocktail table because we had remembered what the owner told us: "Be at your table by two. That's when the birthday cake arrives." And arrive it did, with one huge sparkler and a small candle. The wind whipping off the river blew out Ashlee's candle before she could. I'm not even sure she made a wish.

Soon it felt like all eyes were on us in the club. A tall European tourist and his black girlfriend—who said she was happy to see women like her in Reina—came over to our table to bum champagne off us. We didn't give up a drop, but we did dance with them to some super old hip-hop song that the deejay had dug up. After a few more Turkish men came over to our table to try their hand, three American-looking black men walked up to us and asked us outright, "What are y'all doing here?"

The question made us laugh because if we were honest with ourselves, we had wondered the same thing about them.

"What are y'all doing here?" Ashlee laughed back, tipsy from the champagne.

"We're on tour. I'm a background singer. He's a saxophonist," the chubby dark-skinned one said.

"With who?" I pressed.

Chubs gave me a sly look as if to say he wasn't going to reveal their secret; then he invited us to their table for drinks. Thankful to see similar faces so far away from home, we couldn't follow them fast enough to their table on the second floor of the nightclub.

"Where are y'all from?" Ashlee, in her Maryland accent, asked after we got to their table.

The one with the dreads yelled over the EDM, "Maryland!"

We all looked at each other and gasped. "So are we!"

A collective "Ay!" vibrated from our section.

It didn't take long to find out that they were also from Baltimore, which high school they went to, and who we knew in common.

"If you're a musician from Baltimore, you probably know my brother-in-law. He's a musician."

"What's his name?" asked Mark, the one with the dreads.

"James Richardson."

"Of course I know Jimmy," Mark replied, twisting his wedding ring around his finger nervously.

"That's your *brother*?"

"Yeah," I said proudly.

"Hey, Big Rod! Rod! This is Jimmy's sister!!!"

"Oh, word?" the chubby one yelled over the music. "That's wassup!"

"*You're* related to Jimmy?" a tall, lanky guy, who I found out was another background singer named Shawn, asked. "Cool. Want some Jameson?"

I asked him to pour me a glass with Coke. I hated to go up to other people's tables in a club and bogart my way around as if I paid for it. But he said it was fine to help myself and so I did.

After figuring out more people we knew in common and reminiscing about Old Bay Seasoning, we decided to follow each other on Instagram to keep in touch. But because the club didn't have free Wi-Fi, I could only write down their 'gram handles in the Notes app on my phone.

A few more drinks later and we decided to call it a night. Our George, the owner, got an antique black cab to take the six of us home in style. It wasn't until we were riding comfortably back to our boutique hotel near the Galata Tower that I decided to ask for my black python-skin clutch from Ashlee.

"I don't have your purse."

"Yes, you do. Remember when you said you'd hold my purse because you couldn't believe I brought a clutch to the club?"

"Yeah, I did put your clutch in my bag, but when we went to the bathroom, you asked for your purse back to reapply your lipstick. You never gave me your purse back after that."

My head immediately started spinning. Panic set in. It wasn't the purse that Adam had gotten me for my birthday last year that I was going to miss, or the $100 bill I had slipped in just in case of an emergency. It was my passport that was in my clutch for God knows what reason.

God, this was *not* the surprise I was talking about.

"Ohmygod, you're right. Guys, my passport was in that purse!"

The simultaneous screams let me know that I was in deep shit. I hopped out of the cab, which had only rolled two blocks away from the club thanks to traffic, and went running back inside the club. I ran down the steps to the table where we partied with our new Maryland friends. They were gone. There was no sign of them or the fun we'd just had. The green Jameson bottle that floated diagonally in a silver ice bucket was no longer there and neither was the ice bucket. The clear plastic cups stacked on the table were gone, along with the cup filled with napkins and skinny black short straws. I ran my hand in between the couch cushions just in case my clutch had somehow squeezed in between them. No luck. I hurried back down the second set of steps to where our cocktail table once stood. But among the cornfield of clubgoers I couldn't find our table.

This was impossible. I was screwed.

With so much liquor in my system, I thought it was best I go to sleep and wake up Sunday to figure out my next step. The next day, Ashlee—feeling unnecessarily guilty—and I ran all across Reina in the stark contrast of the morning, looking for my small black clutch. We sat in the security office for hours, shuffling through dozens of forgotten credit cards that were left at the various bars and a couple of purses I desperately wished were mine. I stared intensely at black-and-white grainy security footage and fast-forwarded through b-roll of the prior evening's festivities, trying to spot any sign of my crew and I. Eventually, we gave up and went to the nearest police department to get a report to document that my passport had been lost. I figured I'd need that to get a replacement.

However, the police refused to write a report. I couldn't tell if it was the language barrier that was preventing them from helping me, so I called Cennet, my friend from Columbia who lives in Istanbul. I hoped she could translate for me. Although I never really hung out with Cennet while we matriculated together at the journalism school, she was nice enough to give me her cell phone number when I reached out weeks ago through Facebook. I figured it couldn't hurt to know one native. I dialed her with tears in my eyes, then hurriedly explained my situation without asking if she was busy. Thankfully she wasn't and seemed to feel sorry for my situation.

I would depend a lot on the kindness of others over the next couple of days.

I handed the phone to the police officer and after a few beats, he handed it right back to me.

"Cennet, what did he say?" I asked in my singsongy voice—the voice I get right before I burst into tears.

"He said that he can't give you a police report because he doesn't have grounds to believe that you're actually the person who lost the passport. He has no proof—"

"What?!" I cut her off. "You've got to be kidding me!"

"Well, there's been a lot of passport robberies in Istanbul lately, so they've been cracking down," Cennet said, then paused in thought. "Do you have a copy of your passport somewhere?"

I thought about it. "Yes! The hotel made a copy of my passport when I checked in!"

"Great! Go back and get that, then return to the police station. Make sure you go to the police station where the crime occurred because that's how we do it here. You can't just go to any station."

"Okay, okay. Got it. Thank you!"

When I got back to the hotel, Ashlee, with tears in her eyes, apologized for losing my purse.

"Ashlee, you didn't lose my purse—I did. At the end of the day, my purse is my responsibility and I should know where it is at all times. I don't blame you. I just want to figure out how to get home in the morning."

I plopped down on the bed, emotionally exhausted. Our flight was supposed to leave at 6:00 a.m. Monday and I had no idea how to secure another passport so I could leave the country. I was stuck in fucking Istanbul and the U.S. Consulate in Istanbul was closed. It was Sunday, after all, and when I pressed the "in case of an emergency" option during the phone call—international roaming charges be damned—a Marine answered saying that the consulate would be closed until Tuesday because Monday was Labor Day, and the consulate observed all U.S. holidays.

"But my flight leaves tomorrow at six a.m., sir."

"Ma'am, unfortunately you'll be stuck here until you can secure a passport. Go online to find out how to do that."

"But I already went online! That's where I got this number! Are you sure you can't do anything today? I'm a U.S. citizen!"

"Ma'am, we're closed until Tuesday."

Tears fell from my eyes as I slammed the phone down.

Searching for calm, I opened my Notes app to finally follow the guys we met the night before. Interestingly enough, amid the three IG names was a telephone number, right under shawngreenhouse. Now that I was stuck in Istanbul, I figured I'd text him.

Joi-Marie from last night. I see you put your number in here.

Ur sposed to be here in my hotel room, he wrote back almost immediately.

i'd be no fun. i lost my passport last night.

☹oh shit.

i know! i don't know what to do. i'm stuck until tuesday.

yea i've lost my passport at least twice on tour. you have to go to consulate and pay to get a replacement. go online to get forms.

i called already. they closed til tuesday.

oh no. well we'll be here until then too so if u get bored hit me.

ok

After e-mailing my family the really bad news, I e-mailed my job, telling them I wouldn't be returning on Tuesday as planned. Then I tweeted a snarky remark about my current situation and created a hashtag, #lostqueen, to mark the occasion. I then remembered I had to call my airline to tell them I wouldn't make my flight and asked what my options were before figuring out what hotel I could stay in until Tuesday.

I also texted Cennet to see if she could offer some insight.

Instead, she offered me something better: a place to stay while I was stuck. I couldn't imagine how much more money I would've spent if I had stayed at my current quaint boutique hotel, but I was thankful I didn't need to compute that. Cennet suggested I check out as late as I could that afternoon and try to waste the day by sightseeing. She wouldn't be able to let me into her apartment across town until that evening because she was covering a story for the *New York Times* on some far-flung Turkish island. She had plans to meet a childhood friend for dinner near Instinye, so if I didn't mind crashing I could come with and then figure out how to get a passport in the morning from her Wi-Fi-equipped apartment. She made sure to add that it was perfect for me to stay there because she lived five minutes away from the consulate, where I'd need to go to buy a new passport.

I couldn't type back Where should I meet you? fast enough. I had gone from crying and thinking I'd end up like that girl in *Taken* to praising God for my good fortune.

How was it that I reached out to Cennet before coming to Istanbul? We never, ever, *ever* hung out back at Columbia. I barely hung out with any of my classmates, actually. I was too busy trying to get clips in New York publications and trying to keep Adam happy.

Clearly I was meant to be stranded in Istanbul because although I was stuck, it was a pretty painless mistake. The airline said they'd change my flight for free. AT&T—who called me after I made a flurry of calls to the consulate—said that because it was an international emergency they wouldn't charge me roaming fees, and Cennet said I could stay at her home for free…for as long as I needed. And thankfully my credit card and ID hadn't been in the lost purse. I could easily pay for a replacement passport. Not to mention, I got at least another day of vacation, and who didn't want that?

It was definitely a blip in the matrix, but it was handled. God had already worked it out before I got here. But why? Why was I stuck here of all places?

I had dozed off thinking about what lesson God wanted me to learn in this moment. When I woke up, it was only 10:00 a.m. I still had a full day to spend alone in a country I had never been to before. And I still had to get a police report.

I also had a text from Shawn: what r u doin?

trying to figure that out. u?

we're about to go on a boat

I told him to have fun while I figured out how to get home.

First things first: I had to get a copy of my passport and head back to the police station, nearly twenty minutes away by cab. I chose to walk to waste time. On the way there, I got lost and stopped into a business that looked like it sold computers. I couldn't tell what sort of establishment it was, but I figured I wouldn't get killed inside because the showroom was completely made out of windows. If anything happened to me, everyone on the street would see it. When you're alone in a foreign country, you start to think about random survival tactics. I walked inside and, pausing after enunciating each word, asked, "Does. Anybody. Speak. English?"

Six men stared at me doe-eyed, clearly not comprehending. I was about to turn around and try to find another place to stop into when one man raised his hand, "I do!"

"Ohmygod, great! I'm looking for this police station. I lost my passport and just need a police report."

"Oh no," a tall, burly salesman, who introduced himself as Ahmed, said with sincere empathy.

"I know! I have this map the hotel concierge gave me, but I

can't seem to find the police station...and I don't have Wi-Fi for my Google Maps."

Ahmed took the map I had and tried to figure out how far away I was. Apparently, I was only around the corner, so he offered to come with me, thinking I'd need help. He was right; the police station again refused to give me a police report.

"But I have a copy of my original passport," I said with tears welling in my eyes, waving the black-and-white copy of my lost passport and ticket to getting home and reuniting with my friends and family.

"I'm sorry, but this is the wrong police station. You have to go to the police station in Ortaköy."

"I'm not *there?!*"

"No," he said with indifference.

The police officer, with his freshly pressed royal-and-navy-blue uniform, began to walk back inside.

"This is *ridiculous!*" I screamed at no one, doubling over to grab my knees to steady myself. My tears had forsaken me and ran without permission down my cheeks. Getting help from police in the States just didn't seem this hard! I was stuck! Alone! With no friends and no family and no Wi-Fi! I just wanted to get home!

I forgot that Ahmed was there until he tried to comfort me in his accented English. "It's going to be okay. Let's just go to the police station in Ortaköy. Follow me," he said, warmth in his eyes.

I followed tightly behind Ahmed through the winding streets of Istanbul. I stayed two or three paces behind him. I didn't want to get lost or snatched, so I stayed close. I had sneaked through enough VIP areas at nightclubs back home to know how not to get separated from your party. Older Muslim men stared at Ahmed and me as we made our way. I didn't know if they were staring at me, or him, or if the sight of us together was strange. To Ahmed, it didn't seem to be.

"Are you hungry?" he asked.

The question startled me. I hadn't eaten all day, but I'd starve if it meant getting a police report so I could get another passport.

"Yeah! I mean, no... that's okay. I just want to go home."

The sun seemed stronger today than normal. As we walked to a better area to grab a cab, I started to feel sweat running down my back. Sweat beads were gathering at the nape of Ahmed's neck too.

We hopped into a yellow cab and Ahmed took the front seat. I couldn't tell what he and the cabbie were talking about, but he often pointed back to me and said the word *passport*, so I knew they were talking about me. When we hopped out, Ahmed paid without hesitation. I tried to protest, but it was pointless. Ahmed was already strolling into the Ortaköy police station, which looked much nicer than the last one.

I felt the seriousness of this moment. This was my last hope. If they refused to give me a police report for whatever reason, I'd be fucked.

After filling out a form I barely understood, I was told to wait in a brightly lit room. Three police officers, who didn't look older than twenty-four, sat on the left talking about something on one of their cell phones. I stared at the tan linoleum floor while I waited for something to happen. Then a handsome man with really dark hair entered the room, wearing a perfectly ironed police uniform complete with a hat. He sat down at a really big wooden desk opposite me. It looked like a desk I'd seen in *Law & Order*.

"You lost your passport?" he asked, looking at me skeptically.

"Yes, I was at Reina. I put my purse down and never saw it again.

My passport was inside. I have a copy of my passport here. I work for an international news network," I hurried out.

"Let me see that." He spoke like royalty, while pointing at my black-and-white photocopy.

I stumbled out of my seat to walk the three feet to his desk. I watched as he inspected the crisp photocopy. Then he called out in Turkish to one of the three police officers, who also inspected the sheet. When that police officer sat down, another one got up to do his own inspection. This continued until all three officers examined the document. Seemingly satisfied with this "investigation," I was told to leave the room to get a police report.

"Oh, thank you! Thank you!" I said, bowing as if I were meeting a person from Japan.

Walking out of the police station, with an extra bounce in my step, Ahmed turned to me with a smile on his face and asked, "Now can we get Shake Shack?"

*Chapter 23*

can you get here in 20?

It seemed like an incredulous request, considering he was at Hammerstein Ballroom and I was in Harlem—almost a hundred blocks away.

I lied and texted back, yeah, and quickly requested an Uber.

It had been three weeks since I discovered Shawn's number in my phone after that incredible, crazy, drunken Turkish night. Now he was in New York City, another one of his tour stops. Shawn had been texting me all night and all day, reminding me that he'd be in the city—he texted when he got offstage the night before and when he took a shower before boarding the bus. He texted on the bus to complain about getting motion sickness, and he texted to explain why he couldn't call—because he didn't want people on the bus listening to our conversation. He texted when he arrived in New York, he texted when he made his lunch plans, and he texted when he headed to the venue before the show for sound check. He thought he'd have time to grab a bite to eat with me, but when he told me he couldn't earlier that day, I booked an interview. And so now here I was, all the way uptown to interview rap-per Troy Ave in advance of his debut album, *Major Without a Deal*, rushing to get downtown to spend a moment with Shawn.

Since we met that night in Turkey, Shawn had flown to Aus-tria, Germany, the Czech Republic, Portugal, and even Israel, keeping me up to date along the way. We didn't talk about much. I didn't know his favorite color. I didn't know if he was a basketball guy or a football guy. I didn't know if he had any siblings or the way he likes his coffee. It just seemed like he needed someone to remind him of home. Although I didn't know much about him, besides the fact that he has really pretty eyes, I sort of felt honored to be that for him. Every night I'd ask him how the show went, and every night he'd say, "It's over." And every night I'd pray that he was being facetious and was actually cherishing the experience.

where r u

It was Shawn.

I typed back another lie. 2 blocks away. about to hop out.

That seemed to satisfy Shawn for about two minutes, until I got another text asking the same thing. Thankfully, the traffic gods parted the string of yellow cabs on 34th Street and my lie turned into the truth. Funny how lies do that sometimes.

Shawn looked skinnier than the last time I'd seen him. The tour lifestyle must've been making him shrink. Wearing a ripped-up black tank top, jean shorts, and some shoes that looked very European, I heard Shawn's voice before I even saw him. He was telling me to hurry up and walk faster so we could get inside. His rushed words never stopped tumbling out of his mouth when he hugged me, letting his hand linger too long on my lower back, then grabbing my hand to pull me through meandering tourists.

We stopped abruptly at what appeared to be the stage door of the theater, almost a half block down Eighth Avenue. A tall, bald security guard, who looked like he performed for the WWE in his spare time, asked, "Badge?" Shawn held my hand while he raised his proudly. He then whisked me past Baby Hulk Hogan before he could utter another word. I didn't realize my heart was beating incredibly fast at the fear of getting caught without a badge until I was safely in the standing-room-only theater.

"Are you good right here?" Shawn said, looking genuinely concerned.

We were standing too close; squished together as fans politely and impolitely squeezed by, trying to get as close to the stage as possible. "Jordan's girl will be with you, so you won't be alone," Shawn said, pointing to a shorter light-skinned guy, who I'd later find out was the band's keyboardist. A woman, who looked completely disinterested in the conversation, held on to his hand. "If you stand right here, I can see you from onstage, okay? So just wave if you need me."

He was talking to me as if I was his baby girl whom he was about to let sleep over at a friend's house for the first time.

"Okay," I replied.

Then Shawn pushed me. Hard. He pushed me so hard, my arms flung straight up as if I had just caught the Holy Ghost. I grabbed the side of my ribs in anguish. It didn't help that the push, which caught me completely off guard, made me trip on my black-and-gold sandals. I grabbed my sandal for fear that the strap had snapped. It hadn't. Thank God.

When I looked up, my face turned from confusion and anger to horror because I saw him. It was a man puking his guts out and instead of it landing on me—which if gravity had any say in it, it would've—it landed on Shawn. He looked as if he had just gotten green slime poured on him like on one of those Nickelodeon shows. But it was puke—warm, pinkish, chunky puke. His face lit up a mixture of embarrassment and disgust. He pulled his black ripped tank top over his head, and threw it into the trashcan, conveniently nestled in the corner of the venue. It landed with a splat.

"Yo, my man! Are you fucking kidding me? Yo, get him *outta here*. Where is security?!" Shawn said as he whisked behind the black stage curtain. He returned with Baby Hulk Hogan.

"Who? Where'd he go? Where is he?" Hulk Jr. said, looking right, then left, then right again.

I tried—along with a couple of strangers who saw the puke perpetrator—to help Hogan find the guy, but he had vanished just like that.

I guess he really wanted to see the concert.

Shawn didn't even say goodbye as he huffed away, running behind the curtain probably to a bathroom. Jordan went with him. I had barely introduced myself to Jordan's girlfriend, whose name I discovered was Laurita, because I was so worried about Shawn.

I had to text him. are you alright?☺

no! I can't believe we couldn't find his ass to kick him out.

don't worry about that. just wanna make sure you're good.😔

yup.

By the time the house lights went down, my feet had begun to stick to the floor thanks to all the spilled drinks. At first it was a single screech, but then the fans' screams eventually rose to a fever pitch. The band, including Laurita's boyfriend on the keyboard, began playing. But the man of the hour had yet to take the stage, so the fans started chanting his name. Eventually, in a volcanic eruption of applause mixed with cheers, he—let's call him MJ—appeared onstage.

When MJ performed his first few songs, I barely noticed Shawn onstage. But after I spotted him, I couldn't help but notice him. The funny thing was, I saw him noticing me too. That would be impossible, though, right? With those lights shining so brightly into his eyes onstage? There was no way he could see me. Still, I felt his eyes staring into me from all the way across the theater. There were thousands of people in the Hammerstein Ballroom, but he was looking and singing directly at me. Even with him so far away I could feel my entire body heat up.

"Do you aaalll know him?" an older woman with blond hair asked Laurita and me while pointing her rhinestone-encrusted acrylic nail in Shawn's direction. Her thick New Jersey accent poured over us like the beer from music-loving strangers on my arm.

Laurita answered for the both of us. "Yeah, we know the guys in the band."

"Ooooohh, because he's looking ovah heyere!" she screamed over the music, which was so loud it seemed to vibrate in my insides.

I couldn't help but smile. I had nothing to do with Shawn being on that stage, but I oddly felt special. Perhaps I was proud of him.

But I barely knew him.

I was so aware of Shawn staring at me that I could barely sing the words to my favorite R&B songs, so I tried my best to do a cute two-step. And when my favorite slow jam came on—MJ's hit song from 2006—Shawn pretended to feel the song so much that he extended his arms out like an eagle taking flight. But his left hand really gave me a thumbs-up. I stopped dancing suddenly. It was the smallest of gestures and if I wasn't staring right back at him, I probably wouldn't have noticed. But I did. He was asking if I was okay.

The fact that he managed to pay attention to me with so much going on was beyond flattering. It was humbling. I nodded, believing he could see it, and then raised my hand with my thumb standing at attention, just in case he couldn't.

There is an art to making someone feel special—even if for a moment.

Clearly Laurita had done this before, because when the concert was over, Baby Hulk Hogan lifted the black curtain to let us back behind the silver barricades. Walking at a sprinter's pace, I followed Laurita's backpack as she bopped along the backstage hallways. I felt bad that my eyes were open for any sign of MJ. Laurita led us upstairs to the dressing rooms.

"Jordan told us to meet them here because they're getting changed."

"Okay, thanks."

I looked down at my phone. I thought it was odd Shawn didn't text me directly. So I texted him:

with laurita.

i know. coming

By the time he bounced downstairs, it felt like a tornado had hit the room. The guys were running off the adrenaline from their performance and were talking a mile a minute. All the excitable chatter started to blend together, becoming indistinguishable. I only knew it was time to go because he grabbed my waist. "C'mon. We're all going to the bar. Shots."

I guess it was stupid to think I'd get alone time with him.

The cool September night air hit my face in a welcome reprieve. "Y'all, Drew is meeting us there," Shawn said to no one in particular, referencing another musician who played the piano for a popular late-night show.

No one knew where we were going, but after walking a couple of blocks, we ended up in an Irish pub. Shawn was at the bar, buying the first round, and I was trying my best to stay interested in the table's conversation while he was gone. And to ignore Jordan and Laurita, who were full-blown making out at the table. Drew and I struggled to make conversation.

I don't do well in awkward situations, so I walked over to the bar to pretend to help Shawn carry the shots back to the table. He thought I was being thoughtful.

"You'll be in Baltimore this weekend, right? I think the tour will be there at the same time," Shawn said.

"Oh, yeah. It's my cousin's birthday party in Annapolis. You remembered!"

"How can I rearrange my schedule? Shoot, I was going to see some people," Shawn said aloud. But he was really talking to himself. His eyes darted back and forth in pensive thought.

Wait—would he really rearrange his whole schedule to see me again? A guy like this, on tour with MJ, would go out of his way for me? He's probably slept with so many women in the last month! It seemed like he was doing a lot just to spend a moment with me. And as flattering as it was, I couldn't set myself up like that. Not right now. As much as I liked him, I remembered what my sister said about different types of men: some are for right now and some are for forever. In my mind, Shawn had *right now* scribbled in bright red ink on his forehead.

"Well, her birthday party is in the afternoon. Come over for breakfast."

"Can you cook?"

I smiled.

## Chapter 24

Shawn was still on tour. It had been nearly two months since he stopped in New York City and nearly two months since our breakfast "date" in Baltimore. (Can I call it a date if we didn't actually go anywhere?)

I did my best in the kitchen, considering the last time I cooked for a man it ended in an argument about overcooked noodles. So while getting my hair done, my hairstylist Aisha and I brainstormed a menu I couldn't mess up and settled on eggs, waffles, bacon, scrapple, and fried oysters. Mixed fruit was also on the menu…so if he arrived and I wasn't finished cooking he could at least start eating something. That was Aisha's idea.

My planning paid off because Shawn was beyond impressed. He hadn't had a home-cooked meal in months thanks to globe-trotting, and since my parents were out of town that weekend, we had the whole house to ourselves.

Picking up a strawberry with his fingers, Shawn asked, "So what do your parents do?"

"My mom's a preacher. My dad's retired."

"Word? I'm a PK too," he said, referring to himself as a preacher's kid. "Waiiiiiiit . . . wait! Is that scrapple?!"

I didn't understand why Shawn was so excited. Yes, it was scrapple. Scrapple was my favorite breakfast food, so really I sneaked this on the menu for myself.

"That's my shit. I just tweeted that the only thing I wanted while I was home was a piece of scrapple."

The coincidence tickled me.

"How do you know this song?"

My favorite song that summer was playing through my parents' Bose speaker in the kitchen. The music was so loud it carried throughout the open floor plan. I had been playing the song on repeat for the past few weeks.

"It's my favorite! Duh," I teased, throwing an oyster into a mixture of Old Bay Seasoning and flour before putting it into a sizzling hot pan of grease.

"I'm singing background vocals on this song," he said demurely. "That's why I asked."

"Oh," I said, pretending to concentrate on cooking.

It'd be the second coincidence of the morning and for some reason it made me feel nervous. I didn't want to move too fast with Shawn.

We ended the "date" out on my parents' patio, overlooking the lush green treetops in the backyard. I thought back to the last time I was out on that same patio with my father, when the trees only had bare branches to remind them of memories past. I was comforted seeing those same trees in full bloom. It reminded me that everything indeed has a season.

Although I had spoken to Shawn every week since then— discovering the answers to every question I had about him and learning that we had so much in common—I hadn't seen him. He was bopping around Europe and texting me along the way.

So, I busied myself with work. I interviewed actor Tony Goldwyn about a new TV show he had created called *The Divide*. I went to the *Love & Hip Hop* reunion show taping, and almost got pushed by burly security guards when rappers Joe Budden and Consequence began fighting backstage.

I brought *Hit the Floor* star Kat Bailess into our studio to chat about the show and ended up falling in love with her Southern accent. I even did a phone interview with Russell Simmons after his annual charity gala in the Hamptons, Art for Life, and later interviewed Trina and Towanda Braxton about their hit show, *Braxton Family Values*.

I chatted with Eric Stonestreet about his show *Modern Family* and asked him if he thought the ABC comedy could tie *Frasier*'s Emmy Award–winning record. He told me they could. Then I stopped into Central Park to interview Enrique Iglesias backstage at his outdoor concert.

Hours after I interviewed rapper T.I. in Times Square, I had coffee with a young journalist who needed advice on getting her start in the business. The next day, I had an interview with SWV—but lead singer Coco didn't show up—and later that evening went to Big Sean's album release party near Wall Street.

Another week, I met Keke Palmer in Times Square to talk about her Broadway debut in *Cinderella* and later invited Ray J into our studio to ask him why in the world he would appear on *Love & Hip Hop: Hollywood*.

And before *Scandal* returned to TV for the fall, I got a chance to talk to Kerry Washington again, this time about her collection with The Limited. She even complimented me on the sweater I wore that night on the red carpet. When I told her my Chanel-inspired sweater was from Forever 21, she couldn't believe it.

I also…um…oh, fuck it: I went on a date with Adam. But let me explain. It was his birthday, for God's sake!

Although I had asked Adam for space, what that looked like for him was calling every three days instead of every day. When he wasn't calling, he was sending me short random e-mails about a couch from Target that was on sale or the fact that my favorite singer, Alice Smith, was performing at the Bowery downtown. Adam was still trying to be my friend, although I had told him repeatedly before we broke up, and even afterward, that ex-boyfriends don't get the luxury of my friendship. That's a luxury because I'm a damned good friend.

Whenever Adam was most proud of me—like if I learned a new meal or looked really good for a date—he'd say stuff like, "Well, the next guy will appreciate this," or "Your husband better appreciate what I did." I always told him to be careful about how he joked around because one day it could become his reality. And now that it was, he was obviously having a hard time coping.

Because I loved him, I appeased him. I more than appeased him; I missed him. Although for my sanity's sake, and my heart's sake, I probably needed real and tangible space. But I couldn't help but appreciate the moments when he reached out, because oddly enough, I was happy he hadn't moved on just yet.

So when he texted me the day after his birthday, upset that I didn't wish him a happy one, instead of criticizing me, he unnecessarily blamed himself.

"I always spent my birthdays partying with my boys—I should've spent them with you," he said. His words were full of sincerity and doused with regret.

"Adam...," I sighed.

"No, no, I want to say this. I should've spent them with the woman I love. I should've spent them with you."

I didn't know what to say. What do you say when you finally hear what your heart has been waiting to hear for years?

I'm a celebrator. I love celebrating anything, but birthdays most of all. It's probably because my mom always made our birthdays feel extra special. Growing up, my birthday felt like Christmas and New Year's Eve combined. It was truly a holiday. My mom would hide surprises around the house and would remember the one time we whispered we really wanted that Sega Genesis game and we'd be amazed that she knew our heart's desire. She was an expert at making us feel special and I always wanted to pass that on to him.

But year after year after year of complaining about not being able to take him out on his birthday proper, I had adjusted to figuring out which day—before or after—he'd want to celebrate with me. And now that we'd split up, *now* he wanted to spend his birthday with me? It felt anticlimactic.

"Are you busy Friday?"

"Why?"

"I figured we could go out for my birthday," he said, adding before I could object, "C'mon, it's for my birthday." Inserting a joke, he went on, "It's not like you got me a present."

Although I didn't want to, I laughed. "Fine! Let's do it. Where are we going?"

"It's a surprise," Adam teased. "Just wear comfortable shoes."

Adam seemed to be in a good mood when he picked me up from my apartment on one of the warmest days in October. Thanks to global warming, it was a balmy 81 degrees. He usually didn't like when I drank too much but suggested we stop at the liquor store to create our own cocktails to sip on while we walked around the secret location. Adam got a bottle of Don Julio and he bought my favorite Riesling, RELAX, while I waited in the car. I poured half the bottle into a tall Styrofoam cup that the guy behind the liquor store counter gifted while we drove an hour and a half without ever leaving New York. I didn't even feel like guessing where we were going. It just felt good to be in the moment, on an adventure, on a date with Adam again. Once we got to the edge of Brooklyn, it was pretty obvious we were going to have a Coney Island good time.

We did Coney Island as if neither of us had ever been to the theme park before. We started off by grabbing Nathan's hot dogs—fully loaded with chili and cheese on mine and sauerkraut and ketchup on his—with a side of cheese fries. It was a terrible idea because, right after, Adam dared me to go on a roller coaster. I take dares very seriously and so there we were on the Thunderbolt, the Island's newest loopy attraction, trying not to throw up hot dogs and cheese fries. Every other ride—and we tried a lot of them—seemed like a letdown after that, so we decided to race go-karts. I don't know if I had really won, or if Adam let me win, but I talked shit about crossing the finish line before him for the rest of the evening.

"Let's take a selfie," Adam suggested.

I stopped in my tracks. Adam hated photos. Adam hated selfies. He hated camera phones. He hated Twitter. He hated Facebook. He hated Instagram...and now he wanted to take a selfie?! Talk about a 180. But I didn't hesitate to take a quick snap of us, cheek to cheek. Ordinarily, I'd send the photo to the group text message my mom and my sister were on, but I didn't think they'd approve.

As the sun set, we walked down to the pier. Fishing rods balanced on the gray wooden planks. A blue crab crawled across my feet. I jumped up, laughing hysterically. When we reached the end of the pier, I leaned over, pushing my face into the bay's breeze. I watched the sun dance on the water's ripples in delight. I looked out, trying to find the exact spot where the sky kissed the water—the horizon.

Horizons have always fascinated me because the harder you seek them, the farther they appear. You could spend a lifetime trying to see what's beyond the horizon, but you'll never know. It's funny that so many people are fascinated with seeking something they'll never find. Turning back to take a peek at Brooklyn, I spotted a couple stealing a kiss right in front us, reminding me of what Adam and I once had.

"Wasn't this fun?" Adam said, implying more than his words allowed.

"It really was," I said honestly.

I knew what he was getting at, and unlike the fish on the other end of the lines beside us, I wasn't taking the bait. Sure, today was fun. But all today proved was that we could play nice, something we had been doing for months—avoiding each other's hot buttons and walking around our relationship as if it were a booby-trapped land mine.

Despite an amazing date, I had to listen to myself. Some call it an inner voice, but I call it something more familiar than that. It was God. I had heard this same voice the day after Valentine's Day when I woke up and asked Adam if he had real intentions for our relationship. I had heard the voice nudge me loudly, screaming even, after years of quiet prompts and inside-voice suggestions. It was the same voice gently rubbing me on the back now, telling me to not get swept out to sea.

It was the voice of my spirit. It was relentless, decisive, and sincere in its instruction. It did not make me guess or try to solve a riddle. It was plain. The voice was humble—it never bragged about what it already knew or made me feel bad about continuously questioning it. It never said *I told you so.* The voice wasn't me but it was part of me. Although it had to compete with so many thoughts constantly running through my head, the voice always came through crystal clear. It corrected me kindly. It corrected me patiently. The voice often told me in seconds what would take years to figure out. And when I didn't listen, it would repeat itself without tiring.

That voice told me a while ago, *No, this isn't it. This isn't your happily ever after.* I tried to tell the voice it was wrong because I loved him and he loved me and we worked so well together. So I ignored it because I didn't know how to end a relationship when I was happy.

When the voice didn't speak—and sometimes it would go mute—I sought it in prayer or meditation. Not some sit-down-and-fold-your-legs-type meditation, but the meditation one can have by simply appreciating what's around them in silence. I'd walk home with earbuds in my ears, but with no music playing, looking at the beauty of creation and meditating on it. I'd stare, looking at the bright green leaves blowing in the wind, appreciating the sun fighting its way through the clouds, breathing in fresh air as it blew past me in communal silence...as much silence as New York City would allow.

Sometimes the voice would butt into my conversation to gently correct me, but for once, I didn't mind. Because the voice had no ego. It didn't seek to make a point. It just wanted the best for me.

The voice felt better than any comforting words from my mom

or friends or even prophetic strangers. It felt better than a freshly washed and dried comforter, or ice water, or warm chocolate chip cookies, or getting your eyeliner perfect, or walking on the sunny side of the street.

I had already wasted years trying to put a square peg into a round hole, thinking I'd never get any other pegs to take an interest in me—let alone marry me. This time I was finally ready to listen.

"Want to do this again?" Adam asked as we walked back to the car. He normally didn't ask questions he didn't already know the answers to, so I could tell he was making a point to be vulnerable.

With the sun now set, the air turned cold.

"We'll see," I managed, hugging myself and rubbing my arms to keep warm. "We'll see."

While Shawn was in Iceland, he texted me that he'd be flying into John F. Kennedy Airport and asked if I could meet him there. He said from there he'd be riding all the way down to Maryland and asked did I want to come with. Apparently the tour manager had booked everyone's flights to arrive in New York, so he decided to take a car service the rest of the way home. He had a few weeks off from the tour, since Thanksgiving was three weeks away, but he wanted me to be the first person he saw. The thought scared me, since I was trying to keep this light, but it also endeared me to him.

when do you come in? I replied.

Tuesday.

Tuesday. As in a workday, Tuesday? This is why we could never work. Didn't he realize I worked? I had a job! Did the other girls he messed with not have full-time employment? How could I possibly meet him at the airport and ride with him the three hours to Maryland? I was not one of those groupie chicks who didn't have a job and claimed she was a student. I had to *work*.

But life is so short. I would regret not going. Should I go? Could I get off Tuesday? But if I went down there, I'd have to get off Wednesday too, and I couldn't be out of the newsroom for two days. I couldn't go! See?! This was why we couldn't work. Our lifestyles were completely different.

On one hand, I loved that Shawn's life provided a total antithesis to mine, which at times felt boring and ordinary. On the other hand, I truly couldn't live like this. At the end of my life, though, I'm not gonna think about the times I went into the newsroom. I'm going to think about the times that I created memories. I should totally go. Would I look pressed or too eager if I went? Who cares? Okay. I was gonna go but I wasn't spending the night. I couldn't take off Wednesday. I'd leave in time to make it to work on Wednesday. I've done crazier things.

ok. just text me your flight information.

"You're *leaving*?!"

I met Shawn at the airport that morning just like he had asked. I didn't want to tell him that I'd have to turn right back around after driving the three hours down to Maryland so I could make it to work in the morning. Not after the wonderful ride down we just had in the backseat of a black Lincoln town car, drinking our own mix of Hennessy and airport juice in two cups I stole from the Dunkin' Donuts inside the terminal. I felt like Beyoncé in the "Partition" music video, and when I looked up for air I finally noticed a little gray-and-black camera in the right corner of the car. At the sight of it, I leaned over and kept kissing Shawn.

I spent the afternoon trying to learn how to ride his skateboard, which was extremely hard to do in calf-high boots. In his rooftop loft in downtown Maryland, overlooking the Arts District, I held on to him as I shakily coasted on the skateboard and found it surprising how encouraging he was.

He had the perfect artist's hangout: original paintings of Marvin Gaye and Jimi Hendrix hung on red exposed brick in his living room opposite his large flat-screen television, which he mainly used to play video games.

An acoustic guitar, unplugged, stood upright thanks to a stand in one corner, while another skateboard occupied the other. His refrigerator was empty besides a jug of water and a nameless bottle of vodka. The label was already torn off. There were no perishable items in his cabinets and when we had first walked in from our road trip, it took a couple of hours for the place to cool down. The air conditioner hadn't been turned on in about a month, after all.

We spent the rest of the afternoon living in light. He sang. I listened. We read. We danced to old songs my mom and dad used to play. He played video games while I took a nap. I was making us another round of drinks in the kitchen when I heard him call out from the living room, "Did you miss me?" I told him I did, but I was unsure if that was actually true. I hated that I couldn't believe the things coming out of my own mouth.

It felt like a much needed vacation, but I had to get back to the real world. I had to catch my train and head back to New York.

"Seriously, you're leaving?" Shawn asked again.

I don't think he meant to sound so upset, but he did. He looked horrified with his mouth hanging open, standing in the middle of his kitchen, wearing sunglasses, a basketball jersey, shorts, and tall white socks.

I didn't quite understand his reaction. I thought he'd prefer me to leave.

"Yes, I have to be at work tomorrow at seven."

"Oh, please. I've had earlier call times," he volleyed. "You have to leave *now*?"

"Well, the last train that leaves tonight is in fifteen minutes. The next train isn't until three a.m. Do *you* want to take me to the train station at three a.m.?"

Shawn huffed, his entire upper body contracting with exasperation. He stormed into his bedroom to grab his jacket. "Could you *at least* grab some shoes for me?" he said without so much as glancing in my direction.

He had turned bookshelves into a large display for his extensive shoe collection. I couldn't even count the pairs of Jordans, Adidas, Air Force 1s, and Air Max's, but if I had to guess, there were close to 150 pairs of shoes lining the walls of his living room.

"Which ones, Shawn?" I yelled, utterly overwhelmed by the choices.

I felt him storm past me. He muttered "Good for nothing" under his breath and I pretended not to hear it. He probably said it loud enough for me to hear and start an argument, but I wouldn't give him the satisfaction tonight. My train was leaving in thirteen minutes and I wasn't going to miss it because of three pissy words.

Instead, I went mute. I was quiet when he snatched his car keys from my hand and when he held open my car door so I could get inside. I was even quiet when he kissed me good-bye at Baltimore Penn Station. And even more quiet when he texted me the following day to make sure I got home safely.

# Chapter 25

Thank God the movie theater was pitch black. I didn't want my girls to see I was wiping away tears. I'm not a big crier, but for some reason watching Nate Parker and Gugu Mbatha-Raw in *Beyond the Lights* portray two people who fall in love after one tries to commit suicide sort of hit close to home.

After spending less than twelve hours in Maryland with Shawn, I was back in New York and back to my reality. A girls' night at the movies was exactly what I needed to decompress. Not to mention, I was preparing to interview Nate later this week, so I had to see the romantic comedy. This movie was significant for Nate because it was the first time he was the leading man in a film and I couldn't wait to ask him how he felt about pulling it off. He pulled it off so well I didn't want to go home and sleep in my bed alone that night.

"Joi, we're grabbing a drink. Come on," Ashley boomed in her South Florida accent.

Ashley, a fellow writer, was my girl. She had become part of my New York City hodgepodge family after we met at Columbia.

There were only a few of us black girls at the Ivy League institution when I graduated, so we became fast friends.

"You know I can't," I whined.

I hated to always be the party pooper, but I never stayed out too late because I was not a morning person.

"Not just one drink?"

"One drink turns into three drinks turns into Joi is late for work tomorrow. No one has to get up earlier than me...," I trailed off. I was repeating myself. Ashley and Leah, my other Columbia black girl bestie, had heard my excuses before and were probably sick of hearing them as much as I was sick of giving them.

"Next time," I lied.

I hugged them both, then began my trek to the subway down two of New York City's historically lengthy avenues in the crisp fall weather. The sun had already set since it tended to retreat behind the skyscrapers a bit earlier these days, which meant I was walking alone in the dark. I picked up my pace as I made my way, making sure to look behind me every third building I passed. It was something my grandmother taught me to do—I grew up in Baltimore, after all. The leaves had yet to change. Looks like they were being stubborn this season. I reached into my purse to pull out my purple-and-white pashmina that I got in Istanbul. I wrapped it around my neck like the young Turk who sold it to me in the Grand Bazaar taught me—a double loop with a loose knot at the end. I had also asked him to teach me how to say *yes, no, thank you,* and *cheers* in Turkish. Too bad as the months went by I didn't remember my lesson in language. Of course, except how to say *cheers: şerefe.*

I figured the long walk from Ninth to Seventh Avenue would

fly by quicker if I called someone, so I decided to ring my sister and update her on Shawn. Plus, I hadn't spoken to her since I got back to New York and I'm sure she was worried about me. She hadn't heard from me since I sent her a picture of Shawn's place when he was out grabbing dinner. I immediately felt bad about it afterward.

"He said *what* to you?!"

"Yeah. That's what he said," I told my sister, recounting when Shawn said I was good for nothing.

I told Jasmine that although I've managed to stay somewhat detached from Shawn for self-preservation—"I mean, he is on tour for goodness' sake"—I admitted to one small gesture to apologize for jetting back to New York so quickly. When I spent the day with him in Maryland, he complained that his tooth was hurting, so after I left that night, I overnighted Anbesol to him since he had never heard of the tooth-numbing product. I knew after our little fight he wouldn't go to CVS to get it like I had suggested.

My sister cut into my story to ask, "Why did you get him *anything*?"

"I actually don't know. I guess I like taking care of him...when he lets me."

"Joi," she said tersely with disapproval.

I told her that when I got on the last train leaving Maryland that night he actually looked a little sad. But the next day after I received an e-mailed notification from USPS alerting me that they had delivered my very thoughtful package, Shawn never texted me or even called to say thank you. When I asked, Why didn't you say thank you? he replied that he was just about to.

"Right," Jasmine said, also not believing him. "Did you look him up in Case Search yet?"

"Case Search" was our nickname for Maryland's judiciary case search, the website that allows you to look up public court records.

Each state has one. In this day and age, I don't seriously date any-one without looking up their name in the state where they live. If they've gotten divorced, have had child support issues, paternity tests, or even a traffic court appearance, it'll show up there. It's bet-ter to know what you're getting yourself into.

"Yes, girl. He's clean."

"Good," she said with emphasis.

Actually, Shawn had been nothing but nice to me, going out of his way to see me when he could, I told her in his defense. But even I couldn't overcome my common sense...that eventually if I tried to be in a serious relationship with this man he'd probably cheat on me with some random groupie in some random country. I'm way too Baltimore to deal with that. I'd more than likely be giving so much of myself to make his dreams come true without the same in return. Let's be real—he never even asked about my family, how I was raised, who my best friends were, how I liked my coffee.

Before I ran down the subway steps to catch the train back to Harlem, my sister said what I had already been thinking: "Well, Joi, not everyone is forever."

"Word."

When I got to the newsroom early the next morning, I was just about finished drafting my questions for Nate Parker. I decided that an extra pass at Google for everything Nate Parker couldn't hurt. That was when I stumbled across his Wikipedia page.

I read through all the stuff I already knew—like that he was born in Norfolk, Virginia; the latest hit films he's starred in; and that he's been married for years now. However, not even three paragraphs down, it detailed an incident that happened while he was a student at Penn State in 1999. According to the website, Nate, along with another wrestling teammate, was accused of raping a student who had passed out. He was eventually acquitted two years later, but the mention still gave me pause. How would a woman who had gone through this feel reading it? It was a story that could've easily been buried on his editable Wiki page. Or did Nate leave it there displayed prominently on purpose?

I had to ask.

After our interview was over in the studio, I walked Nate and his publicist to the elevators. I told Nate—who came dressed in a black leather jacket, jeans, and more facial hair than I've ever seen him sport—that I had one more question to ask.

I spilled all my thinking about the matter—from stalking him on Google to prepare for the interview, to randomly clicking on his Wikipedia page and stumbling upon him being accused of rape back at Penn State and the gnawing feeling I had because I didn't understand why it was displayed so prominently. This was one of the tougher parts of my job, trying to remain unbiased.

He let me talk. He didn't interrupt me and he didn't rush me, even when I stumbled around a few times out of sensitivity to him, and the topic, and the fact that it wasn't really any of my damn business.

After looking at the floor for most of my inquiry, when I had finally raised my eyes and asked him why he had left that incident there at the top of his biography, he looked at me squarely and said: "I don't run from anything."

That was all he could say before his publicist rushed him into the elevator. Her pink manicured hand was on the back of his black leather coat. She had already told me he didn't have much time; he had to be on time for his interview with Tom Joyner, which was happening in a nearby studio.

"Are you slammed? If you wait here, we can talk about it more," he offered with sincerity.

"Sure," I lied. I knew his publicist wouldn't bring him back and I had to get back to my desk anyway. So after five or so minutes of waiting idly, that was what I did.

Nate's directness wasn't lost on me, though. His face never lowered, his eyes never squinted even as I fumbled around repeatedly, trying to pace myself through all the details.

Was there anything to be learned from this incredibly emotional conversation—especially after my own experience in Istanbul?

When I got back to my desk on the far side of the newsroom, I had my answer. And it was a lesson I thought I had mastered as a journalist. If anything, I had to ask. That was half my job, right? To ask and then relay the information. Even if I wasn't satisfied with my question and even if I wasn't satisfied with the answer, I ask. And continue to ask.

# Chapter 26

W*amp! Wamp! Wamp!*

At the sound of my iPhone alarm clock, Arista sighed loudly. The nerve. I willed my body to roll over to look at the clock. It was 7:00 a.m.—on a Saturday. But I had to get up. I had a hair appointment.

Now that I was single, I cared much more about my appearance. It's taken up much of my spare time—time I would otherwise spend lying on the couch, writing, or watching my shows. I could meet my future husband anywhere—walking to the train, at the grocery store, at the coffee shop that I frequent at 129th and Lenox, leaving work, shopping at Zara. I didn't know when God would send him, so I wanted to be prepared at all times, which was why I was up at 7:00 a.m. to go thirty minutes deep into the Bronx to get my hair done.

"You know you have gray hairs?" said Princess, who was flat-ironing my natural hair, turning my light fuzzy locks into straight and shiny strands.

"Yeah, I *know*. I saw one peeking out behind my ears."

"It's not just one! It's a *lot*. The good thing is they're in the middle of your head."

"I suppose that is good," I mumbled while scrolling through the latest postings on Instagram.

"Have any plans later today?" Princess asked, keeping the beauty shop conversation going. I wonder if hairstylists are trained in creating conversation. They always seem to be good at it.

"Yeah, actually. I'm going to the Jingle Bell Tour in Jersey with my friend Kim."

"Oh *word?!* I wanted to go to that."

"I really don't want to trek to Jersey, but at least there'll be good music."

Shit. Shit. Shit. Shit. Shit. According to his Instagram, Shawn was in Jersey. Shit. Apparently, he was on another tour—the Jingle Bell Tour. Great.

I had stopped responding to his text messages right after Thanksgiving. Should I text him? No. He probably didn't want to hear from me anyway. It had been weeks. It was damn near Christmas.

"So what do you think?" Princess asked as she turned my chair around to face the mirror.

"I LOVE it," I squealed, running my hand through my hair, which was still warm thanks to the miraculous effort of the flatiron.

My hair in all its perfection made my face look completely bare without makeup. I thought, *I hope I don't run into my husband on the subway ride home.*

Kim and I were late. We could already hear the screams from ladies about to lose their minds when we arrived at the Izod Center in

New Jersey, which surprisingly is only about thirty minutes away from Harlem. By the time we found our seats in Section 106, the house lights were already down, the band was already jamming onstage, and Trey Songz, one of twenty-two performers that night, was already working the stage, singing my favorite song from his latest album, "Cake."

Shawn still didn't know I was in the audience for the sold-out show when he took the stage with another R&B singer. Although I struggled with whether I should text him, I thought it would be odd if I was looking at him and didn't hit him up—even if I was one of 19,000 screaming fans.

Looking at him up there on that stage, one of two background singers, reminded me of when I first saw him perform and how he wouldn't stop staring at me. Right now, with dozens of rows of screaming fans between us, Shawn couldn't see me. I could see him, but he couldn't see me. Interestingly enough, I've always felt that way. I could see him, but he couldn't see me. He didn't seem particularly concerned with getting to know me, but that didn't stop him from wanting to create a future with me. He would say random things like "I want to get you pregnant." I remembered asking him, "So you don't wanna get married first?"

"Who does that anymore? I'm just ready to have babies."

"True." I'd nodded, thinking how backward yet common his thinking was.

I snapped a couple of pictures of Shawn onstage and decided to text them to him. I figured it'd be better than a "Hey! I know you've been texting me and I've been ignoring you but I'm looking at you onstage right now" text message.

I was up on my feet dancing with the rest of the crowd, when I felt my phone vibrate in my pocket. What in the world? It was

Shawn, who immediately texted back...from onstage. Wait—shouldn't he be singing right now? I didn't even see him look down at his phone. The thought of him texting onstage made me laugh uncontrollably. It was so Shawn.

"What, Joi? What's so funny?" Kim asked, thinking she missed something that happened onstage. And I guess she did.

"Girl, I texted Shawn. Why did he reply right away? He's so crazy."

"Def," she said, throwing her hands up in the air on the singer's command.

really, from onstage? I replied to Shawn with a smirk. I missed his carefree attitude, especially because it seemed that lately I cared a lot about everything.

what section are you in?

106.

see you afterward.

And for the first time in a long time, I was looking forward to it.

"Let's order Thai," Shawn said.

We were back in his hotel room after the show.

I felt Kim judging me the entire time we drove from the Izod Center in New Jersey to his hotel in midtown Manhattan. But I had to see Shawn. Perhaps I wanted closure. Or perhaps I just wanted our spirits to brush up against each other one more time.

"Are you gonna sleep with him?" she asked in my mother's tone.

"*No!* It's not about that. He owes me an explanation. I don't know why he would ever treat me like that. He needs to know he can't treat women like that. I'm getting closure."

"Well, just make sure your legs stay closed too," she chimed on cue.

Kim didn't know just how easy that would be. The last time I saw Shawn was over Thanksgiving, and it was a shit show. At the time, Shawn didn't have anyone to overhear his conversation on a tour bus any longer since his run had ended, but he still texted me as if his iPhone didn't have a call button.

We were both in Maryland to spend the holiday with our families, and I still felt bad from the last time I visited and had to turn right around. So this time, after a night of sleeping on the air mattress in the computer room, I headed downtown to his place. I planned to stay as long as he wanted—well, at least until Sunday night. I still had to get back to work Monday. I raced over after Black Friday shopping with Mom, Jasmine, and baby Brandy, and after packing a small black duffel bag. If I had taken my large pink suitcase, Arista would've gotten suspicious and would've started whining by the door. It irritated me how smart she was.

By the time I got to his loft, it was nearly midnight. We watched the sun come up as he told me how his best friend was murdered while on another tour. I had heard about it days before—it was front-page news on every entertainment website. The last time Shawn was in New York, we bumped into his friend at the airport. The three of us promised to do dinner together soon. Life didn't even warn us that that'd be a promise left unfulfilled.

I just let him talk. I didn't even have the right words to say to console him anyhow. What would make him feel better? What would make anyone feel better? So I listened. I found myself calling him babe, which not only surprised him, but also surprised me too, as we did what we always did—listened to music, some of it his, played video games, and drank.

I must've fallen asleep on the couch because when I woke up, I was still in yesterday's clothes and Shawn was nowhere to be found. After I made my morning trip to the bathroom, I peeked into Shawn's bedroom to find him brushing his hair. I watched him curiously, standing in a fresh shirt, as he put on his two gold rings. Then he pulled his two wooden necklaces over his head and sprayed two puffs of cologne meticulously onto his neck. I guess we were going somewhere. Great, because I was hungry.

"Are you hungry?" I asked. "I'm starving."

"I'm sure you can get food at your momma's house," he said matter-of-factly.

*Offensive* would've been the mild adjective to describe how I felt in that moment. I was irate's older cousin. More so, I was embarrassed to even be in this situation at my age.

"Okay, Shawn."

"What? Is something wrong?" he pressed.

"It looks like you have somewhere to be. Don't worry about it," I said angrily.

"Oh! You're *mad*," he said in fake surprise. "I just thought you'd do like you did last time."

"Is *that* what this is about? You don't have to drag me all the way over here to prove a point," I yelled at him, eyes squinted. "If you would've told me you had something to do today, it would've been fine."

"I didn't feel like I needed to explain. Whatever, you're just mad you got turned out only to be sent home. Admit it."

Ignoring his cruel words, I replied, "Shawn, next time, just tell me you have somewhere to be so I can plan accordingly."

Even if he thought that was how I felt, why would he be so comfortable in making me feel that way? That was the part that really stung.

We hadn't talked since then. I was hurt, but I was even more hurt that he had a point. I get it. He was still upset that I left so suddenly last time…but I had to go to work! Couldn't he understand that? If anybody could, surely he could.

Shawn was waiting for me in the hotel lobby when I arrived. The tour bus had just pulled up, and the dancers, musicians, and Shawn had just gotten off and grabbed their luggage from underneath.

He sang, "Joiiiii," in the tune of Frankie Beverly and Maze's hit song, "Joy and Pain," when he saw me. Perhaps I was the only one still harboring ill feelings.

I could feel the other roadies, who had just gotten off the bus, staring at me, wondering who I was. I refused to return their looks. I was embarrassed to be there, at the hotel, especially this late. I felt like a groupie. Shawn didn't seem to notice as he led me up the winding purple-carpeted stairs of the hotel to his room, which was the size of a shoe box—very New York.

"Let's order Thai," Shawn said as he swiveled around in the hotel's black desk chair. I sat on the opposite side of the room, on the corner of the bed.

We decided to ignore the elephant in the room while we ate. We didn't even turn on the television; we were too busy catching each other up on the past couple of weeks. I always felt at home when I spoke to Shawn…when he wasn't being an asshole. We enjoyed the same things: good food, music, books. He appealed to the very artistic side of me that most people would call me weird for indulging in.

"Did you ever read that book I gave you?" I asked him.

Instead of answering, he pulled out his designer backpack with gold studs. Unzipping it revealed *Glow*, the Rick James autobiography that had come into the newsroom only to be left in a pile of unwanted CDs, DVDs, and books received by all the editors. I'd grabbed it off the pile before anyone else could take it home, knowing Shawn would appreciate it.

"I haven't finished it, but I'm reading something else now."

He pulled out *The Tao of Wu*.

"What is *that*?" I asked, wide-eyed.

"You know, RZA, from Wu-Tang. He wrote this book about how he went from Staten Island to, like, the fucking Wu-Tang Clan. The shit is so deep. He's so smart, man. He breaks down, like, life principles."

I grabbed the book from his hand and fanned the pages with my fingers. When my finger stopped on a random page, I could see Shawn had underlined something: "A good man will see the goodness in himself." I wondered what drew him to that sentence.

"You should totally buy this book, Joi. He talks about honing and mastering his art and how he had a vision for Wu-Tang to be so much more than a group. Then he started Wu-Tang from his basement... It's mad inspirational."

I loved when Shawn got excited about art. It made me excited about art.

Although Shawn wasn't the touchy-feely type, he motioned for me to come sit on his lap. Instead of wrestling with my common sense, I surrendered to the moment and followed his instruction. He wrapped his arms around me, which seemed even skinnier than the last time we'd seen each other, and held the book out in front of us. Then, like a schoolteacher, he began reading.

I sat and listened to him read aloud, playfully telling him to read faster or slower, depending on how much I wanted to annoy him. Instead of getting irritated with me, which he seemed to do quite easily, he laughed. Feeling his warmth and sipping on his intellect made me want this moment to last forever. It made me want to love him.

After three hours, we had our first lull in conversation, which made the hotel room's silence in the dead of night really loud. So Shawn turned on his own music, a project he had been working on for months when he wasn't on tour.

"Have I played this for you?" he asked, before playing a song that sounded like sweet caramel.

*Was that a rhetorical question? He knew I hadn't spoken to him in weeks. He knew I hadn't heard it. Was he getting me confused with someone else?*

"I *love* this," I said instead, bopping my head to the mid-tempo beat. I smiled while looking at the hotel's purple carpet. If I'd looked into his eyes, I'd be a goner. I didn't want what I said to Kim to be a lie.

"You're so cool when you're not an asshole."

"You mean when *you're* not an asshole," he corrected.

I looked up and saw the elephant in the room give me a head nod.

"I've never spoken to you or treated you like you've treated me," I said with an even tone. The last thing I wanted to do was start an argument tonight. Especially after the lovely time we were having, eating, drinking, listening to music, and reading.

"Joi, I come home from being away on tour for weeks and who did I want to be with? You. I asked you to come with me to Maryland and you literally up and left! You couldn't even stay. You treated me like I was some bird."

"Shawn, you know I had to be in the newsroom early the next day. I had an interview."

"Oh please, no interview is that early." Shawn wasn't finished with me: "You set the tone for this relationship. You never opened up. You never stayed over...and then you got mad when I treated you the same way?"

"Shawn, I just wasn't ready for what you wanted. I had just gotten out of a five-year relation—"

"Stop. Don't tell me. *Please*," he said, rolling his eyes with disgust.

"Why? You never wanted to know. *That's* the issue! You never wanted to know anything."

I found myself yelling and I really didn't want to. I was sick of arguing with someone I wasn't even in a relationship with.

Shawn picked up his guitar, which was leaning against a corner of the room. He started strumming chords I had never heard before but that sounded beautifully familiar.

"You know," Shawn said with an air of reminiscence, "I was with Mark and his wife the other day. You remember him? From the tour. We were all sitting around, talking about church people...You would've fit right in."

I sighed. Here I thought he was the bad guy and clearly I was. Shawn wanted something from me that I just wasn't ready to give.

"You know what, Shawn? I'm sorry. I misjudged you. I misjudged you based on what you do for a living...I couldn't take you seriously. You travel too much. You're on tour all the time..."

"Not all the time..."

"Right."

I felt like I should say something else, but I didn't know what else to say.

"So are you gonna stay the night?" he asked invitingly.

"I can't. I actually should go," I said, picking up my coat and pashmina.

Although I really wanted to stay, to see what it could be like, I left. The fact is that I could love Shawn, but I foresaw our life together and it wasn't at all what I wanted. He would want so much of me—calling out on random workdays, midweek trips to meet him in a random city—without giving me exactly what I needed in return. If I decided to be with him, my days would be spent supporting his goals and his dreams since they seemed to be on the edge of fruition and I knew I'd eventually resent him for that. Also, it felt so easy for him to cut me down—too easy. He didn't fight fair and I just wasn't ready for another heartbreak. My heart was still healing from the last time I had trusted someone enough to hand it to him, and it wasn't strong enough to deal with blatant disrespect.

Since Adam and I had broken up, any sort of jab didn't feel like a jab; it felt like a one-two knockout punch. Surely I could forgive Shawn for what he did, especially since from his perspective I had done the same. And in fact, I had forgiven him; otherwise I wouldn't have gone to his hotel. Still, it seemed that since Adam, I felt pain from men much deeper. My heart was still raw, still healing, still needing intensive care.

The pain from my previous heartbreak had formed an unexpected keloid. I just didn't expect my scars to heal that way. I had to make a decision to move past the pain that was eating my heart. It was stealing my future. It was even stealing my smile.

My mother texted me the other day and asked why I stopped smiling in photos. Of course I hadn't noticed. I thought I was giving my best sultry look, but my mom didn't see it that way. She saw the void in my eyes. And so I looked back on my Instagram timeline and sure enough, I went from smiling—almost showing my entire thirty-two—to a tightlipped smile to a smirk. My smile had indeed disappeared, inwardly and outwardly. This pain was corrupting my core.

This second wave of pain was surprising. I thought that when I found my happy again, it was mine to keep. I didn't expect the pain to keep coming back to me like an unreachable itch. I thought I had moved on. I was dating, working out, eating again... instead of having wine dinners. I was happy. I had found it. But like a merry-go-round, I had returned to a place of pain.

My pain was a phantom limb pain—pain from something that was no longer there. Perhaps I needed to decide that today was the last day I would recognize it. It was the last day I'd give it a name. If I ignored it, one day I'd no longer recognize it and I'd no longer know its name.

As for Shawn, I think I will always, until after the universe dries up and it explodes into a new one, have a soul tie to him. We just had one of those connections. He felt like college love or even a first love—relationships you knew wouldn't stand the test of time. It was everything I wanted it to be: noncommittal, so much fun, sunny, warm, don't know if we ate, don't do the dishes, don't stay long, we are the best of times, the sunny side of the street, teenage love. We weren't grown-ups; we didn't even want to grow up. I loved it. After so many years of desperately caring, it felt good to choose not to. I refused it so wholeheartedly that I couldn't see what stared back at me—a lovely person. I don't mean that dismissively. I mean Shawn was a person who was full of love, capable of love, seeking it and needing it. I was so busy trying not to care that I didn't see that he actually did.

I'd like to think that one day I'll be married, he'll be doing what he does, our kids will be grown, and we'll run into each other back-stage at an awards show that I'm hosting. He'll have just performed his hit single and we'll give each other a head nod and that'll be it. Deep down, I think we both knew that we just wouldn't have survived each other's love.

## Chapter 27

I was a half block away from the subway entrance, but I could feel the train rumbling into the station. I quickened my pace. I didn't want to wait another three minutes underground for the next train to come. Plus, singer Jill Scott was coming in today and I was not at all prepared.

"Excuse me!"

I thought it was someone trying to push past me because I wasn't necessarily running to catch the train this morning, but I was hurrying as best I could. Being on time be damned.

I turned my head slowly—because you never know what you're going to get in Harlem at 6:47 a.m.—and discovered the "Excuse me" was from an older woman, dressed like she was headed to work too. She clutched her heavy briefcase with one hand. It strained her so much that the veins in her arm had started to pop out. She peered over her clear-rimmed glasses that didn't hide her left eye, which was a bit lazy. I caught myself staring at it when she asked, "Do you want me to zip that up?"

"Oh! Um, yes," I said with a flush of embarrassment.

It was the zipper on the back of my J.Crew dress, which I had given up on before I left the house only ten minutes earlier. I'd tried to zip it up as far as I could with my arm cranked at a ninety-degree angle behind me, but the zipper had only been pulled halfway up my back. So then I reached over my shoulder, stretching as much as I could—even standing on my tiptoes as if that'd give me any leverage—but the zipper refused to budge.

She lightly touched my back as she zipped up my silver-and-navy-blue polka-dot dress that was probably too short for the newsroom.

"That used to happen to me when I didn't have anybody," she said with a smile.

I looked down and mumbled a quick "thank you" before I picked up my pace again. There was another train making its way into the station at 135th and Lenox, and I didn't want to miss this one.

The train, at this hour, was unsurprisingly empty except for the few schoolchildren in their navy-blue-and-white uniforms accompanied by their sleep-deprived parents. I found a seat and let out a huge sigh as I placed my Marc Jacobs leather tote on my lap when I noticed someone staring at me.

I met the stare and discovered it was a small brown boy with the saddest eyes. A tiny blue polo shirt was tucked underneath his miniature blue cardigan. He clutched his blue-and-green plastic backpack devoid of books as his penny-loafered feet kicked to and fro wildly, matching the rhythm of the train. The subway was moving steadily toward 125th Street, but because he was so small, his body flailed around in the seat. His mother, standing over him, put her knee in between his legs so he wouldn't fall out.

But how did his eyes get so sad? He couldn't have been more than four or five years old and it looked as if someone had whispered all the lessons of life in his ear—like he knew all the disappointments to expect. He looked as if someone had told him Disney fairy tales were just that. Like he knew Santa Claus wasn't real and the Easter Bunny would be totally weird if it were that huge in real life. He looked like he knew girls weren't actually gross and that a girl would eventually break his heart. He looked as if he already knew he wouldn't marry his college sweetheart and that he'd cry when he had to leave her for a new job in another city. He seemed to know that he'd marry the second-most beautiful woman he'd ever been with and that they'd struggle to stay together after the first miscarriage. He seemed to know that eventually he'd have two kids and he'd have a favorite. His eyes said that his mother, who had once held him up by her knee on the train, would slip and fall and die the same year his dad was diagnosed with cancer. It looked like he knew all of it and he was already beaten down by it.

So I smiled.

I smiled until his smile struggled to find its legs and I smiled until it stood up and became a full-blown curled-up smile. But it didn't stay. It collapsed in a heap like a baby doe's legs. I kept smiling, but thinking it might be weird if his mother should catch me, I looked away. But I kept smiling even when I changed my glance to let him know that my smile was unconditional. My smile refused to stop smiling because I had known much of what he already knew, but I still found it in me to hope.

"Do you all have water?"

"Absolutely!" I said with a spring in my step. I ran out of the studio where Jill Scott sat patiently at mic three, waiting for our interview to start.

*Why didn't I have water ready?* I thought as I ran down the curved hallway to where the bottles of water sat idly on the floor still in their plastic wrapping. By the time I ran back, I was out of breath.

"It's not cold, but...," I said as I handed her the bottle of water.

"Hmm, I wanted ice water."

"We have ice!" I cheerily volunteered.

"And snacks?"

"No...no snacks. I can show you to our vending machine, which is right next to our fridge with ice!"

She smiled politely and followed me out of the studio. Heads turned as the Grammy Award winner floated through the ordinarily mum newsroom in glittery black pants. My brain was racing. Now, what do I talk to Jill Scott about?

Usually when celebrities come in for an interview, I have three questions on deck. That's the amount of time it takes to get from the elevators in the lobby to Studio 9. "How's the weather outside? I've been in here since seven a.m. so it's always chilly when I walk in." Then it's "How's your day going so far?" followed up by "Do you have many interviews after this?" Then we sit down for our interview. I escort them back to the elevator with some random anecdote from the interview or with a question I didn't get to ask during our stroll inside, but Jill had thrown me for a loop. And now I'd have to find something to actually talk to her about.

"Ooooh, M&M's," she gushed. Her manicured nails danced on the glass of the vending machine, making a *tap, tap, tap* sound to a rhythm I couldn't hear in her head.

"I know, right? But I hate peanut M&M's," I said nervously.

"Oh, I love them! I'm getting them."

"I'm trying to reduce my sugar intake. I told myself I'd start eating healthier by thirty," I rambled in another nervous submission. "Plus my favorite food growing up was cotton candy. I need to do better."

"Where did you grow up?"

Again, her curiosity caught me by surprise. The normality of it all. This was freakin' Jill Scott, one of my top five favorite singers of all time. Jill sing-my-pain Scott. The Jill Scott I listen to when I want a good cry—"Hear My Call." The Jill Scott I listen to when I want to feel on top of the world—"Golden." The Jill Scott I listen to when I want to feel sexy—"Crown Royal." She had no idea where her songs and her voice had been in my life.

"Baltimore. You?"

"Phil—"

"Oh! Right," I cut her off abruptly. "Philadelphia. I knew that. Do you have everything? Ready?"

Jill came in to promote her new Lifetime movie, *With This Ring.* It was a movie about three unmarried women who vowed to get married within a year. I had already watched the film on my laptop in bed the evening before to prepare for the interview. Although I had enjoyed the film—even wanting to be friends with the three characters all seemingly dying to get married—*With This Ring* was everything that I hated about society. Placing the burden of marriage solely on women as if the coming together of two people in love and law was their responsibility alone. When the (socially acceptable) reality was that women don't ask themselves to get married; their mates decide. Their mates choose.

"Have you ever been engaged?" I asked Jill with the tape rolling.

"Yes, a few times."

Oh, right. How could I forget about her song, "He Loves Me (Lyzel in E Flat)"?

"What happened?"

"It just wasn't right," she said in her familiar breathy saccharine voice. "I'll put it to you like this: You can hold your stomach in for four hours, but you can't hold it in forever."

My stomach dropped. There it was. That was it. That was what I had been feeling with Adam. I was trying so hard to be picture perfect for him, for our families, for our friends so that we could be the perfect couple, but I was uncomfortable. And tired. I was tired of pretending this was the right fit for me. I didn't know how to properly explain it before this very moment, and here, Jill Scott put it into one finite sentence for me.

Although my family didn't need any convincing, it was hard to explain to friends that after loving this man for so long, I no longer thought he was the one.

"Why don't you just get back together with him? Do you really want to start over again at twenty-eight?" Kim once asked me.

It was a damn good question. Who wanted to start over at twenty-eight? I wanted to have kids soon so that my sister's daughter and my children can be close in age and grow up together and become best friends. Why would I leave the man I love...for what? For the hope of something better? Does life even work out that way?

Jill brought me back to reality. "You have to be who you are and you have to genuinely love who you are in order to have a lasting marriage," she continued. "Getting married is one thing; staying married is something else."

I felt the lump in my throat. It felt so big I thought Jill could see me straining to breathe through it. I looked down at my notes to ask the next question, but Jill had more to say.

"I'm older now so I see a little bit better than I did before. The longest I'll date someone is for about nine months. Actually, it's more like six months."

"Really?" I said excitedly, leaning forward. I had told myself I'd never date anyone for five years again and here Jill was saying I only needed less than a year to truly know.

"There's no need for me to waste my time or anybody else's. I know by then if we're compatible enough for a relationship," Jill said confidently.

I nodded at this statement like Jill's own personal Amen Corner.

"If you make it over six months," she continued, "you have done something. I must *really* like you."

Although Jill wasn't in a rush to end our interview, her publicist was, as our twenty-minute talk had turned into forty-five minutes and she was about to be late for her sit-down with HuffPost Live.

"I'll walk you all out," I said, holding the studio door. Once we got a few paces down the hallway, I asked a question I hadn't gotten to earlier: "Do you have many interviews after this?"

# Chapter 28

I had been dodging Adam for days, so I finally invited him over.

He had been calling and texting nonstop since our date at Coney Island, saying he wanted to drop off an early Christmas gift for me. He was upset that I hadn't made time for him in the weeks following our trip to Brooklyn. And he was right. I hadn't made time for him. We weren't in a relationship any longer. We used to be. He had me. He had all my free time and he didn't know what to do with it. Now, months later, so many tears later, another heartbreak later, he expected me to drop all my plans for him? That wasn't fair—and I wasn't going to do it.

Although he wanted to come over the evening before, Shawn was in town for a few hours to record a song with my girl Jilly from Philly. So I lied to break our "date" to see Shawn. I told Adam I had to work a red carpet. That seemed plausible. So Adam came over as I packed to head to Maryland to spend the Christmas holiday with my parents.

I expected him over by 4:30 p.m., figuring I'd be home from the newsroom by then, but he was early. So early I ran into him, struggling to get a huge box out of his car, while I was walking the dog outside my building.

"Need help?" I asked him.

He looked amazing. Perhaps he had just come from work because he looked wedding-ready in his tailored blue suit, purple tie with matching pocket square, and brown double monk-strap shoes.

He had a twinkle in his eye I hadn't seen in a while. Seeing him look excited about whatever was in the box got me excited about whatever was in the box. I missed seeing him this happy. I missed him. I wanted to wrap him in my arms and nuzzle his neck, gently kissing it, but I couldn't—and *wouldn't*.

"Nope! I got it," he said proudly, although he was barely able to carry the brown box up the two flights of stairs into my apartment.

Whatever was in the box was heavy. When he placed it on my red-and-orange area rug, in front of my tan leather couch, which was slowly falling apart because I bought it at a cheap furniture store in the Bronx, it made a thump.

Arista circled the box excitedly before jumping all over him. I wasn't the only one who had missed Adam.

"What is *in* this, Adam?" I said. I couldn't contain my excitement and didn't mind when a smile appeared on my face.

Adam was prepared. He had his presentation orchestrated. Instead of answering my question, he continued to smile and pulled out a piece of paper. It shook violently back and forth in his hands like Arista's vacillating tail. He steadied his hands long enough to hand the white folded sheet of paper to me.

Admittedly in my excitement, I skimmed the short note, which he had typed. I caught the phrases *you always credited your grandmother Ida as your inspiration . . . so I tried to imagine what a young*

*Ida's desk would look like...in an interview, your mother described* *what type of typewriter she used...I searched high and low for one...* *I hope you can pass it on to your kids.* Then he signed his initials in blue pen.

After reading the letter, I looked up at Adam, who was looking back at me. We both had tears in our eyes. As for mine, the tears came, but they didn't fall. I couldn't find the words to thank him. Conveniently, they were written right on my face. It was the most thoughtful gift someone had ever given me.

Adam knew how much I loved my grandmother Ida and how I found my life oddly mimicking hers as I've gotten older. I used to tell him often how I'd watch her sit at that typewriter growing up, writing entertainment stories for her father's paper, the *Afro American Newspaper*. As a child watching her, I never realized I'd grow up to be just like her—an entertainment journalist. In my ten years of getting to know her, she had the most profound impact on my life and I just wish she could've seen where I had gotten and how much she was a part of my success.

Adam told me it took him a couple of days to find this type-writer on eBay. After negotiating a fair price, it arrived at his house in Jersey, where he then polished off the former owner's dust and grime and stories.

It was the perfect gift. If Adam could "get me" like this, he could get me. If a man wanted me this much, I should just give in. Isn't this what I wanted all along? I was ready to wave my white flag and give in. Enough was enough. He admitted to e-mailing my mother to tell her how much he admired me and to thank her for raising me. (I hacked into my mother's e-mail and deleted the note. She didn't need to be involved in our relationship.) Not to mention, he posted a rather emo message on Facebook—something he'd never do. I should just give him another chance, although I never give third chances.

"Thank you, Adam. Thank you," I said, hugging him. Unbridled tears fell and landed on his tie.

I felt like he had more to say, but he didn't say it. Instead he pulled out another sheet of paper. Adam looked down at the floor nervously. I could see him trying to steady his breath. He then uncovered another white box, big enough to fit a pair of shoes inside it.

Ohmygod, could this be it? Was he finally going to propose? I pushed down the hope that had started to bubble up in anticipation.

Adam again had his presentation down to a T, this time handing me the note to explain the next gift. I skipped the typed words and looked toward the bottom. There was no sign of "Will you marry me?" Instead the note explained why he bought me a white sweatshirt with the words *Editor-in-chief* stitched onto the front. His note, again typed, said he always knew I'd chase after my dreams and how he didn't want me to stop, unless I wanted to.

I let out my breath, which I had been unconsciously holding in during his presentation. *Of course*, I thought. Why would I expect any different? Why did I expect him to propose now? With another faux proposal under my belt, my disappointment didn't even stick.

"Adam, stay while I pack. You shouldn't leave after this," I said.

I opened the door to my bedroom. Arista rushed into the room as if she owned it. Crap. It was already after 5:00 p.m. and my train left at 6:30 p.m. I had to get out of here in thirty.

I rushed into my walk-in closet to pull out my pink luggage hidden on the back wall. Rushing over to my wooden dresser, I opened the top drawer to pull out three Victoria's Secret underwear with their corresponding bras and plopped them onto the bed. Clearing off the top of my dresser, I threw my deodorant, lotion, and makeup remover wipes onto the bed as well. I picked up a velvet jewelry sack to place two pairs of earrings into it and a cocktail ring. I was just about to plan my weekend's outfits when Adam interrupted my rushed packing.

"What is that?"

"What is what, sweetie?" I said, falling back into old patterns.

"Is that a condom wrapper?"

I didn't need to turn around. Before Adam came over, I thought I had cleaned up from the evening before when Shawn was here. I guess I hadn't and in the worst possible way our lovely afternoon of tentative reconciliation was destroyed. I turned around anyway and, yup, there it was, defiantly shining at the bottom of my bed.

I have never been more embarrassed. The ugly voices in my head shouted loudly: *You're a whore! You're so mean! How could you? Are you fucking serious? How could you treat someone like this?*

They shouted so loudly I couldn't even hear what Adam was saying, although I'm sure it was something similar. I didn't dare look at him. It would hurt my heart too bad.

"Who are you fucking?"

"Adam…"

"WHO ARE YOU FUCKING?"

"It's really none of your business." I cowered. My voice was shaking with embarrassment, terror, and fear.

He punched the wall. I looked away.

"I knew you weren't working. Usually you'll tweet, check in, post photos from the red carpet. Last night? Nothing! You lied to me to see some *asshole*?"

"I didn't lie," I lied.

The voice—interrupting my drama—reminded me: *He's not even supposed to be here. You could've avoided this,* it said in the calmest of manners, *if you just had followed directions.*

"That was supposed to happen," I said to no one, looking down at the floor.

"It was? You *wanted* to hurt me?"

He misunderstood, but I was too exhausted and too embarrassed to explain that my disobedience was causing my life to spiral out of control—in more ways than one. I had lost this fight. Not with Adam, but with the universe. I could not go back to Adam despite the constant attention, thoughtful e-mails, and gifts. The universe was telling me to end this relationship for good, and if I didn't, it would fuck my life up. Enough was enough.

"No...no...," I said with an unknown calm. "I would never do this to you intentionally. I'm so, *so* sorry, Adam. This was not on purpose."

I laughed at the absurdity of it all to keep from crying.

"The universe does not want us to work this out...it just doesn't," I said, forcing my body to pick up clothes and place them in my luggage. The mechanics of packing was the only thing saving me from completely falling apart right now.

"I love you. I can look past this," he said.

That response surprised me. It was way too understanding. Plus, how could I respect a man whom I had so blatantly (even if accidentally) disrespected?

"I just don't think *I* can," I replied. "Adam, your gift was beautiful. It was the most thoughtful gift I have ever received...but I think it's best we just continue to move on."

"Well, give me the photos!"

Perplexed, I asked what photos he was referring to. Apparently,

Adam had noticed that I had conveniently hidden the photos of us that once hung in the corners of my apartment—the silver frame of us on my nightstand, the three photos on my corkboard from the photo booth at my cousin's wedding, another frame on my TV stand.

"Adam...I apologize...I have to go. It's five thirty. If I don't leave now, I'm going to miss my train."

I watched Adam and he watched me as I crouched down to zip my luggage and roll it into the hallway. Reaching into the hallway closet, I grabbed a pee pad for Arista to relieve herself in case she had to go before my dog walker came to get her later that evening. I then ran to the bathroom to grab the razor I almost forgot. I would not stand still. I could not stand still. I could not face him.

Catching the hint, Adam said, "Fine."

I let out a small sigh of relief when he began walking out, but then he turned around in such haste that it startled me. "If I would've asked today, would you have said yes?"

"Were you going to?"

Ignoring me, he angrily repeated, "If I would've asked today, would you have said yes?"

I looked down at my ringless hand—well, not entirely ringless. It held my mother's large amethyst cocktail ring. "I don't know, Adam. I guess you'd have to ask."

"I thought you wanted to get married," he said, his words filled with confusion and exasperation.

"I do. I did...I just don't know anymore. Should it be this hard to figure out?"

I was rambling and I never rambled. It was more of a question for myself. It never seemed this hard in the movies. It always seemed like a pleasant surprise, not something that couples discussed and debated at length. I didn't want to feel like I was convincing Adam to propose to me. That's not a good story to tell our future kids. Honestly, if I still wanted to marry him, I'd know. Right? I just didn't know anymore.

"You're lost. You really are a lost queen," Adam said, interrupting my thoughts before walking out.

And for once he was right.

# Chapter 29

He didn't deserve that. Nobody did. I couldn't blame all the things he didn't do, he didn't say, the gifts he didn't give—nope, not this time. It was my fault.

I didn't listen to the trusted voice in my head, and my insubordination was starting to play itself out in my life. If I truly trusted myself and what the universe had already told me—that Adam wasn't my happily-ever-after—then I wouldn't have put myself in this situation. Although I knew what I had to do, it was becoming harder to do it. Adam's regret wasn't making the process of unraveling any easier.

My traveling habits carried me through Penn Station—I grabbed a caramel latte at the Dunkin' Donuts, like I always did; bought a fashion magazine from the stand, like times before; and rushed to the gate when it revealed itself on the board like the words on *Family Feud*. Those habits were the only things that got me to my train on time because shame had taken over my entire body.

I felt like a piece of shit. I tried to remind myself that I was single and didn't owe anyone an explanation, but that reasoning wasn't even good enough for me.

Why did shame make us feel so bad? Why did we let it make us conform to the shadows of discretion? Why did it make us tell half-truths and only one side of the story? Why did we let it make us run and hide?

I couldn't do that anymore. I had to own this. If not for me, then for Nate Parker, who offered me free advice: Don't run from anything. I wouldn't let my shame burden me with regret. Instead, I'd use it to leave behind the woman I no longer wanted to be and help shape me into the woman I wanted to be.

I have lived my life through men. From my high school sweetheart, to Gary, to Brian, to Shawn, and even Adam. When I think of my life, it isn't marked by personal accomplishments; it's marked by who I was in love with at the time. I have lived my life through the lens of men—how they saw me, what they chose to love about me, and why they wanted to be with me or not be with me—and now because of it, my entire life was spiraling out of control. I wanted the courage to live a self-defined life, not a life defined by what others thought of me, or how they liked my hair, or my fiery attitude, or my long legs. Or if they wanted to marry me. I wanted the courage to become the authority on me.

I had let someone's rejection of me take away my relationship with them and my relationship with myself—the love I had for myself. What a terrorist act. I don't even recognize myself. I don't know the woman I've become. This woman who would hurt a man she loved more deeply than the ocean. This woman was ugly. And although she wasn't intentionally malicious, her carelessness hurt just as deep. And sometimes careless hurt is worse than intentional hurt.

Finding an empty seat on the Amtrak train, I took out my white cell phone charger and plugged my phone in. It was almost dead thanks to the nonstop vibrations that had taken over its soul. My phone had been buzzing since Condomgate. I didn't dare look at it. I knew who it was.

By the time I made it past Wilmington, Delaware, I had gathered up the courage to look at the text messages from Adam. I stared at his nonstop stream of thoughts—some angry, some loving, some remorseful—but I only read the two instructing me to check my e-mail. I sighed and followed his scavenger hunt–like instructions. This time, I wouldn't skip or skim. I'd read every nasty word...if he even took it there. I wanted to feel every emotion. I wanted to feel the hurt, the shame, the guilt, the anger. Because I never wanted to be in this situation again—hurting others, hurting myself.

I have never felt so low as I did just now. You've never lied. You've never played dumb. I don't even know who you are anymore. I just want to love you or at least look at you from across the room, knowing you are still one of the best women I've ever loved. No need to respond.

So I didn't. Shame had silenced me.

I wouldn't speak to Adam for a couple of weeks, until I returned from my weekend with the family and made it through a whole other week of work. But if I thought Condomgate would define the end of our story, I was wrong.

Adam was sincere when he said that he could forgive me and look past what I had done. I wasn't sure if he was referring to the fact that I had practiced safe sex with someone else or left the remnants of that fact for him to see. I really hoped he meant the latter. But how did I know? Because he sent long-stemmed red roses to my job. In our five years together, Adam had never sent flowers to my job.

It felt odd. Confusing, to say the very least. But if this was a gesture of his forgiveness, I'd take it and I immediately called to properly thank him.

He answered on the first ring.

"Adam, I just want to say I'm sorry again for what happened. I promise you, when I asked you to stay, I had no idea that was going to happen. I just feel really crappy for ruining such an amazing moment," I forced out in one breath.

"Joi, I love you. We can move past this. If you want to."

I then became acutely aware that I was still in the newsroom and people could overhear my conversation. I looked around to see if anyone was listening, but mostly people sported headphones and others looked intently at their screens working or pretending really hard to look like they were working. Still, I got up to walk to the ladies' room for just a bit more privacy.

Adam, hearing my shuffling in silence, must've remembered my directive. "Oh. Right. You don't like to talk at work," he sighed.

"No...but I called you...to say thank you. The flowers are lovely, really."

"Listen, why don't we pick a date to meet up once and for all and decide if we really want to do this or not?"

"What do you mean?" I asked as I power-walked through the maze of sad gray cubicles and out to the floor's lobby.

"I feel like we should take a few weeks, think about our relationship and then decide if we get married or not. Let's really think about what we'd be throwing away here. I've thought about it. I've owned my shit. You've owned your shit. Let's just think about it and see."

"That sounds fair," I said, opening the ladies' bathroom door. "Let's pick a date . . . how about January thirteenth?"

"That works. I'll send a calendar invite." Adam paused, then added nervously, "Should I bring a ring?"

"Adam," I started levelly, "if this is another attempt at a joke, now is probably not the right time."

"No!" he said too loudly, then corrected, "No . . . it's not a joke. *Should* I?"

Sensing he was genuinely curious about where I stood on the subject, I took a deep breath and thought about it. But the more I tried to think about it, the more upset I became. Why should I have to tell Adam if he wants to propose to me or not? Why didn't he know after five years of being with me? I knew or at least thought I did. Adam had to make this decision for himself. By himself.

Finding the right words to say, I asked, "What do you feel like you should do?"

"I don't know . . ."

I rolled my eyes. I felt the familiar wave of frustration that I hadn't felt in a very long time. It wasn't welcome any longer.

"Adam, you have to figure this out for yourself. Do what your heart tells you to do."

In what seemed like curious timing, Adam said one of his clients was calling him on the other line, so he rushed off the phone. Sure enough, when I returned to my desk from hiding out in the ladies' room to finish our conversation, I had a calendar invite from him. The memo line read: "To put an end to the bullshit."

How eloquent. But why did I feel like January 13 was D-Day?

# Chapter 30

why did you post that?

It was Adam interrupting my Friday night, which I was spending on the couch warming up beside my space heater. I thought I wouldn't hear from him until D-Day. I thought wrong.

huh?

I was playing dumb, but I knew exactly what he was referring to. I had just posted an old selfie to Instagram.

My iPhone refused to take another selfie, claiming it had run out of storage space. So in an effort to clear up more space for more memories, and forget memories that had been inexplicably captured, I found myself stuck on the couch, reminiscing and deleting, reminiscing and deleting. Photos that I thought deserved a second chance, I e-mailed to myself or texted it to the other person featured in the photo. Then I ran across one photo that I snapped back when I was with Adam. I had been heading out with my girlfriends. My hair was swept to the side perfectly, my skin looked radiant in my hallway's warm lighting, and the buttons on my flannel girl-next-door shirt had somehow popped open, revealing what little cleavage I had. It was the perfect sexy, but not too sexy, selfie.

In my quest to be his Michelle Obama, I didn't dare post it. Instead, after I snapped the photo, I sent it to Adam. He had replied with a discouraging ?? When I asked him about his response days later, he expounded on his theory that people who take too many selfies are narcissists and psychopaths—instead of girlfriends letting boyfriends know you're thinking about them even though you're about to turn up with your girls.

Now he said: the photo.

Adam didn't even have Instagram, so clearly one of his friends snitched. But it didn't matter: I wasn't with him and I can do what I want. I had to remind myself of that. Plus I looked good! Not to mention my text messages were so dry recently. Shawn had gone ghost, which didn't surprise me, and although I took Ashlee's suggestion and joined two dating apps—Coffee Meets Bagel and Plenty of Fish—I was bored. I was hoping my sexy snap would jump-start some type of conversation…just not the one I was having right now.

your caption says you're headed out. who are you fronting for? he texted in rapid succession.

well, technically i am headed out.

it just doesn't seem like you to post such a seductive picture, especially one you sent to me privately. i hope you're not just doing this to hurt me…or worse, for attention.

I could feel the anger creep up the side of my neck. He didn't have the right to check me anymore.

i'm completely confused as to why you jumped to the conclusion and thought my posting a picture that I liked of myself on my Instagram account had anything to do with you. i'm sorry you assumed as much. it's not directed at you. it's not directed at anyone for that matter, I lied. i honestly didn't think the photo was that suggestive, especially to warrant this. most of my friends told me my hair looked good, which it did.

The ellipses on my iPhone let me know that despite my response, he wasn't done typing. you need that much attention? did i do that to you? did i make you lose your self-respect? it's an old pic, #lostqueen. just say you're thirsty for likes and i probably seem wack for this and then we can just laugh it off.

And then more came: i just want this whole thing to be over in due time. on jan. 13 we can celebrate. either to a new beginning or to the great years we had.

I typed *y-u-p*, complete with a period at the end, then sank back into the couch.

I expertly flipped through the hundreds of cable channels while trying to avoid that damn *Say Yes to the Dress* marathon on TLC and stretched my toes, which were wrapped comfortably in hand-crocheted socks that I bought in Istanbul for five U.S. dollars. My couch must've felt really good because before I realized it I was waking up in the middle of the night. Arista grunted as I got off the couch to blow out the scented candles, which I had accidentally left burning on the television stand. I said a silent prayer, thanking God that I didn't burn down the entire building as I walked into my bedroom to get a proper rest.

Before I lay back down, though, I noticed I had two text messages: one from a guy I had met at a dance party in Brooklyn earlier that year, saying, hey! cute pic! and one from Cody. Lost for words, I guess, Cody just sent a rosy-cheeked smiley face. Looks like the photo had worked!

❧

The next morning, my one-bedroom apartment had been turned into an arts and crafts station. Off-brand markers in ten colors rolled around my dark hardwood floors that needed to be stripped, sanded, and lacquered again thanks to Arista's frequent accidents. Poster board in bright neon yellow, neon pink, and white created a new area rug in my living room. A glue stick that no one could seem to find was playing hide-and-seek, and a huge tube of gold glitter remained untouched.

I finally texted Cody back in the morning—just to make it clear, if he hadn't already realized, that he was not a priority—asking how his Saturday was going. It seemed all was well on his side of Harlem. When he asked, I told him what I was up to: creating posters because my sorority sister Sloan was running a half marathon this year. The more-than-thirteen-mile route wound through Central Park and we planned to cheer very loudly for her as she ran out of Harlem and back to midtown and across the finish line.

I chose the neon-yellow poster board while Lindsay and Kaya, my sorority sisters who were set to join me that afternoon in the frigid temperatures, fought to see who would get the neon-pink poster. Lindsay won.

As I crafted my inspirational message for Sloan to see while she ran past us—I eventually came up with *Sloan Yaaaas! Love #FA05*, denoting the semester all thirteen of us crossed the burning sands and became members of Delta Sigma Theta Sorority at the University of Maryland, College Park—I saw my phone light up.

ur such a good friend, Cody texted. i would never stand out in the cold to cheer on anybody.

I had been hearing that a lot lately. Kaya had said the same thing once we realized we were both bridesmaids in Lindsay's upcoming wedding.

Out of our line of thirteen, two were already married and I just so happened to be in both weddings—distinctly lovely affairs in Chicago and Philadelphia, respectively. Lindsay made three and now I'd be in her wedding too, after she asked me by handing me a pink decorative macaron with the words *Will you be my bridesmaid?* written in cursive on a small piece of paper inside. The fake treat was a nod to the fact that she had gotten engaged in Paris. It was just perfect.

Aside from my type A personality, which makes me great at planning things like bridal showers and bachelorette parties, I cared about my friendships. They gave back to me what I gave to them. Before Drake made the term famous, I truly had no new friends. I have known my closest friends since I was three, four, and even nine years old. They had become more than friends. They were sisters, family. When I became a Delta, I took the sisterhood part very seriously, especially since I've always wanted to be a Delta. To me, there was no other option.

My great-grandmother Vashti Turley Murphy was one of the sorority's twenty-two founders. Growing up, the allegiance to the community-service organization was so strong my grandma Ida wouldn't even let me wear pink—the color of our sorority's "rival," Alpha Kappa Alpha Sorority. My mom would let us march around her bedroom, singing Delta songs like, "*Oh, just to be, to be a Delta girl, the finest in the world,*" stopping short of letting us throw up the sorority's triangle-shaped hand sign. I couldn't wait to join and have my very own sisters or sorors.

"What do you think about this?" Lindsay asked, proudly holding up her sign, which read: *Go, Sloan! Run like you stole something!*

We all burst into laughter.

"It works! It works!" I said.

Making our way to the marathon route, we stopped into Dunkin' Donuts before finding a place on the path to look for Sloan. Although it was the perfect day for a half marathon, with bright blue skies and the sun uninhibited by any clouds, it was still January and very cold—not to mention windy. We found a spot right near the corner of 110th and Adam Clayton Powell, but the wind tried to ruin our papered encouragement. A stationed police officer had to chase down my sign as it escaped my numb fingertips, and Kaya's sign was ripped in two.

We were so busy trying to hold on to our signs and keep our bodies in constant motion for warmth that we didn't even see Sloan run up behind us. "Giiiiiiiirls," she squealed. She looked like pure exhaustion in her black running gear. But she still had enough energy to fix her Oakley sunglasses that kept sliding down her nose at every pace. Her gray-and-black scarf was tied expertly around her neck.

"Sloan, here!" I handed her ChapStick for her lips. Thanks to the wind, they looked like she had dived lips-first into a powdery donut.

"Thank you, girl," she said, rubbing her lips together in relief. "How long have you been standing out here?"

"Not long at all, thanks to that trusty marathon app. I don't know what people did before technology," Lindsay said. "We knew you were only twenty minutes away."

"So true! Let's take a quick picture before I continue," Sloan rushed out before reminding us that she was celebrating later that night in her midtown hotel room.

"We'll be there," I said, holding out my arm for the selfie.

Sloan lay coffin-still under the covers of her hotel's king-sized bed when we arrived later that evening to her suite. Her husband, Kyle, opened the door to greet us, while her mother, father, and a family friend occupied the couch. They were engaged in a heated conversation we weren't privy to. Grown folks' business.

After saying our hellos, Lindsay, Kaya, and I made our way to the foot of the bed, carrying small plates filled with cheese, M&M's, and different cuts of salami Sloan had ordered before we arrived.

I got up from the bed to refresh my glass of wine. "Does anyone else want more?"

"Sure!" Kyle said.

I poured two glasses of Shiraz and piled my plate with a different assortment of cheeses and chocolate. I was making sure not to spill my plate, which sat atop my and Kyle's cups, when I felt my phone vibrate in my back pocket.

"Ugh, who is it?" I said to no one in particular.

Placing my bounty at the foot of the bed, I grabbed my phone to discover it was my friend Mia from back home. I wondered what she could want from me on a late Saturday night. Soon I'd realize she didn't want anything at all but to tell me Brian, my Brian, had gotten engaged.

"Yeah, log onto Facebook. He just announced it," she said matter-of-factly.

"What chick did he get engaged to?"

"I actually know her. She's pretty...I saw it on her feed before I saw it on his. She's a nice girl," Mia said sympathetically.

I rushed Mia off the phone to fill everyone in on the bad news.

They all remembered how Brian and I dated off and on throughout college. We finally broke it off—well, he finally broke it off by dumping me a week before Valentine's Day. *Why do I always get dumped around Valentine's Day?*

The story goes like this: I had randomly bumped into Brian on the Metro in D.C. while I was transferring from the Green to the Red Line. I was already running late for work—I had a part-time job at a D.C. nonprofit during my senior year—but was pleasantly surprised to spot him waiting on the platform. So I rushed down to him.

He proceeded to tell me that he had done a lot of thinking over the weekend after going to church, and God had told him to get his life together. He told me he loved me, he cared for me, but he wanted someone better for me—he even admitted how odd that sounded. Then we hugged for a good two minutes, which was awkward for me because back then I hated any sort of public display of affection.

Although I didn't cry when we embraced, the tears came out of nowhere after he let me go. Thank God I had on sunglasses that morning. He must've known; God must've known before I left the house how my morning was going to go. Damn, why didn't God tell me? At least I could've prepared myself.

When he told me his spirit felt happy after telling me—or whatever the hell he said—I knew I couldn't argue nor convince him otherwise. Perhaps it was better this way. God knew I wasn't going to let him go on my own, so he had Brian do it.

After he dumped me on the platform, we had to ride the uncomfortable twenty minutes deeper into D.C. together…but not together. Before I got off at the Farragut North stop, I told him, "And to think I was gonna ask you to be my Valentine."

"Damn, Joi. I'm an asshole. I forgot about Valentine's Day," he said.

I shrugged. He grabbed my hand and we *never* held hands. By the time I had walked off the train, I knew it was over.

I hadn't talked to him since then, except for the occasional happy birthday and Merry Christmas text messages he'd send me. Eventually, I wouldn't even receive those. Over the years, Brian and I had gone from strangers to friends to lovers, and back to strangers.

Why did I feel sick all of a sudden? My stomach was churning and it wasn't from the hoards of cheese I had just stuffed in my mouth. Brian was getting married? My Brian…I had to see what this woman looked like.

Facebook didn't disappoint. Thanks to all the likes and congratulatory comments, it was at the top of my feed and the first thing I saw when I logged on. Mia was right—she was pretty… really pretty, which made me feel even worse. I couldn't even hate her. If she was ugly, I would say, "Oh well, great! He got what he deserved. At least he isn't doing better than me." But no…he chose well. In the photo, they looked happily into each other's eyes. I studied Brian's gaze. It was the same way he used to stare at me. It pained me to look at him looking at someone else the same way he used to look at me.

It didn't seem fair.

Brian and I dated for the better part of four years, so of course we spoke about what our lives would be like as a married couple. He was super handy, always dragging me to Home Depot to fix his washer and dryer or a random light switch in his basement condo. I knew I wouldn't have to waste money and pay a handyman if something should break in our future home. He was great at saving money, buying his own home only one year after he graduated from college. He was a family man, speaking with his mother daily, a quality I adored about him.

But he kept me in competition with other women and I couldn't deal with that. There was always someone else. I never asked, but when he told me the front window of his car was bashed in and asked if I did it, I laughed, told him no, and told my friends he got what he deserved. Some woman had done the dirty work for us all.

Before I found out Brian was engaged, I hadn't thought about him in years. I didn't want him, but at the news of his engagement, I was pissed. There was this feeling of *want* and *what if* and *what happened* that I couldn't scratch out.

"Good riddance," Sloan said at the news. She raised her plastic cup, meant for water but filled with wine, clinking it with Lindsay's. The two giggled devilishly at each other.

"You *guys*! This is Brian we're talking about. *Brian! My Brian!*"

"Joi, you don't want Brian," Lindsay corrected.

"I knooooow . . . I know, but . . ."

"You just didn't want him to get engaged before you."

*Ding! Ding! Ding!* Lindsay had hit the nail right on the head. It wasn't a competition, but it sure felt like one. Honestly, if I were happy in my own relationship, I wouldn't have given two shits about Brian's engagement. But I wasn't, so I did.

"Ugh, you're probably right. But we *did* talk about getting married. I don't feel bad about missing out on him. I feel bad at missing out on a future we spoke about."

"Joi," Lindsay said as if she wanted to say this for the last time, "you *don't* want him."

She was right.

In that moment I begrudgingly decided to let go of what could've been, then clicked "Like" on his engagement status.

I had come to such a place of peace that I was surprised to hear from Brian a week later.

On a random Sunday night, when I was tucked coffin still under my own covers, I saw his text come in after midnight. It was definitely too late for him to be texting me—even if it did only say, Sup? If Brian couldn't respect the new boundaries in his life as an engaged man, I would do it for him.

Instead, I responded the next morning at 6:25 a.m. with Hi? I was up getting ready for work. I secretly hoped I would annoyingly awake him from his sleep.

I didn't. He was already at the gym. Damn.

Very random, I know, he wrote back with perfect punctuation. But you were on my mind. If I may, how have you been?

No, he may not. Is he freakin' serious? But you know what—my curiosity got the best of me. What did Brian want?

Random indeed! I replied, adding, Congrats on the engagement. She's pretty! Much hasn't changed. Still working in NYC. Still have my dog. Still happy.

I scrolled up to see the last time Brian and I had exchanged text messages. I wasn't surprised to see that it had been two years since he had wished me a happy birthday. Before that, he had wished me a Happy Easter and said if I was ever around he'd love to catch up. I hadn't responded to that text.

That's great. I didn't know you worked in NYC. I'm sure she is still a happy pup. I'm glad you're happy. Not surprised by that. You stay happy in most cases. Also, thanks! You taught me a lot. I didn't know it at the time, but you did.

Oh, here we go. Brian wanted me to take the bait. He wanted

me to reminisce with him. He saw my "Like" on Facebook and took it as an invitation back into my life. Sadly, he was mistaken. I'd be lying if I didn't say it felt good, though. Brian proved my theory that they always come back. Always. And here he was, coming back...for what? I still didn't know.

Yeah, I've been here for about four years. What did I teach you exactly? I asked.

Wow! Has it been that long? Time flies! Money: Don't chase it but do what makes you happy and it'll come in abundance. Love: We loved each other. You were way more mature than I was and put up with a lot. It's okay to trust and tell the truth no matter what. Friendship: It's special and if a person is a real friend they will be there no matter the issue or time. I knew that for dudes but not women. Sex: It's okay if you don't remember, but I do.

Out of respect for your fiancée, I'd rather not respond to that last part, I replied, rolling my eyes. But that's a lot! I'm glad everything worked out.

Tuh! If he thought he was going there with me, he had another thing coming.

You must've thought I was awful. We haven't spoken in years.

Well you were. Haha! It's cool tho. Time heals all. And I tend not to befriend exes so it's nothing personal.

Time does heal. You know what? I'll just jump out and ask... Can I be your friend again? Not that I wasn't but could it be actually acknowledged again?

What the entire fuck? Why did Brian want to be my friend all of a sudden? Especially after he just asked another woman—a seemingly good woman—to marry him? Was he freaking out about walking down the aisle? Did he want a squadron of exes at his emotional disposal just in case he was making the biggest mistake of his life? Did he want to clear his conscience or right his wrongs before committing?

Unfortunately for him, he didn't get the luxury of any of that. I was not here to be his friend. I was not here to soothe his fears of his (hopefully) eternal commitment. I was not here to be his emotional sounding board for when he had issues at home. I was not here to clear his conscience. He had followed the universe's instruction and broken up with me. I didn't fault him for that. The universe had already sorted it out in both of our favors. So what more could he want? This was the end of the road for us. That day on the Metro nearly a decade ago was the end of the road for us.

It's not that we're not friends. We're cool, I lied.

As long as we're cool. I'm good.

We've been cool for a while, I lied again. You need to clear your conscience or something?

No. I just thought about you.

Oh, okay. I didn't know if this was in the Man Handbook that before you walk down the aisle you right your old wrongs. This is like the second convo I've had like this with an engaged ex. Interesting.

No, no handbook. Who? Ray?

Oh no, he did not just bring up Ray. Ray was the guy I briefly dated right after him, the one he wasn't happy about when he found out about it through mutual friends. Ray also went to college with us and we were all just one degree of separation. And, yup, like Brian, Ray was now engaged, but to an unfortunate-looking girl from our school. So no, I didn't freak out like I did with Brian. Plus, I never loved Ray. I could've, but my heart wouldn't allow it because he didn't want to commit. And after dating Brian, I wasn't about to put myself through another relationship where I was a girlfriend in practice but not on paper.

Ha! No, not that engaged ex.

I was actually referring to Gary, the preacher. After he walked down the aisle a couple of years ago, we had a similar uncomfortable conversation.

I tend not to think about the past, I typed. I'd rather look forward to creating new memories. That's what life's about.

So insightful.

I couldn't tell if he was being sincere or patronizing.

Well, enjoy the gym. We'll talk soon friend!

Another lie.

Cool. Later!

# Chapter 31

That's *such* a nice ring," Mike, who had slowly but surely become my work husband, gushed.

He was staring at my mom's mammoth amethyst ring, with an ornate 24-carat gold setting. I was clutching my black coffee mug decorated with caricatures of *The View* cohosts while reading this week's *Hollywood Reporter*.

"Thank you! It's my mother's!"

"It's a cocktail ring, right? It's beautiful."

"It is! I tend to keep it on...even in the shower. Because I lose things and if I lose this ring, she'll kill me."

"I'd kill you for her," Mike teased. With that, he bopped back to his side of the newsroom.

Honestly, I might've given Mike some context clues that I was cutting this conversation short. I put my mug down, closed the magazine, and turned back to the computer to finish Googling actor Chris Messina since he was coming in later that afternoon.

I didn't mean to be short. Mike didn't know he had hit a button.

Yes, it was a cocktail ring and no, I wasn't drinking any cocktails in the newsroom. But ever since my sister was proposed to five years ago on Christmas Day in front of our entire family—even Arista was there—I felt my hands needed—at all times—some type of bling.

My sister and I did everything together. Okay, correction, whatever my sister did, I begged and pleaded and bartered and convinced someone, anyone, that I could do it too. Most of the time, it worked. When Jasmine enrolled into Bethel Christian School's first grade, I threw such a fit—even clinging to the headmistress's leg, according to my mother—that although I wasn't potty-trained, I was admitted to pre-K. When she first got rounded acrylic nails with a French tip in high school, I somehow walked out of the nail salon with squared cobalt-blue nails with four designs. And her black Samsung flip phone—her very first cell phone—was in the same AT&T bag as my orange-plated Nokia. So when she got engaged, it felt odd that I didn't do it with her.

I suppose that was why she was so invested in my relationship with Adam. Yes, I'm sure she wanted to see me happy as her sister, but I'm sure part of her—as part of me—wanted a buddy to step into this next period of life with.

But life doesn't happen like an after-school special.

When she got engaged, I subconsciously started trying on rings and ended up falling in love with my mother's cocktail ring. It was such the opposite of an engagement ring that people would barely be able to connect my growing insecurity with my new jewelry—that I would never take off. Because of its size, it often garnered the same amount of attention as an engagement ring. While it was true that my mother would kill me if I lost her ring, what's closer to the truth is that I didn't want to go without my rounded 24-carat security blanket. Or perhaps it was my rounded, golden pacifier.

*Rinnnng! Rinnnng!*

I answered my desk phone in my best white voice—or at least that's what my friends growing up would call my flexible cultural intonation—and told Chris Messina and his publicist that they could come upstairs to our studio on the eleventh floor.

When I opened the translucent door to let *The Mindy Project* star into our lobby, I was struck by how handsome he was, even though he was a lot shorter than I had imagined. He also had more gray hair than I'd noticed when he played Mindy Kaling's love interest on the small-screen comedy.

"Come this way, Chris...How's the weather out there? Freezing, I'm sure. I haven't been outside since this morning."

I dabbed the corners of my eyes with my burnt-orange pashmina. I wiped away the tears quickly, hoping no one in the newsroom would see.

I had just sent an e-mail to Adam, saying our meet-up next week—D-Day—was no longer necessary because I had already made up my mind. I didn't want to be in a relationship with him. I didn't want to work on us. I didn't want to marry him.

Perhaps it was the easiest way out or perhaps I didn't want him to try to change my mind. Either way, there was absolutely no turning back now.

It felt like a page out of our book. I had been physically wrestling with the decision as the days stampeded toward January 13. Without me noticing, the thought of Adam had begun to put me to sleep every night and wake with me each morning.

When I realized I'd only agreed to D-Day out of fairness and not because I was unsure of what was in my heart—that I was ready to move on—I decided that instead of being fair to us, I'd be fair to myself. To my heart.

So I drafted the e-mail.

I told him how he was undoubtedly the best boyfriend I had ever had. I told him how I constantly prayed for God to send me a man who treated me as well as my father did, and then he sent him. I told him that he checked all the boxes on my list. I told him how my life had been the past few months since we split and how my entire world was rocked when he walked out of my apartment that day in February. I told him how I felt the rug was pulled out from under me, along with my dreams of being a wife and my dreams of being a mother to our unborn children. I told him the memory of that still hurt.

I told him how I was happy he was honest about being burned out. I was thankful that he told me then, instead of after walking down the aisle.

I told him I was shocked when he asked if he should bring a ring to D-Day and how I was happy that he was finally ready for marriage but that matrimony wasn't exactly our issue. I told him there was a deeper issue of "lack" in our relationship that hadn't been addressed. I told him I understood how difficult it had been to address what's missing because I didn't want to come to the table and have the conversation. I told him how the focus shouldn't be on the ring; it should be on the relationship. I told him how I couldn't work on that right now because I still felt beat up and couldn't bring myself to suit up and get back on the field after getting wiped out the last two plays.

I felt over the past few weeks our interactions had grown increasingly tense. I told him how worried I was for him when he told me his pride no longer had a place in the relationship and that he would do whatever it took to get me back. I told him his strategy of constantly calling and texting and e-mailing was in fact causing me severe anxiety. I asked him if he had realized he'd texted me nine times back-to-back without a response from me. I asked him if he thought that was healthy.

I told him I loved him. I told him that as much as I wanted to help him through this, I couldn't because it wasn't my job anymore. Not because I didn't want it to be my job, but because he didn't want it to be my job anymore, and I've come to accept that. I hoped that he would come to accept his new role in my life too—as my friend.

I told him that if I based this decision strictly on how much I loved him, we'd be getting married next year. But I wasn't. I was listening to this small yet familiar voice.

Even after we set a date for D-Day, I prayed about our relationship constantly, because it just didn't seem logical to throw away so many years with a person who I loved so hard. But I knew I'd have to make a decision one way or the other soon, so I asked the voice for confirmation.

Days later I got it while sitting in my kitchenette. The voice told me to look up and what caught my eye in between the George Foreman Grill, still in its white box, and my miniature Crock-Pot was my yellow-boxed plastic wrap. The word *GLAD* jumped out at me and sent a chill down my spine. My physiological reaction confirmed my spiritual awakening. *Be glad*, the voice said, then repeated, *Be glad*.

I do not believe in coincidence. I do not believe in chance. I do not believe the ancestors have left us here to figure life out for ourselves.

I believe the universe desires to give us what we want. I believe the universe is designed to lead us down paths we cannot foresee in signs and symbols. I believe the ancestors will whisper the code to unlock the desires of our heart. But only if we have the courage to listen.

I closed out the e-mail, telling him that I had respected his decision last February and now he'd have to respect mine.

# Chapter 32

Living in New York gives you this false sense of closeness to complete and utter strangers. Like the rabbi who complimented me on my manicure right after I left the shop. "Don't worry, they look nice," he shouted amid inspection. Or the subway teller who opened the door for me when the train pulled up and it was late at night, when trains only come in twenty-minute intervals, and I was struggling to find that damn subway card at the bottom of my bag. Or the dude on the corner who always offers to help carry my groceries. I obliged once—after I had already said no—and he politely walked me to the steps. He didn't dare walk up. Or the two Spanish-speaking ladies on 139th who I can count on being outside, playing dominoes or cards or celebrating one of their babies' birthdays. I always speak to them when I walk by. I don't know their names and they only refer to me as "baby." They often throw out compliments on my look that day and I reply with a heartfelt "Thanks!" never losing momentum in my stride. Regular encounters with strangers, who are living too close to ignore each other.

Although it felt charming on any other day, today I had to escape. I couldn't sit still.

For the past five weekends, I've been avoiding. First it was for a bridal shower, then a speaking engagement during D.C.'s Blogger Week, then a birthday party, then a bachelorette party, and now I was headed to D.C. on the 6:49 a.m. Northeast Regional Amtrak train to visit my niece. That was what I was telling myself. That was what I would say if anyone asked.

I didn't want to sit still. Subconsciously, I think if I stayed in one place long enough, I'd start to miss Adam. So now I was headed to D.C. to see my niece. Even though I was staying for only thirty-five hours—I'm on the 5:40 p.m. train tomorrow right back to New York's Penn Station—the distraction was well worth it.

By Saturday night, I was drunk on my family. Everybody was in a good mood. I was in such high spirits Sunday morning on that February day that I even cooked breakfast for everyone—scrambled eggs, fried hash browns, bacon, and scrapple. That was after my niece woke me up by jumping onto the bed and laying her solid thirty-pound body onto mine while she polished off her morning bottle. I even poured myself a mimosa with my breakfast and no one batted an eye. We ate on the patio before Mom jetted off to a church about sixty minutes away to preach their Women's Day.

After breakfast, Jasmine and I opted to instead listen to gospel radio as we made our way to the W Hotel in D.C. The boutique hotel, which sits across the street from the White House, was hosting a Valentine's Day party in their rooftop lounge and I had made it an appointment on my two-day agenda.

I texted Ashlee as we drove into D.C. Coming?

Not going.

☹☹☹

i'm on my way to baltimore to meet my mother. every party is the same. blah. nothing excites me. there are no men.

fine!

I tossed my phone in my purse as I poured the champagne that I stole from the refrigerator into a blue plastic cup, making sure to tip the cup forty-five degrees so the bubbles wouldn't fizz. It might've been in a blue cup, but I still made sure to pour correctly.

Baby Brandy was with my parents for the afternoon, so my sister—on this rare occasion—had two free babysitters. She was giddy to get some time off from being a mommy and a wife.

It's funny how much the social scene in D.C. had changed and how so much of it remained the same. I moved to New York because I had covered D.C. nightlife on my blog—DC Fab!—for so many years that I could walk into any party or club or restaurant and at least know three people. I was sick of seeing the same faces. But in a not-so-ironic twist, I now cherished seeing familiar faces when I came home to the DMV—the area known as D.C., Maryland, and Virginia.

Jasmine and I walked into the hotel's POV lounge, which sat atop the W. It offered Instagram-worthy views of the White House and the Washington Monument on the terrace, which was enclosed with thick plastic draping during the winter. In our just-purchased cocktail dresses, we spotted our favorite bartender, Marilinda. Linda, as I liked to call her, was too busy chipping away ice from a block of the frozen stuff behind the bar to notice us when we strolled up. Little ice flakes flew up into her false eyelashes at every jab she took. Once she got enough of it shaved off, she expertly poured it into a tall glass for a cocktail on the hotel's new winter menu. I stared at her from across the bar, waiting to catch her eye. When a smile appeared on her face, I knew she had finally recognized me.

"Linda! How are you, doll?" I yelled like a Real Housewife, leaning over the bar to give her an air kiss.

I met Marilinda through Ashlee. They were roommates at George Washington University.

Taking a quick scan of the room, I also spotted RaShawn, who hosted a party with me years ago during Congressional Black Caucus Week. I saw Brandon, who used to date one of my sorority sisters, and a makeup artist who I follow on Instagram. I also spotted my friend Ian and the guy who created Broccoli City Festival, one of D.C.'s rare summer music festivals.

Interrupting my inspection, Jasmine tapped me twice on the arm and handed me a drink, crafted by Linda, inside a pink flamingo floatie.

"What is it?"

"Oh, I don't know. I just told Marilinda to make us whatever."

"How much do we owe you?" Jazz yelled to Linda over some generic techno track the deejay was playing.

"That nice gentleman behind you said it's on him," she said with a smile, pointing at someone.

I whipped my head around so I could see if the nice gentleman was cute enough to flirt with since I was in debt with my free drink anyway . . . and noticed it was my friend Richard.

"Richard!" I yelled, showing my obvious disappointment that

I couldn't flirt with my married friend of over a decade. "Thank you! You didn't have to do that."

"Richard says you've known each other for a while," Jasmine said, making bar talk.

"Since BlackPlanet," I yelled back.

"Don't mention it," Richard said. "Y'all hungry? Want to order food?"

By the time we sat down, our party of three had grown to a party of five. My girl Sunni, who was also one of the most popular radio personalities in the District, had joined us along with her friend.

"Catch me up, Joi. I haven't seen you in months," Sunni, a modelesque dark-haired Bosnian purred. She spoke with a slight New York accent. She said it's because when she moved here from Bosnia, she watched television to learn English and everyone spoke with a New York accent.

"Well, I'm single," I announced.

Although it had been a year since Adam and I had broken up, it was the first time I had said it aloud, comfortably. Everyone dramatically adjusted in their chairs while my sister nodded knowingly, wondering what I would share next.

"What *happened*?" Richard said with empathy.

Over brunch, I ran down how Adam had said he was burned out. I told them how he wouldn't stop calling and e-mailing and texting—even after breaking up with me. How he sent flowers to my job in a last-ditch effort. I left out the part about Condomgate. I even explained why I wrote my very detailed e-mail a week before D-Day and how Adam responded right away, explaining why he had to just give it one more shot and ask if I was sure. I told them how he admitted that when he broke up with me, he was preoccupied with his own survival but later realized how much breaking up a second time must've been hard on me. I told them how he felt disrespected and angry and slighted. "What! What could *he* be angry about?" my sister cut in. Ignoring her question, I continued. I told them how he felt it necessary to point out all my flaws to help me correct them. How he later realized this wasn't the only way to love and apologized. He claimed he had changed and was now willing to love me how I needed to be loved. I told them how he admitted that he pushed too hard and was tough on me because he wanted to create a stronger, more loving partnership. I told them how he said he knew I was a good girlfriend, but he just didn't know how to ask for help.

"But what did he *do*?" Sunni asked, squinting her eyes to understand better.

"You know, honestly he didn't *do* anything," I said. "He's not a bad guy at all. It's not like I caught him cheating on me. He wasn't abusing me or using me. We got along great."

"Huh," she offered. I could tell the thought *This girl is crazy to let go of a good man* was crawling toward her lips.

"Sometimes you don't need a smoking gun to decide whether you want to stay with someone," I clarified.

"But if two people are in love, why can't you just make it work?" Sunni asked.

Her question was so simple. Her proposition so innocent. I thought about it for a while, stalling with, "That's a good question." After another bite of my burger, which I hoped would soak up the three Marilinda-made cocktails that were now in my system, I finally knew how to explain it.

"I just knew it wouldn't work," I started. "Almost like knowing you're putting the right shoe on your left foot without even glancing down. It just didn't feel right."

The table murmured, "Mmm."

"Plus, God confirmed it. He told me I should've left a long time ago. I just didn't want to listen."

"I'm not religious, but I feel you," Sunni's friend chimed in.

"I blame hope!"

"Who's Hope?" my sister screamed. Her Baltimore-bred attitude seeped fire into every word. "I thought you said he wasn't cheating! How did you find out?"

She didn't get it.

"No, *no*." I shook my head. "I broke up with Adam because I had hope...that I could be happy without him and that I could get what I wanted without games, without manipulation, without convincing."

"Y'all want to be married so badly," Richard teased.

"Won't you hush!" I yelled back, laughing.

"Well! You want me to hook you up with someone?" Sunni said cheerily, changing the mood from what was to what could be.

"Eh, not really. I've been dating, girl. We broke up last February."

"Ohmygod, *a year* ago? I had no idea!"

I shrugged, picking up my burger and licking the remnants of pepper jack cheese that had begun to drip down my hand before taking another bite.

All of a sudden, my cocktails were hitting me at once and I had to break the seal. "Anyone else need to use the restroom?" I asked the table, standing up. Everyone shook their head no, so I trekked inside by myself.

After peeing for what felt like four minutes, I finally left the stall to wash my hands. With the warm water pouring over my hands and my mom's giant cocktail ring, I started singing the "Alphabet Song." I read somewhere that to fully wash all the

germs accumulated on your hands with soap, you have to sing all
the way from A to Z.

Sometimes ridding yourself of something takes a while.

I made the mistake of checking my bank account balance on
my trusty iPhone app after I had cozied into a seat on my train,
heading back to New York. Crap. All this traveling only left me
with $213.45 and I still had ten days left until I got paid again.

I had to stop running away. If not for my sanity, then for my
bank account.

Something was gnawing at me. It had been pinching me in the
side since I left brunch at the W Hotel earlier that day: I didn't tell
my friends the full story of why Adam and I didn't work out.

The truth is, I wasn't ready to be a wife. I definitely wasn't ready
to get married to Adam. I was so busy asking Adam if he was ready
to get married that I never really asked myself if I was ready. And
I wasn't.

The worst realization is that you're not ready for what you
thought you deserved.

When I looked at my life—took a hard, criticizing look—I
didn't like what I saw. For starters, I felt that I was immune to any
real failure because of how I was raised. A miracle best describes
my childhood. I knew I was extremely blessed and had an arro-
gance that somehow I'd never *really* struggle. But life will humble
you and remind you that you're not better than anyone.

Not to mention, deep down, I thought I wasn't good enough
for Adam. Now, whether he made me feel that way or if I felt that
way all along is inconsequential—because at the end of the day I

thought I fell short. I knew this because I agreed to change who I was to be with him. Hate belly button rings? No problem! You hate my clothes? Fine, I'll accept your gifts with pleasure and pretend I like them. I was never the woman to bite my tongue, but with Adam, I did. I won't be the woman to remember to keep lemonade in the fridge even if it was his favorite, though I tried and failed on many occasions. I'm not the woman to cook a meal without almost burning down the kitchen at least once, but I did, because it's what he expected. I volunteered to change in order to fix problems instead of addressing them. I jumped at the chance. I didn't even fight for me to exist. Clearly, I didn't love myself enough as is, like I said I did to anyone who would listen. I robbed him of the opportunity to really know the real me and potentially robbed myself of a deeper, more understanding relationship with Adam. Somehow, instead of confronting myself, I resented him for being the reason for my changes.

But starting today, I would no longer be the woman who hides the very essence of myself to make someone else feel visible next to me.

I was so focused on becoming Adam's wife that I wasn't appreciating my life right here, right now. Instead, I obsessed over other people's lives and relationships, seeing if they were happy in love or not. I compared my relationship to other people's and if theirs was doing worse than mine, I felt better about myself. I was relieved when other people broke up because it meant that I wasn't alone in my failure; it meant that perhaps I wasn't unlovable and instead the whole system was designed for failure.

But what would my life be like if I lived in the moment instead of in the next one? Life could be filled with fewer anxieties if I never thought about what's on the next page. Life could be easier to handle if I remembered that dreams are designed to shift, change, and even dissolve. But that doesn't mean your faith has to. The universe wanted me to live up to the calling placed on my life, but I'd have to wait. And enjoy the wait instead of being discouraged by it.

I could have easily placed the blame on the slow deterioration of my relationship solely on the person who walked out of my apartment that day. But perhaps, in a couple of years, I'll be sitting in bed again, watching another man walk out the door if I don't truly assess my part in the split.

I looked out the window of the speeding Amtrak train, darting my eyes back and forth as they landed on different hues of foliage that lined the railroad tracks. Eventually my eyes shifted in dimension and suddenly I saw my reflection in the window. I recognized the young woman in the reflection, but she didn't look like herself. She still looked good on the outside, but she had miles in her eyes. I saw a woman who wanted an undying love—a big, great, unconditional type of love. It's not because she watched too many Disney films growing up or because she thought she had it all together. She didn't. She just knew that she was worthy of real love even in her shortcomings—her flashes of anger, her substandard cooking skills, her bad memory, and her garden variety of other annoying habits.

Right there on the train, I told the universe that I was ready to work on myself. I was ready to roll up my sleeves, tie up my boots, and get to work. I didn't want to run and hide and mask myself with random relationships anymore. I wanted to confront myself.

"God," I approached him with my inside voice. "I'm ready. Prepare me, God, for your will and your way. Guide my steps in becoming a better person, a better daughter, a better sister, a better aunt, a better friend, and a better sorority sister. God, tell me what to do to prepare myself to be a wife. In Jesus's name I pray, amen."

When I opened my eyes, slightly lifting my head, I knew what I had to do. After all, it was only right. I needed to make a list of the type of wife I wanted to be. In hindsight, I worked backward. Instead of making a list of what type of husband I wanted, I should've made a list of the type of wife I wanted to be. Because doesn't a healthy marriage start with me?

Writing in the Notes app on my phone, I typed the first things that came to mind. After thirty seconds and without much thought, I realized I had a sizable list.

1. Be loving
2. Be caring
3. Be kind
4. Be respectable
5. Stop cursing
6. Stop gossiping
7. Stop holding on to anxiety
8. Smile, even for strangers

Equipped with my new list, I could now begin my quest to become a Mrs., by first becoming a better version of myself.

# Chapter 33

Yellow was my grandmother's favorite color. I didn't know that when she was alive. I only discovered that fact when I was ten years old right before her funeral.

It wasn't the first funeral I had attended. It seemed that I had been attending funerals for my entire life since my mother—at the time—was the pastor of the second-largest church in Baltimore. I was always at a funeral, or waiting downstairs at a hospital, or waiting in the car while my mom went into someone's home to pray with them.

I knew the funeral rituals, even at ten years old. I knew that people wore black or white. I knew that the casket was already there hours before everyone sat down: "Don't go in the sanctuary. There's a body in there," was an oft-heard warning, and I knew to expect a long processional down the aisle with those paying their last respects to the deceased's family. I knew at least one person wouldn't be able to hold it together and would wail loudly. I knew that before Mom gave the heavenly bound their eulogy, the family got a moment to see their loved one just one last time before the casket lid had to be closed for good. And I knew that at the gravesite, the casket would remain aboveground until the family left. Too many times, that old auntie would jump in, proclaiming, "Take me with you!" And they'd have to get her out somehow.

So when Mom said that instead of wearing black—or white—to my grandma Ida's funeral that we'd be wearing yellow, I asked why.

"It was her favorite color," she explained as if I had already known.

Although I had carefully selected blue as my favorite color, painting my childhood bedroom and adjacent bathroom different shades of the hue, I would later come to be a yellow enthusiast after I graduated from college.

Why did I wait so long to switch teams? Perhaps because I missed my grandmother in my unconscious mind. But in my conscious mind, my grandmother was everywhere in my life. It felt like her spirit was leading me somewhere great.

I remember the first time she actually sat me down at her card table to teach me how to write my name. After figuring out how to play her favorite card game, pinochle, I learned how to write in block letters and in cursive *Joi-Marie McKenzie* on wide-ruled white paper. The fact that I became an entertainment journalist was no coincidence either. She had been the entertainment editor of the *Afro American Newspaper* for decades and was literally on the job the day she died. She passed out inside the Baltimore Convention Center while covering For Sisters Only, a one-day women's conference, and later died at a nearby hospital.

Friends marveled at the time I dedicated to reading and even made fun of me for color-coordinating my bookshelf in my apartment. But curling up on the couch, in long socks, sipping black tea, and reading a book felt like a natural part of the day. My grandmother had a whole room in her Baltimore row house full of books, and my mother—her only daughter—would later have an entire study wall of books in our home. I stored my own collection of Sister Souljah, Omar Tyree, Terry McMillan, and Eric Jerome Dickey on my desk in my childhood room. Plus Grandma would make us walk to the Enoch Pratt Library on North Avenue from her home on Ruxton Avenue weekly to check out new books to read.

Had I known that I'd eventually become a writer, I might've paid more attention to her while she sat at her Corona typewriter, pressed up against the wall. I might've asked more questions about that photo taped to the back of her door. The one where she's wearing a shimmery black dress, dancing with the beloved pre-scandal version of Bill Cosby.

I had become so much like my grandmother in so many ways it felt right to adopt her favorite color as well.

So as I prepared to go to the senior prom of bougie blacks living in New York—the Black Ivy Alumni Gala—I painted my nails in our favorite shade.

"Is this the Black Ivy Alumni Gala?" I asked a young lady, similarly dressed in an LBD and heels, outside the address provided on the confirmation e-mail.

I feared I had the wrong address since I was greeted by bulletproof-looking faded blue doors. Last year, when I came to the Black Bougie Nerd Prom, I was greeted by an ornate hotel lobby that could rival the one in *Home Alone 2*, complete with shiny wooden floors and sparkly chandeliers at every other glance. Not to mention the endless buffet of eligible black men with Ivy League degrees. I guess I was expecting much more.

"Yeah, girl, this is it. I was thinking the same thing," the gorgeous caramel-skinned woman said. She adjusted her coat, tying her wool trench a bit tighter before opening the heavy blue door and walking inside. She held the door for me and we both dared to see if all the dressing up was worth it by walking inside.

I texted Kim and Ebony, my publicist friend whom I knew from working in the industry, to see if they were already inside. Meanwhile a hostess handed me two red drink tickets.

"I see you're VIP," another hostess said. Her head was buried in the Excel sheet, printed off to easily check in the hundreds of expected guests. She wiped away the bangs that had fallen into her eyes before grabbing a wristband for me.

"I am?" I asked, shocked.

It wasn't that I hadn't been a VIP before; I just didn't know I would be deemed very important tonight. After all, I only came to see who was here. I wasn't expecting to meet my husband tonight or anything, but I did manage to put on the flirty black-and-white dress I bought from İstinye Park, an upscale mall in Istanbul.

I felt my phone buzz in my black clutch. Upstairs, Kim replied.

The hostess placed the green wristband carefully around my left wrist and explained that VIP was on the second floor.

After walking up a few steps to arrive at the main ballroom, I did a quick scan of the room before determining how to get upstairs. I didn't recognize anyone—not a single soul—and it was too early to tell if that was a good thing or a bad thing.

The gala was a total downgrade from last year. The year before, I networked, sipped on cocktails, took loads of iPhone pics. Now I found myself in the middle of what felt like a nightclub. The music was way too loud to network and people sat uncomfortably in silver or black couches instead of Chiavari chairs.

If I knew it was going to be a party-party, I would've stayed home. I had done the club scene. I was tired of it. I hadn't even set foot in a proper nightclub in over four years.

I finally spotted a black iron staircase through the red, green, and blue uplighting, which reflected off the furniture that looked like it belonged in the home of an avid *Star Wars* fan. Walking up the stairs in my three-inch Zara heels, I became acutely aware of how clumsy I was. I clutched the railing in fear of making a complete fool out of myself.

It was pretty easy to find Kim on the second floor, which consisted of two black leather couches. One was occupied by an older set—they looked like they could be my parents' friends—while Kim held court on the other. Everyone already had a round of drinks, including Kim's date for the evening and another one of my sorority sisters, Alicia, who was handling the press list and had invited us.

"Get a drink! The bar is open!" Kim yelled over a hip-hop track. She raised her glass in the air with an encouraging smile.

I followed her instructions, turning to the bar before attempting to fit on the couch.

"What are you having?" the bartender asked. She kept her eyes on me, while her body moved at a rapid, expert pace as she stacked crystal-looking plastic cups behind the bar.

"A vodka gimlet, please!"

"We only have these cocktails," she said, placing a small framed drink menu in front of me.

Every drink looked too sweet for my taste—flavored vodkas, rums, liqueurs. I had given up my favorite drink, an apple martini, a couple of years ago when my body betrayed me. I could no longer gulp down sweet cocktails without feeling beleaguered in bed the next day.

"I'll take the Black Ivy," I said, grabbing two singles from my purse for her tip. When I looked up, I caught Jason's eye.

I met Jason at a wild dance party on a crazy summer night in Brooklyn with Kaya. Although she usually didn't invite me to parties like that, because she knew I'd be ready to go home after ninety minutes, I decided to join her that night. When we walked up to Berg'n, an indoor-outdoor beer spot in Crown Heights, we could already hear the music blasting from outside. By the time we made it inside, the party was raging. For some unknown reason—perhaps it was the swigs I took from my Hennessy-filled flask, which I had sneaked in—I was in a dancing mood, which is completely out of character for me. I don't typically like to rub up against strangers when I'm dancing. The last time I danced like that was when I partied in Hammerjacks back in Baltimore every Sunday with DJ Quicksilva and K Swift on the turntables. But I circled my hips tightly underneath me anyway, dancing to the summer's song of the moment.

I was lost in my own groove when I felt two hands envelop my hips. I stepped forward in protest. I was too drunk to be angry, but I pretended I was anyway when I turned around to confront Mr. Hands.

"Excuse me?" I said with a smile. My hips continued their sway side to side, side to side to the beat.

"Oh, I'm sorry. I didn't mean to upset you," Jason said, licking his lips. "It's just that my friend wants to talk to you."

"What?"

I wasn't playing coy. I really couldn't hear him over the speaker that was now playing Lauryn Hill's "Lost Ones."

"My boy wants to talk to you!"

"Who?"

Jason, who was a bit shorter than me at a respectable 5'9",

pointed to his tall friend, who stood at 6'3" behind his left shoulder. He was playing with his skinny dreads that he had pulled back tightly in a ponytail away from his face. The tall friend, sensing that we were talking about him, looked over in anxious hope.

"So why didn't he come over and just say hi himself?"

"I don't know," Jason said, laughing. "He asked me to do it."

"Well, too bad for him. I don't want to talk to him. I want to talk to you!"

That #FlaskLife made me a bit bold, but it was the truth. The "shy guy" routine never worked on me anyway. (If you have no idea what I'm talking about, watch the film *The Five Heartbeats*.) If you were too scared to speak to me, how could I expect you to confidently lead our household? I needed a confident man—like Jason. Not a shrinking violet like his tall friend.

"Oh word," Jason said, laughing.

I turned around, grabbed his hands, and started to match my hips to his on the rhythm. Lauryn crooned over the crowd, "*You might win some, but you just lost one,*" and the timing wasn't lost on either of us. We looked at each other and laughed. In fact, we laughed all night. We were pretty much inseparable until his boys texted him that they were leaving. When he hit me up later that evening, he said his boys made fun of him the whole ride back to the Bronx, where they lived.

"Jason! What are you doing here?" I smiled genuinely, leaning down to hug him.

"What am I doing here, heartbreaker? I should be asking you that," he said.

"Heartbreaker? What are you talking about, Jason?"

"We went out a few times. I thought we were building something and then I never heard from you again."

"The phone works two ways, Jason," I said. It was the default answer for anyone feeling slightly guilty that they never did respond to that last text. Jason was right. I did curve him and thankfully he respected it.

Jason was a great guy: He had a great job in Connecticut, had his own place, a nice car—not that it mattered to me, but it did feel nice to ride around in a Mercedes-Benz with black leather interior—and he was super respectful. But he was low on my roster. Plus, I got super busy working, dodging Adam and catching trains to meet Shawn.

Jason knew the game and he wasn't buying it. Hell, I wasn't even buying it.

When the bartender gave me my Black Ivy, Jason put five dollars down as tip for me.

"Look, can we be friends again?"

"Of course. Let's properly catch up," I said. "You were always so busy!"

"Well, I do work in Connecticut. But"—he let out a sigh—"I'll make time for you."

"Joi!" Alicia, my soror, cheerily bounced into me at the bar.

"Hey, Alicia!" I said, hugging her. I shot her a look that said she was interrupting something.

"You know Jason?" she asked anyway.

"I do. I do," I answered. Jason and I looked at each other, wondering if we would reveal our past.

"How do you know each other?" Alicia pressed. Why did she even want to know? Was she interested in Jason?

"I've known Jason for a minute," I dodged.

"Oh right. I forgot you know everyone! Well, we're over here if you need a place to sit," she offered.

"Thanks, girl," I said, and turned my head back to Jason. I wasn't finished with our run-in.

"You should probably go," he said, disappointed. I guess he didn't want our run-in to end either. "She's over there waiting for you."

I rolled my eyes on the inside and looked over to see Alicia idly standing there, waiting for me to wrap up the conversation. So I nodded and followed her to the black couch where Kim was waiting. Ebony had also walked in and sat down unbeknownst to me.

"Why are we sitting up here?" Ebony asked no one in particular.

"Because this bar is open. Downstairs it's not," Alicia said.

The whole group understood.

"Well, girls," I said, hinting at an announcement, "I've decided I'm giving up gossiping."

The three of them looked at me as if I had said I was giving up on life itself.

Kim, breaking the awkward silence first, simply asked, "Why?"

"Yeah, we like you just the way you are," Ebony quipped, laughing. "Giving us the tea."

"Honestly, I just don't like how it's making me feel. Like, why is everyone coming to me to find out this and that about so-and-so's boyfriend or husband?" I explained passionately. "Why am I always keeping tabs on what other people are doing? Do I not have my own business to take care of? I just can't do it anymore."

"Well, people open up to you. There's nothing wrong with that," Kim reasoned.

"True. But I don't like how it makes me feel, you know?"

They nodded.

"Listen, I'm telling you all this so you can hold me accountable," I said. "And it's not just gossiping. I'm not cursing anymore. I want to be more kind. Actually, let me just show you this list I made."

I pulled out my iPhone from my black bejeweled evening bag and opened the Notes app, where my list of betterment was stored. I handed it over to the ladies, who passed it back and forth among themselves.

"So how long are you doing this for?" Kim asked.

"I'm gonna start with forty days," I explained. "We'll see after that."

"As long as you don't give up gossiping forever, we're good," she retorted.

"Oh stop," I said, laughing.

After a few more rounds of free hangover-inducing cocktails, Ebony suggested we do a lap around the room downstairs. I readily agreed. After all, I put on a new dress and no one was going to see it sitting on a couch in VIP. After taking an Instagram-worthy photo—which took several tries and one filter—we found a vacant cocktail table near the dance floor to rest our drinks on.

We looked around in an effort to see if any cuties had wandered in while we were upstairs but discovered we had no such luck. We did, however, notice a small crowd encircling a woman. I didn't see her dancing, the usual impetus for a circle to be created at a party, so I wondered what they all were looking at. Some women even had their camera phones out. I moved over slightly to get a better look.

A beautiful petite brown-skinned woman wore a racerback cocktail dress. Her sandy-brown dreadlocks were swept up in a bun and I wasn't sure if she just couldn't get all the dreads in the bun or if she had purposely left some dangling. Her look was complemented by silver earrings that hung delicately from each ear. I looked for something out of place—maybe some toilet paper stuck to the bottom of her shoe or her dress hem caught in her underwear—but she looked great! I didn't get it. What were the ladies gawking at? It wasn't until she turned around that I got it.

On her back was a sign—a laminated sign—that read I JUST CAME HERE TO FIND A HUSBAND. She secured her declaration of codependence using two black ribbons, wearing her sign proudly like a backpack.

"Excuse me, I *have* to take a picture of this," I told the unnamed woman.

Without even so much as a word, she turned around so I could get my shot. I immediately posted it to Instagram. My caption? "She's playing no games. #blackivyleague #blackivygala."

Her boldness was laughable yet honorable. While she wore her thoughts on her sleeve—well, her back—the rest of us snickered and snapped pictures. But we all felt the same way. It was why the women gathered around her to stare and it was why I took a picture to share with my followers.

For some reason, society told women that if we didn't find our husbands—and not the other way around—then in some way we were defective. But society also told us, "Don't be desperate! Let the man chase you." It was an impossible situation to be in. It made becoming someone's girlfriend and eventually someone's fiancée and later someone's wife a sly activity, done with the illusion that you're not doing anything at all. Marriage, if you let society tell it, was supposed to fall into your lap. It's not to be chased down or sought after. But when has anything in life ever happened that way?

Back at my apartment, I couldn't wait to get into my pajamas. I rolled down the thick black tights that held my shrinking tummy fat in and flung them with one foot to the other side of the room. After hanging up my dress, I took off both my silver hoops, then looked down at my hand.

It was time. It was time to take off my mom's cocktail ring. I didn't need it anymore.

Sure, I wasn't the woman with a sign on her back, but I might as well have been. If I was going to work on myself, to become a better person not for someone else but for me, I had to let go of all the things pacifying my fears.

I had to rock the ring back and forth to get it to loosen up and slip over my knuckle. I placed the ring in my jewelry box on my dresser and instinctively rubbed the spot on my finger it now left bare. That place was fleshy and a little lighter than the rest of my hand. Who knew I had gotten such a tan this summer?

It was time. It was time to let go of everything I wanted my life to be and start embracing who I was right now: a beautiful work in progress. It was time to accept that my life may not end up how I dreamt it sixteen years ago and that's okay. It was time to accept that life wasn't the same as six years ago, a year ago, or even six months ago, and it never would be again.

I've always wondered why life loved change. I've worn my hair in the same drop curls in the same shade of chestnut brown for twenty-nine years. (There was that one awful experiment in high school when I tried to give myself highlights from a box I bought at the grocery store and my brown hair ended up being striped with burnt orange. I looked like Halloween in springtime.) I've always ordered a no-foam caramel latte from Starbucks when it was cold and an extra-caramel, caramel Frappuccino when it was hot. I've had the same friends since elementary school, not because I haven't met equally dope people since then, but it's a lot easier to go through life knowing and accepting all the things you don't like about a person rather than discovering for the first time what annoys you.

But life continues to change and evolve and morph. Why?

I've thought about this over, and over, and over again—how despite the need for consistencies in life, every now and then there is pleasure in the outlier. I have finally come to the conclusion that it's not that life loves change. It loves beginnings.

Beginnings are awesome. Everything amazing happens in the beginning. Hello! New baby smell! Everyone loves the smell of a baby! Or what if you never felt that feeling you get on that very first date? The deliriously pleasurable nail-biting anticipation feeling. Or remember on the first day of school when you were so excited to wear the new shoes Mom bought you and told you not to touch until the very first day of school—remember that? Or the unexplained peace you feel watching the sun rise. It peeks its head above the horizon every single day, but can you turn away at the sight of it? Or when you first got that idea to start your own business, one you had no business starting, your friends and family would tell you, but that feeling of knowing and yearning and excitement outweighed all logic. Or even that first sip of a cold Pepsi. Everyone knows that if you open a can of Pepsi, the first crisp sip is the best of all the sips. Face it: Life loves beginnings.

It felt completely unfair that my life got turned upside down when Adam decided he was burned out. It felt like the universe was punishing me for something untold…perhaps even undone. I had played this hand right; I was supposed to collect the books, but I didn't. And what's worse, I never would. I was dutiful, encouraging, sexual, and even shape-shifting to become the perfect girlfriend and later the perfect wife for this man, and everything ever sold to me in life told me that I'd be rewarded with a diamond at the end of it. And I wasn't. What the fuck? I mean, what the eff. Ugh, God help me with this no-cursing thing.

But I was looking at it all wrong. My life didn't end that day when he left; it had only just begun. The universe was painfully course-correcting me to my own new beginning. I couldn't see it at the time. I couldn't see it under my hurt and tears and even under the many men I filled up empty days with. I wasn't cherishing the beginning because I was stuck focused on the ending.

I grabbed the sweatpants that were on top of my hamper and put them on. Finding my scarf where I left it that morning, dangling on my full-length mirror, I began the intricate process of wrapping my hair before I called it a night.

I almost started to criticize myself—why did it take me so long to figure this part out?—but the tiny voice gently bumped me with its hip, rubbed my back, and said if you didn't feel the loss, you wouldn't appreciate the gain. If you didn't mourn the ending, you wouldn't cherish the beginning. I was in desperate need of a new start, a jump-start even, and I didn't even realize how broken down my car was on the side of the road. I was incapable of getting out of the car and leaving it, because despite its busted-up bumper and stalling engine, I loved that car. I loved it so much I'd rather be on the side of the road with the car than leave it to get in a new one and arrive at my destination. The universe wanted me to get what I wanted. God knew my heart's desires, and because he's never left me, or let me fail, or let me end it all, he created the blessedness of the beginning.

It was the spark of something new that pushed me forward to keep at it, despite all convention not to touch the stove again because it was hot and it had burned me before. It was that spark that gave me hope and it was that spark that would bring my covenant spouse eventually without any games.

*Chapter 34*

It was only March, but I was already carefully crafting a rather lengthy e-mail to my boss, detailing every single vacation day I wanted to take that year. After three years at the network, I had gained five more vacation days to a grand total of fifteen, but it didn't matter. Those days would be eaten up by the four weddings I had been invited to and the four weddings to which I had happily denoted *yes* as my RSVP. Although I did have a trip to Iceland planned with two of my forever friends, my wedding schedule meant that the majority of my vacation days were going to be pirated to celebrate other people's happiness.

My mom thought I was crazy when she called that Saturday morning to check on me. My mini Keurig machine had already brewed a cup of coffee. I tiptoed quickly back into bed, the floor cold from winter's breath, and placed my mug on the wooden bedside table before jumping back under the duvet.

"Joi, you *can* say no, you know."

"Mom! It's not like I was invited to four *random* weddings. These are my friends! I'm in Lindsay's wedding, so I have to go to that one; then my other sorority sister is getting married, and the other two are real friends—like slept over my house, let you have a sweater, know all my business type of friends."

She wasn't buying it.

"Mom, you just don't understand. Do you even remember what it was like when all of *your* friends got married?"

"I remember!" she said, pretending to take offense. "But, baby, remember, your friends will understand that you can't be everywhere at once."

"True, but then it'll be like, '*Oooh* why can't she come? Is she *hating*? She went to *her* wedding? Why can't she come to mine? She ain't that busy!' I can hear it now. I just can't skip any. I'm just gonna suck it up and be broke for a year."

"What a life you lead," she said sarcastically.

I couldn't help that all my friends were getting their happily-ever-afters at the same time. I'd just have to deal.

"Gasp!"

My mom's advice on how to get out of at least two weddings—that I had no intention of taking—was chirping out of my phone's speaker while I was scrolling through Twitter. My mentions were going crazy. For some yet-to-be-discovered reason, I had nearly thirty notifications. I tapped to find out what witty tweet had finally captured the love and attention of my thousands of followers. Scrolling down, I found the genesis of the activity: Common had retweeted me.

"What, sweetie?" Mom asked. "Is everything all right over there?"

"Oh! Sorry! Yeah, Mom! Everything is fine! Common retweeted me!"

"Common did what?"

"He retweeted me! On Twitter!"

"Oh," she managed. "Girl, I thought something happened to you."

"Mom! Something *did* happen to me! I went to a party last night downtown at this place called Tao. Super-cute place. Plus it was open bar. Tanqueray all night. Common was there. He performed for like five minutes—which was a bit of a letdown—but he just retweeted my photo!!!!!"

"Moss doesn't grow under your feet, girl," she said before rushing me off the phone. Apparently, she was about to cook breakfast for Dad.

"Bye, Mom," I sang, still staring at the photo. I tried to figure out what made Common retweet it. It wasn't really that spectacular. Half of his body was covered up from the silhouettes of industry types, who were invited like me to the invitation-only event. It was even sort of blurry.

Perhaps it was my caption. With two gin cocktails in my system, I had listened intently to the rapper thank sponsors and then motivate the crowd with a few words before he performed his hit "The Light." Wearing a white hoodie, zipped all the way up, with matching jeans, Common told the crowd about the time he was nominated for five Grammys. He said he just knew that he'd win at least two of them, so he prepared a couple of acceptance speeches. But finding out in the pre-show—the part of the show that doesn't get aired on television—that he hadn't won two, he just figured, "Well, I'll cram my acceptance speeches in the last three."

Eventually, he realized he actually hadn't won in now four categories and there was only one category left: Best Rap Album. And when Ludacris announced the winner, Common told the crowd that he was halfway out of his chair when the Atlanta rapper yelled, "Kanye West!"

Common said he was feeling down on himself when Kanye called him the next day and told him, "Let's get back in the studio and work on getting you that award." And the very next year, he did win. Common said it didn't matter how much he believed in himself or that he believed that he deserved those awards. In order to get the reward for all the years of hard work put in, he had to earn it.

So he reminded the crowd, "If you really wanna be great, you have to face the challenges." And my caption was born.

The next month, he won an Oscar.

I was sleeping blissfully when I felt a slight nudge. I couldn't tell if I was dreaming it or if it was really happening until I heard a familiar voice. "Joi! Joooooooi, waaaake uuuuup!"

It was Kaya, standing over me, fully dressed.

"What tiiiiime is it?" I grumbled out.

"Nine fifteen!"

I grabbed the down comforter and pulled it over my scarf-wrapped head in dramatic fashion so she would get the hint.

"Shouldn't you be headed upstairs to get your hair done?"

"No, I'm doing it myself," I yelled from under the lavender-scented sheets. "I only need to get my makeup done. I'll come up a little later. It's going to be a long day."

Kaya and I were sharing a hotel room in Philadelphia. It was Lindsay's wedding day—a perfect August Saturday without a cloud in the sky—and I was exhausted. I had been out of town for the last five weekends for wedding festivities. First it was my sorority sister Jade's bridal shower in East Baltimore; then it was Lindsay's bachelorette party in Las Vegas; then it was Yodit's rooftop bridal shower in northern Virginia, followed by Jade's bachelorette party in New York—at least I didn't have to travel for that one. I had to skip my other sorority sister Ashley's thirtieth birthday party to be able to afford trekking to Philadelphia for Lindsay's bridal shower last weekend. And now her big day, seven days later, was finally here.

Mom was right. She was always right. I should've said no to something.

I wanted to be thrilled that love was in the air, but I was already sick of wedding season and I hadn't even been to my first wedding yet. I was worn out from spending hundreds of dollars on the pre-festivities and I'd probably spend hundreds more on travel alone. A week from now, I'll be at a Virginia winery for Yodit's Ethiopian Orthodox wedding, followed by my friend Madie's Maryland countryside wedding, followed by Jade's Chesapeake Bay–inspired wedding right on the edge of a dock.

I budgeted to spend only $17 a day this week so that I could afford to stay in the hotel I just grumpily woke up in. It was why I wasn't getting my hair done by the hairstylist Lindsay had specially ordered to come to her hotel room for the bridal party. I couldn't afford to pay $60 for someone to curl my hair...I could do it myself for free. But that's what you do for people you love. That's what you do for your friends.

I was the last bridesmaid to make it upstairs to Lindsay's massive bridal suite, which was busier than a bee colony. Some girls were staring at themselves in the mirror, inspecting the way their hair was crafted and preserved for the evening's festivities with bobby pins and silver clamps. Others were on the couch, filling their mouths with fruits, cheeses, and muffins from the continental breakfast cart her mother had ordered. Lindsay's future mother-in-law was getting her makeup done by the artist, while her assistant prepped another bridesmaid by instructing her to wipe off her makeup that refused to come off in the shower.

The sun poured into the J.Crew catalog–inspired room through the translucent curtains that offered just a glimpse of downtown Philadelphia. Jill Scott played from the hotel's Bose speaker, while Lindsay sat quietly on the couch with her legs tucked underneath her. Her brown eyes were fixated on her iPhone and her thumbs feverishly moved back and forth, texting someone. I sat down next to her, in the only free space on the sectional, and looked over in nosiness. Aww, she was texting Lamar. Wait…is that allowed? I guess there's no rule on texting your future husband on your wedding day; you just can't see him. They're so cute.

"Joi! Are you ready to be prepped?" the assistant yelled out to me.

Wow, how did she know my name? This wedding was a well-oiled machine and I had been in enough to know that they all didn't run this smoothly.

"Yes! Yes!" I said, hopping off the couch.

"Wait," Lindsay said. She ran over to the closet and pulled out a crisp white bathrobe with my initial stitched on the left side. "Put this on first!"

"Awww, Lindsssss! This is awesome! Thank you," I squealed like a kid on Christmas Day.

If this was any indication of the evening to come, I was going to have a really good time.

The afternoon had escaped us thanks to a flurry of blow-drying, curling, brushing, tapping, gluing, and primping.

There's always that time in a wedding where it seems like you have all the time in the world and then something switches and it's rush, rush, rush. Someone had just flipped the switch at Lindsay's. By the time the photographer knocked politely on the bridal suite to make sure we were all clothed, it was already 3:00 p.m. and we were rushing out the door with our floor-length Amsale gowns in hand. We had to head to the venue early for a quick rehearsal.

A black Mercedes van took us the three blocks to the wedding venue. Who wants to walk when you look so good? The grooms-men, whom we hadn't seen since the night before at the rehearsal dinner, held in a private room at Valanni, had already claimed their seats in the van. By the time we filed out and walked into the venue, a local landmark called the Atrium at Curtis Center, thirty minutes had flown by. Weddings.

I was too busy laughing and talking to notice it at first, but when I saw just how beautiful Lindsay's wedding was set up, it felt like that moment in every Spike Lee movie when the cam-era focuses on one person and zooms in dramatic fashion. It was jaw-droppingly beautiful. From the third floor of this beautifully lit atrium hung white sheer drapes that looked like heaven's gates. They contrasted the black-tiled floor and matching Chiavari chairs. All-white flowers lined the aisle on mini pedestals, which complemented the building's all-white floor-to-ceiling pillars.

A woman who introduced herself as the wedding coordinator tried to grab our attention. She looked as if she hadn't taken a breath since we walked in the door. I felt bad for her…trying to grab the attention of twelve excited adults.

"Guys! Can you line up?" she yelled. "I want to do a walk-through so you know how you'll walk down the aisle. Guys, it'll be a bit dif-ferent. Since the ladies are holding their bouquets, you'll actually hold on to *their* arms."

The guys groaned. "Ew, that looks weird," one said.

One bridesmaid asked, "Yeah, why aren't we holding on to the guys?"

I thought I heard another guy say they'd look like girls.

"I know! I know! It's a more traditional way of walking down the aisle," the coordinator explained. "Line up! By height!"

This was my fourth wedding. At a statuesque 5'10", I knew that I'd be first in the processional after Lindsay's family, so I made my way to the top of the aisle.

The tallest groomsman—a chocolate-skinned guy standing at 6'4"—found me there. I found myself blushing for no reason. After all, our acquaintance was so new. It was still in the box. It still had the wrapping paper on it.

After we ran through walking up, then back down the aisle, past the hundreds of perfectly placed Chiavari chairs that would later be filled by their family and friends, my groomsman, whose name I'd later learn during the reception was Kemuel, asked, "You got it?"

In a rush to head to the bridesmaids' dressing room to take down my pin curls, which had been in overnight for ultimate drop-curl effect, I snapped back: "Sure. This isn't my first wedding."

*Ugh!* I reprimanded myself. *Think of number three on your list: Be kind!* I had been committed to bettering myself for months now. I hadn't cursed in 116 days and hadn't been on a date in the same amount of time. And life still felt full. Those once unbearable moments of loneliness in my apartment now felt like a welcome time-out from my packed social calendar. I smiled with my eyes, indulged in anything and everything that pleased me—biking alone in Central Park, buying two cupcakes just because, and ordering the most expensive glass of champagne—and appreciated life as it evolved in front of me.

"Word," he said, brushing off my bristles. A broad smile cozied onto his face, showing off his charming gap-toothed smile.

"What's so funny?"

"You're just a pleasant surprise, that's all. When we get married, they won't believe how we met. We're gonna have to make up another story because no one will believe us," he explained casually.

"A *surprise?*" I asked, fixating on that one word and dismissing everything else he said.

I looked at him as if he had lost his mind, which I think he did somewhere along the bouquet-lined aisle. He dismissed my nonverbal offense and offered me another smile in return.

Although I wanted to stay on course and without distractions, I couldn't help but notice the hairs on my arms standing up in what felt like a moment I should pay attention to. Trusting that this was a *kairos* moment, instead of resisting it, I fell into it because I finally felt like I earned it.

"Yes, a surprise," he said, unaware of what had just happened. "So, are we going to figure out our new story?"

Taking another look at him, I took a deep breath, smiled, and replied, "Yes."

# ACKNOWLEDGMENTS

This book would not have come to fruition without God. So, thank you, God, for this wonderful surprise.

I'd also like to thank several people who helped me along the way, including my very understanding and loving mother, Vashti Murphy McKenzie, who has said since I was a child that I always had four or five books inside me. (Well, Mom, here's one! Four more to go!) I'd also like to thank her mother, Ida Murphy Peters, and my sister and best friend, Vashti-Jasmine Murphy Saint-Jean. And, of course, her husband, Amos Saint-Jean; my brother, Jon-Mikeal Murphy McKenzie; and my father, Stan McKenzie, who is our rock.

Special thanks also goes to my supportive family members, including Carl Smith, Qiana Jihan Murphy Gabriel, Jonee Brown, Blair Smith, Jake Oliver, Rachael Murphy Phillips Humphrey, Rev. Frances Murphy Draper, my godmother Rev. Dr. Marie Murphy Phillips Braxton, and the entire Murphy and McKenzie families.

I'd also like to thank Rev. Angelique Mason, Kim Sadler, and Rev. Dr. Cecilia Williams Bryant for allowing me to use her very inspiring words in these pages.

I'll forever be indebted to Adrienne Ingrum, who first believed in me beyond my family circle and gave me the tremendous confidence to complete this book. I'd also like to thank the team at Hachette Book Group, particularly Center Street, and more notably my editor

Alexa Smail. Thank you for pushing me beyond my earthly limits. Also, appreciation goes to my cousin Anthony J. M. Jones and photographer Tayo Ola.

I'd also like to thank my support circle, who read early versions of this memoir, including Rebecca Bratu, Ashlee Tuck, and Kimberly Wilson. I'm also so very appreciative of my friends, who at many times during this process restored my sanity, including Anton R. Lewis, along with Leah Faye Cooper, Ashley Calloway-Blatch, Ceylan Yeginsu, Yolanne Almanzar, Lillian Rizzo, Emory Proctor, Jamishia Smith, Addie Whisenant, Tarrah Cooper, Vanessa Dormesy, Mary Ogundare, Sydnee Wilson, Adriene Boone, and of course my line sisters Aurelia Michael, Tia Salmon, Ashley Moore, Erika Hall, Alexandra Tyson, Chelsea Jones Crawford, Jade Steele Hunter, Shamera Wilkins, Jackie Iloh, Felicia Jones, and Felice Leon; with special thanks to Linsey Edwards Drummonds. And I'd be remiss without thanking Mia Fields-Hall, Tiffany Probasco, and the rest of The Fab Empire team, who held it all the way down.

I'd also like to express my appreciation to Steve Jones, Wayne Fisk, David Blaustein, Andrea Dresdale, Christopher Watson, Andrew Kalb, Helena Andrews, Jason Reynolds, and Stephen Hill.

I could not say thank you enough to the unnamed men whose lives have intertwined with mine and are reflected in these pages. I am better for knowing and loving you.

I'd also like to thank those who inspired many thoughts in this memoir, including Sydnie Mosley, Spike Lee, Jennifer Hudson, Kerry Washington, Nate Parker, Chris Messina, Jill Scott, Common, Michelle Obama, Marissa Millet, Vildana "Sunni" Puric, Yodit Gebreyes Endale, and Maaden Eshete Jones.

I'll end this by thanking Lenox Coffee, the place where much of this book was written; Jacob Restaurant, which fed me on many late nights; and musicians like Kehlani, Stacy Barthe, Brandy, Alina Baraz & Galimatias, and Jhené Aiko, who kept me motivated to write.

Oh! And I can't forget to thank my beloved miniature dachshund, Arista.